# Culturally Responsive Self-Care Practices for Early Childhood Educators

The first self-care book designed specifically for the early childhood field, *Culturally Responsive Self-Care Practices for Early Childhood Educators* is filled with helpful strategies and tools that you can implement immediately.

Recognizing that self-care is not one size fits all, the authors present culturally responsive strategies drawn from diverse early childhood staff working in a range of roles across communities and contexts. By tying the importance of educator self-care to goals of social justice and equity, this book advocates for increased awareness of the importance of self-care on both an individual and institutional level.

Through key research findings, effective strategies and personal anecdotes, this accessible guide helps readers understand and engage with the critical role self-care and wellness-oriented practices play in creating strong foundations for high-quality early learning programs.

**Julie Nicholson**, Ph.D., is Professor of Practice at Mills College and Senior Fellow for Childhood Education International, U.S.A.

**Priya Shimpi Driscoll**, Ph.D., is Associate Professor of Education, Chair of Early Childhood Education and Director of the Language Development Laboratory at Mills College, U.S.A.

**Julie Kurtz** is the Founder of the Center for Optimal Brain Integration, specializing in trauma healing and resiliency building for all ages, U.S.A.

**Doménica Márquez**, BA, is Director of Provider Services for the California Child Care Resource and Referral Network, U.S.A.

**LaWanda Wesley**, Ed.D., is Co-Director of the Center for Equity in Early Childhood Education and Director of Quality Enhancement and Professional Development of Early Education for Oakland Unified School District, U.S.A.

# Culturally Responsive Self-Care Practices for Early Childhood Educators

Julie Nicholson, Priya Shimpi Driscoll,
Julie Kurtz, Doménica Márquez
and LaWanda Wesley

Routledge
Taylor & Francis Group

NEW YORK AND LONDON

First published 2020
by Routledge
52 Vanderbilt Avenue, New York, NY 10017

and by Routledge
2 Park Square, Milton Park, Abingdon, Oxon, OX14 4RN

*Routledge is an imprint of the Taylor & Francis Group,
an informa business*

*Library of Congress Cataloging-in-Publication Data*
A catalog record for this book has been requested

ISBN: 978-0-367-15011-2 (hbk)
ISBN: 978-0-367-15025-9 (pbk)
ISBN: 978-0-429-05458-7 (ebk)

Typeset in Palatino
by Apex CoVantage, LLC

# Contents

# Meet the Authors

**Priya Mariana Shimpi Driscoll** is an associate professor of education at Mills College. She directs the early childhood education BA and MA programs and runs the Mills College Language Development Laboratory. For self-care, she enjoys taking long walks with her close friends, taking mindfulness classes and playing board games with her family.

**Julie Kurtz** is a national speaker, trainer, consultant and therapist specializing in trauma healing and resiliency building for ages 0–99. For more information, you can connect with Julie at www. juliekurtz.com. Her self-care word is "walking". She loves walking but also tries daily to walk toward people, places and objects that fill up and restore her reserves and, when possible, walk away from those very things that diminish her soul.

**Doménica Márquez** serves as the Director of Provider Services for the California Child Care Resource & Referral Network. She continuously works to support all home-based caregivers— family, friend and neighbor caregivers and licensed Family Child Care providers alike—through local Child Care Resource and Referral agencies across California. Doménica is learning to find self-care every day through music, dance, play, prayer, humor and being mindful of personal boundaries. She shares in self-care with her daughter through all of the above and any chance they can get to swim, play at the beach, get lost in Tilden Park or create together.

**Julie Nicholson** is a professor of practice in the School of Education at Mills College and Senior Fellow at Childhood Education International. Her research, presentations and publications all emphasize different aspects of equity and social justice in early childhood. Her favorite forms of self-care include her sunset runs through Golden Gate Park, listening to podcasts and laughing with friends and family.

**LaWanda Wesley** serves as Oakland Unified School District's Director of Quality Enhancement and Professional Development of Early Education. She supports a cadre of 200-plus teachers and a dynamic early learning leadership team. Dr. Wesley also co-directs a national leadership fellowship titled *Emerging Leaders for Racial Equity in Early Care and Education*. She describes self-care as an emergent practice to preserve her peace of mind, physical health and journey of spiritual healing.

# Introduction

*Self-care's about doing all of the self-work. It's about how are we nurturing ourselves and letting ourselves grow all the time. One of the wonderful things about the early childhood field is that we're in this mindset of nurturing growth across all these different domains and seeing the child as a whole person. This practice puts us as caregivers in a great position to also sethink about ourselves as whole people, and ask, "Well, how do we grow ourselves creatively, spiritually, physically, as well?". . . . It's finding ways to deal with stress in the moment where you're not taking it into your body. . . . It's a lifelong process.*

*—Encian Pastel, Preschool Teacher*

*Self-care, I think it means that being able to take care of yourself physically, emotionally, socially and spiritually.*

*—Teresa Fuller, Director, Early Childhood Center*

*I'm a teacher and also a mom and I'm also a single mom, so self-care is usually the last thing I get to work on because of everyone else that needs taking care of. . . . I'm learning that I have to do self-care because if I don't, my stress just eats me up and then I'm not as effective at my job . . . teachers are so undervalued already, I think we need to value ourselves.*

*—Elsa Karlsson, Early Childhood Special Education Teacher*

*Self-care is the awareness and the validity of honoring the self, that we are deserving of feeling better, of taking care of ourselves. We're deserving of acknowledging that we experience hardships and that those hardships are worthy of being recognized as something we can learn from and overcome.*

*—Fawzia Saffi, Site Supervisor, Head Start*

## Why Is It Important for Early Childhood Educators to Practice Self-Care?

*You can't pour from an empty cup. Take care of yourself first.*

*—Unknown*

Early childhood educators have very complex jobs. They work long days on their feet with constant demands on their energy and patience—whether they are holding and rocking infants, reading storybooks to toddlers, engaging in imaginary play with preschoolers, building problem-solving and self-regulation skills with kindergarteners or leading programs that serve young children and families. Despite the intense workplace demands they face on a daily basis, early educators do not receive the compensation, benefits, professional development and support they need and deserve given the complexity of their daily work (Lieberman, 2018). Unfortunately, most early educators continue to earn poverty-level wages, and almost half qualify for public support programs (Whitebook, Phillips, & Howes, 2014; Whitebook, McLean, Austin, & Edwards, 2018). Many in the early childhood workforce experience significant stress on a daily basis due to their own family's food insecurity, housing instability, lack of health care and economic hardship (Whitebook et al., 2018).

Adding to their cumulative stress, early childhood educators are working with an increasing number of young children and families who are impacted by toxic stress and trauma (Nicholson, Perez, & Kurtz, 2019; Sorrels, 2015). Working with children and families who are trauma impacted—e.g., as a result of immigration or deportation stress, community violence, child maltreatment, opioid addiction or other substance abuse, homelessness, natural disasters, domestic abuse or other factors—takes a professional and personal toll on the lives of educators, putting them at risk for burnout, compassion fatigue and secondary trauma (Perry, 2014). Additionally, when teachers' stress systems are repeatedly activated, the neurochemicals they are exposed to can have a toxic and harmful impact on their bodies (Cozolino, 2006; Pally, 2000; Stein & Kendall, 2004). Long-term exposure to stress chemicals can result in a variety of health problems, including anxiety, depression, digestive problems, headaches, heart disease, sleep problems, weight loss/gain, diabetes and memory and concentration impairment (McEwen, 2006).

Decades of research demonstrate that consistent, attuned and responsive relationships with children are an essential factor in high-quality early learning programs. Remaining responsive and self regulated with young children, especially those who are impacted by trauma and present complex and challenging behaviors, is a critical responsibility of early childhood educators. Yet even the most committed and skilled professionals may struggle to provide caring and responsive care if their own stress response systems are continually triggered as they worry about paying their bills, supporting the children and families in their care and managing all of the additional pressures currently being placed on the early childhood workforce (e.g., pressure to complete higher education degrees; participate in Quality Rating and Improvement activities and improve the quality of their programs through coaching, training, technical assistance and program evaluation from external raters).

*Given these realities, it is essential that early childhood educators understand the importance of engaging in self-care and that the early childhood field move toward organizing programs, organizations and systems to value and integrate self-care practices and to shift policies and practices to be trauma informed and wellness oriented.*

---

### In the Voices of Early Childhood Educators, Self-Care is. . .

Being aware of what I need when I need it

Being in solitude or in quietness

Putting myself on the schedule

Figuring myself out

Nurturing ourselves and letting ourselves grow

Finding ways to deal with stress in the moment so you do not take it into your body

Being reminded of the joys in life

Feeling loved by people

Listening to myself inwardly

Taking care of myself mentally, physically, emotionally—my whole self

Letting certain things fall through the cracks

Acknowledging that we experience hardships and those are worthy of being recognized

Knowing we are all related/interconnected: everything we do impacts everything else

---

## Self-Care Is Defined in Many Different Ways

The National Association for the Education of Young Children (NAEYC) Focus on Ethics Column (September 2015) described the importance of self-care in our profession and defined it in the following way:

> Self-care is identified as self-regulation of one's needs—physically, emotionally, cognitively, and socially. It is the ability to recognize and identify when you are not having your needs met and planning a course of action that will support you in changing your behavior or circumstances. Why is it important? As one early childhood educator shared, self-care is how you assure that you bring your whole self to your work in the classroom and community in early childhood education.

> *Self-care means being able to take care of yourself physically, emotionally, socially and spiritually. Physically, is being able to eat healthy, exercise, watch your weight, get enough sleep, all of that. Socially, is being able to surround yourself with people that are supportive . . . you feel safe, you have a sense of trust, someone you can communicate and think critically with . . . your emotional wellbeing. . . . If you need support, how do you take care of working through issues in a healthy way? Spiritually . . . whether it's nature or God or whoever, to be able to find time to practice or be surrounded with that . . . it offers such hope and peace.*
> —Teresa Fuller, Director of an Early Childhood Center

# The Problematic Nature of Current Discussions of Self-Care

Although the topic of self-care has been increasing in popularity across the field of education, the current conceptions of self-care and recommended self-care practices are often problematic for the field of early childhood for several reasons:

♦ The literature is *dominated by language, beliefs and prac-tices that are overwhelmingly Western Eurocentric and middle class*. As the early childhood workforce is composed of many individuals who are low income or experiencing poverty, almost 40% of whom are women of color, and a large percentage who are recent immigrants from coun-tries around the world, many of the strategies outlined in the available literature and courses on self-care are not accessible, meaningful or culturally aligned with their lived experiences. Additionally, current literature often does not authentically acknowledge the genuine condi-tions that exist for the early childhood workforce today in their personal or professional lives. Therefore, too often, current discussions of self-care are not equitably inclu-sive of the early childhood workforce.

♦ Current conceptions of self-care too often *perpetuate ideas that educators are responsible for their stress manage-ment while hiding the structural and institutional conditions* in the field of early childhood and across society and that contribute to and, in many cases, create the stress and trauma educators experience. Doing so has placed the responsibility for self-care on the shoulders of the educators—perpetuating a myth that self-care is entirely an "individual" endeavor—without holding programs and systems accountable for the health of a working envi-ronment or the need to provide staff with resources and supports to help them prevent and reduce their stress in the workplace.

♦ Discussions of self-care focus *almost exclusively on the reduction of stress so teachers will be more effective in their work with young children and families*. Rarely is self-care discussed in terms of the intrinsic health and wellness value it provides to the educators themselves, a sig-nificant gap that only exacerbates the injustices they experience.

## Toward a More Just and Equitable Conception of Self-Care: Re-Conceptualizing and Re-Claiming Diverse Understandings of What It Means to Care for the Self

To address these limitations, our discussion of self-care reflects the following commitments:

♦ We acknowledge that *self-care is a culturally informed concept* and that authentic self-care practices are different for each individual, are dynamic in nature and may change over time and differ as a function of an educator's interests, family and cultural background, geography, income/class, religious or spiritual beliefs, age, sexuality, gender, community participation, personal experiences and other factors.

### Culturally Diverse Self-Care Practices

There is more than one way to engage in self-care or to learn strategies that will be effective in caring for and healing the self. Self-care strategies and therapeutic treatments developed to help address stress and trauma are frequently based on Western majority concepts of the self, which tend to adopt an individualist framework. As a result, these strategies carry specific Western-oriented cultural assumptions about the self; relations with others and the framing of conditions such as stress, mental illness and medical interventions or cures (Kirmayer, 2007). In this book, we aim to take a culturally responsive approach to self-care and critique the idea that Western psychological assumptions about the self, others and healing are authentic or appropriate for all educators.

Instead, we emphasize that the way individuals experience the world is always through a cultural lens and that descriptions of "objective" reality or "universal" truths and best practices are actually based in dominant cultural assumptions and may have limited relevance for people who identify with minoritized groups. We note that science itself is not culture free (Sue, 2005). *This is why, in the current book, we add the caveat that some common therapeutic techniques and strategies used for self-care may not be comfortable, relevant or even appropriate for individuals depending on their cultural backgrounds and/or current cultural beliefs and practices.*

For example, cognitive behavioral strategies focused on self-reflection, such as writing out and identifying triggers, may be most relevant to dominant Western European American culture as well as a few minoritized ethnic groups (Vega, Kolody, & Valle, 1998). For others, however, the practice of engaging in identifying conflict, emotions or other types of personal introspection and reflection for problem solving may be uncomfortable. This may be due to cultural differences in having a frame of reference of the self in some collectivist groups or differences in value of "emotional stoicism" whereby reflecting on negative feelings may not be fostered (Ross, 1987). Therapeutic uses of emotional expression may also not be a good fit for everyone, given that there are differences across cultures in how emotion is expressed (Koppelman & Goodhart, 2011).

One way to counteract or avoid ethnocentrism (i.e., evaluating other cultural perspectives and practices based on the standards and customs of one's own culture) in dominant Western perspectives on self-care and healing strategies is to learn about and potentially incorporate healing practices used by a diversity of cultural groups. Some of these approaches may be based on spirituality, including churches and faith-based or Indigenous healers, as well as other types of community-based programs and institutions that encourage and use Indigenous or culturally varied approaches (Aten, Topping, Denney, & Bayne, 2010; Awanbor, 1982; Cervantes, 2010; Gone & Calf Looking, 2011; Parham, 1999; Yeh, Hunter, Madan-Bahel, Chiang, & Arora, 2004; Wendt, Gone, & Nagata, 2014). These may include decolonization-focused[1] approaches, for example, Ayurvedic healing, Mestizo spirituality or African psychotherapy. As we learn about and incorporate these multiple approaches, we are less likely to rely solely on ethnocentric practices (Wendt et al., 2014).

It is also important to note that the research on cross-cultural differences in understanding self-care as well as evaluating the effectiveness of multiple types of therapeutic techniques is quite thin. Most research on these techniques is based on people from dominant Western cultures (Sullivan & Lawrence, 2016; Wendt et al., 2014). Therefore, we cannot generalize the effectiveness or ineffectiveness of different techniques across diverse racial, ethnic and cultural groups.

With these understandings in mind, we offer different ideas and strategies throughout this book, understanding that they may be more or less useful for different individuals and groups. We encourage you to try different techniques and reflect on how they may or may not resonate with your cultural frameworks and belief systems. As you learn about diverse approaches, you can adapt them to your needs. Additionally, if you have found other practices to be useful, we, of course, encourage you to incorporate these as well.

◆ We acknowledge that an individual's experiences of stress and trauma and their access to *self-care and healing resources and supports are* significantly impacted by their social categories of identity (e.g., race, ethnicity, gender, class etc.) and the manner in which they are *impacted by historical and structural forms of oppression* (e.g., racism, classism etc.). Similarly, the types of self-care different individuals desire and/or find meaningful are deeply influenced by the impact of structural and institutional forces of oppression and inequity in society.

◆ We explicitly define *self-care as a foundation of equity for the field of early childhood.* Self-care, we believe, is a necessary practice given the inequitable and challenging conditions early childhood educators face on a daily basis and the profoundly important role they play in supporting young children—especially those furthest from opportunity—during the most critical years of their learning and development. We take an explicit stance that self-care should not be the sole responsibility of educators. Instead, self-care must be valued and embedded throughout programs, agencies and systems serving young children and their families and supporting the early childhood workforce.

> Self-care is an essential professional activity for promoting ethical practice. . . . Self-care is not an indulgence. It is an essential component of prevention of distress, burnout, and impairment. It should not be considered as something "extra" or "nice to do if you have the time" but as an essential part of our professional identities.
> —Barnett et al., 2006, pp. 17, 263

## Goals and Overview of the Book

The goal of this book is to provide early childhood professionals working directly with, or on behalf of infants, toddlers, preschool and early elementary-aged children with the knowledge and skills they need to understand authentic culturally informed self-care, including its critical importance and the diverse ways of conceptualizing and caring for the self. This book is the second in an aligned series of books: Our first book, *Trauma-Informed Practices for Early Childhood Educators: Relationship-Based Approaches That Support Healing and Build Resilience in Young Children* (Nicholson et al., 2019), provides a comprehensive overview of the neurobiology of stress, the impact of trauma on young children's learning and development and trauma-informed practices to support children to build resilience and heal in early childhood environments.

In this book, we shift the focus to early educators, discussing the impact of stress and trauma on the adult caregivers themselves and the many strategies—including but not limited to trauma-informed practices—they can use to reduce their stress, build their resilience and support their own healing engagement. In our next book, *Creating and Sustaining Trauma-Informed and Healing Engaged Early Childhood Organizations and Systems* (Nicholson, Kurtz, Leland, Wesley, & Nadiv, 2021), we shift the focus once more to describe policies and organizational and system-level practices that lead to caring, healthy, healing-oriented programs and environments for early educators. The contents of the three books align and build on one another, and they are all written specifically for the early childhood field.

## The Butterfly Metaphor

Throughout this book, we use the metaphor of a butterfly to represent the transformative learning process early childhood teachers go through in learning about the importance of self-care, discovering the culturally specific beliefs, practices and approaches to self-care that are accessible, authentic and restorative for them and then making the necessary changes in their personal and professional lives to care for themselves.

**FIGURE 0.1** Lifespan of the Butterfly

*Credit*: Alice Blecker

## Why Choose a Butterfly?

Although butterflies have different cultural meanings in different parts of the world, we chose to use a butterfly for this book as, universally, they represent change and transformation. They are also associated with renewal, hope, rebirth, love, happiness and changes that are about to happen in a person's life: changes that are inevitable for growth and for new opportunities to emerge.

We draw upon the butterfly to represent the transformative learning journey—the metamorphosis—that happens when educators increase their self-awareness of stress and its impact on their physical, emotional, social and spiritual health and well-being and become more consciously aware of the importance of integrating culturally responsive self-care in their personal and professional lives. As seen previously, the four quadrants represent important elements of this transformative learning process:

◆ *Caterpillar*. The job of a caterpillar is to eat, eat, eat as much as they can to prepare for the transformation ahead.

  *Applying this to an early childhood educator*: This is the time when educators are gathering different sources of information to influence and inform their learning journeys on such topics as the neurobiology of stress and trauma, burnout, compassion fatigue, secondary traumatic stress and the importance of self-care for job satisfaction and effectiveness and educators' mental and physical health. This information includes research and professional publications and stories of practice. And in doing so, educators are learning about themselves and the cultural values and practices they identify with as well as other perspectives and practices they are consuming that are external to their values.

◆ *Chrysalis*. Having eaten a significant amount, the caterpillar is now ready to enter the transition stage, becoming a chrysalis. At this time, the chrysalis finds a place where it can create a protected space for a period of time while it undergoes its profound transition: suspended under a branch, buried underground or hidden among some leaves. This time can last from a few weeks to a few years. Although it is often difficult to visually detect any change from the outside, internally, there are profound changes happening inside the chrysalis.

*Considering the metaphor of the chrysalis for this book*, we imagine educators having opportunities in protected environments—e.g., through self-reflection alone or in a group at work or outside of work, professional learning experiences, coaching, reflective supervision, communities of practice, completing the exercises in this book etc.—to engage in sense-making regarding the information they have received about stress, trauma and self-care to deepen their understanding of what it means for them personally and professionally and to begin to explore the changes they want to make in their lives as they continue on their learning journey. This looks like educators learning to build self-awareness about the ways their body responds to stress or beginning to question messages they have heard throughout their lives that they have to care for others at the expense of their own health and well-being or practicing breathing techniques that help them to calm down when their stress response systems are triggered. Although "change" is primarily reflected as positive change, there is also the potential for negative changes to occur in a transformative journey. Just as the educator with knowledge and use of self-care can increase her health and well-being, the lack of self-care practices and the buildup of stressors could, in contrast, lead to a decline in mental and physical health.

◆ *Eclose* is the name for the moment when the butterfly first emerges from the chrysalis. As it breaks out, its wings are soft and folded against its body, and it needs time to rest before pumping blood into the wings and then lifting into the air for its first flight.

*Applying this metaphor to educators' learning journeys,* we understand that there is a vulnerability at moments of change, and it takes time and patience to be ready to take flight into a life and intentionally choose or reclaim cultural values, beliefs, practices and opportunities. Yet, once ready, educators can break out of environments, relationships and practices they have discovered are unhealthy and unproductive for them and focus on transforming those things that are in their control so they can improve their health, professional effectiveness and overall well-being.

◆ *Butterfly.* The butterfly, now fully transformed, is free to fly around the environment. It spends the majority of its time searching for a safe place to lay its eggs, allowing the life cycle to start again.

Butterflies represent educators who understand the critical importance of self-care and integrate it into their practice on a regular basis. They understand that caring for the self is not just a nice thing to do but an essential element of professional responsibility and practice. They model self-care practices for others and advocate for the conditions that support healthy workplace environments.

The metaphor of the butterfly *also represents migration,* as many species of butterflies migrate to find food and ensure their survival. Some, like the monarch, migrate up to 2500 miles away. This experience is shared by many in the early childhood workforce in the United States who arrive in the country as refugees, asylees and immigrants from many countries across the globe hoping to find safety, survival and a quality life for themselves and their families.

The previous picture of the lifecycle of the butterfly intentionally represents *more than one butterfly going through a transformative process together*. Although an educator's journey to embrace self-care does have important individual elements as part of the process (represented by the image of the individual chrysalis undergoing its own personal growth and change), we emphasize the importance of positive trusting relationships; interdependence; connections with people, animals and nature and a sense of belonging and participation within communities as central to self-care for most people. As a result, we make this visible in the image by showing the metamorphosis of the individual caterpillar/chrysalis within an environment with others going through their own process of change, a metaphor for educators learning in the context of relationships with children, families, colleagues and other community members and in the context of their environments, including the land/nature.

> *Some people believe that when a butterfly crosses your path, it is a symbol that you should embrace the changes that are about to come into your life.*

We also chose *butterflies as a metaphor for early childhood teachers because of their diversity*. Butterflies are found throughout the world. The Smithsonian reports that there are approximately 17,500 species of butterflies in the world, close to 750 species in the United States alone (Smithsonian, n.d.). Butterflies represent diversity as seen through the wide variation in wing colors, patterns on their wings and the range of flowers and environments they prefer and thrive within. Despite so much differentiation, they also share some characteristics, as the large majority of butterflies live in warm climates, and for those that don't, they migrate during the winter to warmer environments. The different colors and patterns on the butterfly wings beautifully represent the diversity of educators as learners including their intersectional identities—each working within their own program and community contexts, with their specific cultural backgrounds, interests, strengths, learning edges and experiences with privilege and oppression. As early childhood educators, they also share a professional commitment to support young children and their families.

*The lifespan and well-being of a butterfly are entirely dependent upon the larger ecosystem in which they live and the health of their immediate environment.* Butterflies are highly impacted by changes in temperature, rainfall, use of pesticides and loss or fragmentation of their habitat (as a result of human activity, defoliation etc.). In fact, the presence or absence of butterflies is often considered a signal to scientists of the health of an ecosystem. We use this as a metaphor for the early childhood workforce and self-care. Early educators need to work within homes, centers, schools and organizations/systems where self-care is valued and actively supported through policies and practices. Educators will not see the benefits of self-care if the environments they work within are stress and trauma inducing. Like butterflies, educators' ability to thrive or to suffer is significantly impacted by the ecosystem around them. Toward this end, we include a discussion of the importance of self-care for administrators and other staff as well as healthy and healing workplace environments.

*The environment may have differential impacts on the well-being of a butterfly based on the specific attributes of different butterfly species* (Kelly, 2013). Butterflies' wing patterns may help them thrive in certain environments, keeping them safe from prey, for example, through camouflage. Relatedly, not all butterflies will find the same environment to be a good "fit" in terms of safety and well-being (Zhan et al., 2014). We relate this to cultural diversity among early educators, as certain early childhood environments and self-care practices will be culturally relevant and responsive to some educators but not to others. If an educator's work environment differs significantly from their family and home communities, this may cause some educators to be more vulnerable to stress and other negative outcomes as a result of the cultural incongruence with their own values, beliefs and cultural routines/practices. The field of early childhood emphasizes the importance of early learning environments being culturally and linguistically responsive to young children and families; however, this is also important for the early educators themselves. An environment that is not culturally familiar to early childhood staff will be more stressful and less supportive or healing than a program that intentionally strives to be culturally responsive to children, families *and* the educators serving them.

## Chapter Outline

Each chapter begins with an *inquiry question* to model the importance of reflective practice in early childhood pedagogy. In each chapter, we provide definitions of key terms, cite relevant research, introduce educator-friendly strategies for applying self-care in early childhood programs and provide authentic vignettes drawn from diverse individuals working in a wide range of early learning programs and organizations.

Throughout the book, *we use the word "educator"* to represent the diverse range of early childhood professionals who work directly with or on behalf of young children and their families. We understand that many adults who serve our youngest children use a range of other formal titles—e.g., *provider, caregiver, care teacher, care provider, child care provider, teacher aide, instructional aide, home care provider, substitute, volunteer, parent, caregiver* and others. Our decision to refer to "educators" throughout the book is only to provide a consistent term for readers. The <u>content of the book applies to all adults who work directly with or on behalf of infants, toddlers, preschoolers and early elementary-aged children</u>. This also includes administrators, professional development facilitators, coaches, mental health specialists/consultants, inclusion or disability specialists, foster/resource caregivers, family advocates and others working with or on behalf of young children and families.

We include *case studies and reflection questions*. The case studies include narratives of educators' authentic working conditions, including the various stressors they face inside and outside of work; their beliefs about self-care and the various practices they engage in to care for themselves, refresh their energy and keep their sense of hope alive. These case studies support readers to connect the various concepts introduced to their own lives and professional practice.

As a central goal of this book is to reflect a range of culturally informed perspectives on self-care, we worked as a team of authors to *gather diverse stories from a large group of individuals working in the early childhood field*. Specifically, the vignettes included throughout the book were gathered from 44 qualitative interviews and 250 online survey respondents who were invited to talk about a "typical day", stressors they experience at work and outside of work, their definitions of self-care and the strategies they use to reduce their stress and care for themselves. They were also asked to discuss any barriers they face that prevent or limit their ability to engage in self-care. The individuals who so generously shared their stories with us are working in a wide range of positions directly with or on behalf of young children and families, including:

- ◆ Family child care and family, friend and neighbor providers
- ◆ Infant/toddler, preschool, pre-K/transitional kindergarten, early childhood special education, kindergarten and early elementary (1st–3rd grade) teachers
- ◆ Early childhood professors and researchers
- ◆ Infrastructure staff (child care policy council, resource and referral and advocacy agencies)
- ◆ Family engagement and parent education coordinators
- ◆ Administrator/site supervisors and directors
- ◆ Coaches, professional development providers (trainers) and curriculum developers
- ◆ Social workers

◆ Home visitors, early intervention specialists, occupational therapists, speech language pathologists, behavioral technicians and mental health specialists.

Those who shared their stories with us are currently living in ten countries (Australia, Canada, Cyprus, Ireland, Mexico, Netherlands, Singapore, Spain, the United Kingdom and the United States. Respondents in the United States are living in 24 states across every part of the country, and many are first- or second-generation immigrants who came to the United States from Latin America, Europe, the Middle East, Africa and Asia. They range in age from 18 to 60+ years, and they represent the entire continuum of experience, from a novice entering her first year of teaching to several who have spent over 30 years in the field. Collectively they speak 17 different languages (Arabic, ASL, Cantonese, Dutch, English, Farsi, French, German, Hindi, Italian, Mandarin, Nepali, Norwegian, Portuguese, Russian, Spanish, Vietnamese), they identify with various races/ethnicities (30.09% White, Non-Hispanic; 25% Hispanic or Latino descent; 12.03% Black or African-American; 4.55% American Indian or Alaska Native; 4.55% Middle Eastern, Arab or North African; 11.36% Asian) and identify with different genders, including male, female, nonbinary, transgender.

Throughout the book we include *vignettes* that reflect their authentic stories about the stressors they face inside and outside of work, the forms of self-care that are authentic to them and the various barriers they face—and in many cases actively work to overcome—that stand in the way of their opportunities to care for themselves. We intentionally highlight these narratives throughout the book to position the educators as experts of their own experiences and to emphasize their agency and options for resistance, resiliency, healing and empowerment despite the marginalization and forms of oppression they endure working in the early childhood field. We consider the narratives they share a form of *counter-storytelling* (Solórzano & Yosso, 2002). Counter-stories are "a method of telling the stories of those people whose experiences are not often told" (p. 26). Counter-stories are an effective strategy for social justice educators who bring visibility to the experiences of individuals and groups who are often marginalized in society and/or whose voices are too often missing from consideration of the individuals in positions of power and decision-making, conditions that reflect the reality of educators in the field of early childhood.

Chapter 1, "The Impact of Stress and Trauma in the Lives of Early Educators", begins with a discussion of the current realities of the early childhood workforce, including compensation and working conditions, and a description of "a day in the life" of three early childhood educators is shared. Next, we make visible many different types of stress and trauma early educators experience inside and outside of work and connect this to a discussion of oppression. We also describe the various consequences of stress and trauma for early childhood educators and introduce the concept of allostatic load. We explain the importance of preventing burnout, compassion fatigue and secondary traumatic stress. This chapter ends by highlighting the importance of attention to the program/organizational climate when addressing educators' stress and provides a description of what it means to create equitable and safe, supportive and engaging workplace environments for early childhood educators. An oak tree is introduced as a metaphor to represent the image of an equitable health-oriented early childhood environments where the conditions are in place to support educators to work effectively, to grow and learn as professionals, to care for themselves and others and to be active participants in their own and others' healing engagement.

Chapter 2, "Foundations of Culturally Responsive Self-Care", begins with definitions of culture and a discussion of cultural conceptions of the "self" as a foundation for understanding culturally responsive self-care. We then describe research on the cultural neuroscience of stress and provide examples of culturally informed beliefs about healing. Next, we introduce several frameworks that expand our understanding of self-care and position it as a more equitable and inclusive concept and set of practices (e.g., decolonizing self-care, critical race theory, culturally sustaining practice and intersectionality). This chapter ends with the need to see educators' process of discovering culturally responsive self-care practices that are meaningful for them as a dynamic life-long journeys.

Chapter 3, "Building a Culturally Responsive Self-Care Toolbox", begins with a reminder about the culturally situated and individualized nature of effective and meaningful self-care and healing practices. With these principles in mind, the chapter then introduces a wide range of self-care strategies to support educators' health and healing; first, we describe approaches that focus on "tuning inward" and follow this with a description of strategies that encourage educators to "tune outward" emphasizing social connections and community. We end with the introduction of a tool, the Health and Wellness Toolkit, that educators can use to create a self-care plan that is accessible to and meaningful for them.

Chapter 4, "Case Studies: Applying Ideas Throughout the Book to Your Practice", presents five case studies to support readers to reflect upon, discuss and connect to the information introduced throughout the book. The case studies focus on five early educators: Anh Tham, an early childhood mentor teacher and coach; Monique Lee, a large family child care provider; Angelica Chacon, an infant toddler specialist; Maria Sandoval, an assistant director and teacher in a private school and Nelena Alegre, a mental health consultant working in a Head Start program. They each provide some details about their backgrounds and discuss their role, stressors they experience, their personal beliefs about self-care and the culturally responsive self-care practices they find most helpful and authentic to them. Each case study ends with reflection questions to guide educators' discussion of the concepts in the case and how they can apply them to their practice.

The end of the book includes important *resources* on self-care practices, including books, websites and self-care apps.

## Doménica's story

This butterfly indicates Doménica's story

*Vivian Gussin Paley* (1929–2019), a beloved preschool and kinder-garten teacher, author of 13 books and a 1989 MacArthur "genius", known for her keen observations and attunement in listening to young children, inspired early childhood educators to ask ques-tions about their practice and to continually strive to improve their teaching through cycles of observation, documentation, reflection and dialogue. In one of her most well-known books, *You Can't Say You Can't Play* (1993), she introduced an innovative strategy by integrating a complementary but distinct narrative from the main text—a story about Magpie, a make-believe bird indicated through the use of italics—throughout every chapter of the book. Each time readers saw the italics, they were queued to begin reading the evolving story of Magpie, whose adventures both aligned and extended the topics she was exploring in the book.

We draw inspiration from this literary device as both an expres-sion of gratitude for the manner in which Vivian Paley elevated the voices of young children and their teachers and the innovation, creativity and playfulness it introduces into a text. As she did with the Magpie, we introduce the story of Doménica Márquez, a mother, daughter, sister and child care advocate—by the use of italics inside this uniquely formatted textbox. Unlike the Magpie, which was a make-believe bird, Doménica's story is an honest and authentic rendering of her lived experiences, told in her own words. Winding her story throughout the book, readers have an opportunity to read a more deeply contextualized narrative that embodies the many concepts we introduce—culturally situated ways of knowing and being; intersectional identities; experiences of oppression and individual and collective sources of strength, resilience, coping and healing that cross over generations. We invite readers to follow her story and, in doing so, to use it as inspiration for generating your own questions to reflect upon. As Joan Didion (2006) reminds us, *we tell ourselves stories in order to live.* May the stories throughout this book inspire you to live in the ways that are the most meaningful to you.

> *The first time I heard the words—self care and leisure—I was in college . . . I remember feeling like it wasn't something for me. My mom raised me to believe that life, this life, is really about sacrifice and service—after all, that was the purpose she was raised with too. I remember a time I was driving with my parents and I was upset; my mom told me, "Oh, just let it go, move on." She said, "Stop worrying about being happy. Being happy is for the next life." And I said, "Okay mom, well, I'm gonna find the next cliff and I'm gonna drive off because I'm ready to be happy." And she said, "Are you crazy? That's not what I meant!" But I don't think she ever heard her words how I received them—if there's no joy for this life, what is the purpose. I never realized how much I'd been fighting to hold on to that joy, and at times against the one person who believed that if we can let go of hope for it, then we can wait for it to come in the next life.*
>
> *Recently I have been trying to set up boundaries for myself and that has come off as highly offensive to my family, and especially my mom, basically not wanting to engage with certain people at Thanksgiving and just refusing to go because I no*

*longer felt safe or welcome. My mom was really like, "You have to go, you have to go for your in laws." She felt like, "You need to go to be there for your mother in law especially," "It'll make her happy," she said. And I've been sharing all the anxiety that I've been having over going back to the house where they typically host Thanksgiving and I said, "I'm not doing that." I finally asked my mother, "Did you have me for other people's joy? Did you have me to sacrifice me for another person's joy? Is that why I'm here?" Because she was essentially telling me, it doesn't matter if you're uncomfortable just suck it up and go for others. And I think that was the first time that she paused and was just like, "Okay." She dropped it. I've realized that whenever it comes to those kinds of breaking points or having to set any kind of firm boundaries, it's never received as self care, or self preservation. The personal toll is never tracked, but the imposition or discomfort imposed on others is weighed as more important. I can accept now that this is simply how my mom had to survive—fighting the reality that her life was in service of others could've possibly been too much—or kept her from where she is today.*

*I think my parents had a life of sacrifice. They didn't really have time to complain. They had to survive. They had to navigate an entirely new world and then raise their family in this new world. I think self-care is really, it's a luxury, it's a privilege. So, I have to be able to think about what it truly means to me . . . I have to look for it in the daily rituals. I have to see it in our engagement, love, and care for one another, in what looks like work and feels like joy and freedom. I have to see that if I can't be my full self, it's not worth being, and that is my charge, for my survival.*

*My father came as a bracero\* to this country when he was in his twenties. His mother was very ill, he came with his father and his brother and when his mother passed away, his father did not tell him. He didn't tell either of his sons because they had just gotten to the States and so he figured, why? He couldn't afford to go to return to Mexico anyway, and so he just didn't* *tell them. When my father found out, he just cried and cried, he would be working, and just crying all day. His brother expressed just how much he wished he could cry because he just couldn't, he couldn't feel anything. They were expected to repress any vulnerability, any emotions, and I think that was part of it. I can't imagine what that must have been for them, because for me, in recently losing my father, I've been feeling so sick ... just vomiting anxiety, I feel like I'm just wearing this emotional corset all the time, at least when I'm trying to work, or function, or focus. And I just think of how much they (my parents) had to put up with and all the sacrifices. No matter how much I get frustrated at work it's like, "Well, this is still not as bad." And so it's almost a test of my limits to handle the stress. And now, I usually don't realize I've hit the limit, until I've passed my own threshold.*

### Reflection Questions

- ◆ What historical, cultural and family values, beliefs, expectations or norms were passed down to you verbally or non-verbally about self-care?
- ◆ What verbal and non-verbal messages did you receive growing up when you attempted to take care of yourself?
- ◆ What differences or tensions relating to notions of taking care of yourself can you identify between how you were raised and what you may currently believe and practice?

*The Bracero program was established by executive order in 1942; it allowed Mexican citizens to come to the United States to work on farms and on railroads, making it possible for the US economy to keep up with the demands of the war effort.

## Note

1. Decolonization is defined and discussed in Chapter 2.

# 1

# The Impact of Stress and Trauma in the Lives of Early Educators

*What creates stress for early educators and what is the impact on their health, well-being and professional practice?*

**Key Topics Covered**

- ♦ Current Realities of the Early Childhood Workforce
- ♦ Sources of Stress and Trauma Early Educators Experience Inside and Outside of Work
- ♦ Consequences of Stress and Trauma for Early Childhood Educators
- ♦ Preventing Burnout, Compassion Fatigue and Secondary Traumatic Stress
- ♦ Attending to the Program/Organizational Climate to Address Educators' Stress

*Early Educators Across the United States and Internationally Described Their Stressors to Us. . . .*

## What are your biggest stressors?

Lack of energy  Excessive workload
Policies conflicting with best practice    Political climate
Family pressures  Mental health   Family illness  Meetings  Job insecurity
Racism  Traffic  Finances. Money. Bills.  Health
Communication with parents    Lack of recognition    Safety
Not enough time  Social political strains
Long Hours  Deadlines   Lack of work-life balance   Commuting
Lack of resources   Communication with Administration
Disengaged colleagues    Lack of funding    Challenging Behavior
Trauma  Microaggressions  Inexperienced Staff    Unrealistic Timelines
High expectations  Poverty  Lack of support
Housing insecurity    Emails        Single parenting
Under-staffing  Debt  Navigating Cultural Differences
Low pay  No benefits  Language barriers  Ageism
Juggling too much  Paperwork  Parenting
Oppression  Caring for relatives  Discrimination  Needing help

# Current Realities of the Early Childhood Workforce

Working as an early childhood educator is one of the most important roles in our society. It is during the first five years of a child's
life that their brain development is most rapid (Azevedo et al.,
2009; Conkbayier, 2017; Herculano-Houzel, 2009; Rogers, 2011).
Neural growth in the vulnerable and developing brain is strongly
influenced by environmental conditions and a direct result of
the various experiences a child has, whether developmentally
supportive or traumatic and impairing. Through healthy and
caring relationships, play, exploration of their environment
and responsive communication where adults help children feel
safety and belonging in their families and communities, children
develop healthy synaptic connections that become a neurobiological foundation supporting their future academic learning and
social-emotional health. Similarly, early experiences of chronic
stress and trauma can interrupt normal synaptic growth, leading a young child's brain to develop differently, with negative

outcomes that can last a lifetime without proper intervention. This is why the early childhood years are so critical. *Early childhood educators have a tremendously important role in guiding children's healthy brain development.* As Wolfe (2007) explains, early childhood educators not only support young children's learning, they are in a profession that impacts children's biological wiring (cited in Rushton, 2011, p. 92).

Despite the critical and profoundly important nature of the work they do, *working in early childhood is among the lowest-paid jobs in the country,* a reality with significant consequences for the workforce—primarily women, almost 40% of whom are women of color—and the children and families they serve (Whitebook et al., 2018; McLean, Whitebook, & Roh, 2019). The absence of a livable wage and other factors related to poor compensation (e.g., lack of health care, dental care or retirement benefits; little or no paid time off including sick leave, vacation, family leave and the absence of paid time to complete such professional responsibilities as curriculum planning, child assessment and administrative paperwork) negatively impact early childhood educators' sense of emotional and physical health and well-being, as they experience significant economic vulnerability and feelings of worry about how to pay their monthly bills, afford housing and medical costs and even feed their families (McLean et al., 2019). Researchers at the Center for the Study of Child Care Employment at the University of California, Berkeley, have documented the high percentage of early childhood educators whose families rely on public income support and health care programs (e.g., Federal Earned Income Tax Credit [EITC], Medicaid and the Children's Health Insurance Program [CHIP], Supplemental Nutrition Assistance Program [SNAP] and Temporary Assistance for Needy Families [TANF]), programs that target the lowest-earning households in the United States. Specifically, they have documented that one-half (53%) of child care worker families and 43% of preschool and kindergarten teacher families rely on these subsidies, percentages that are much higher than elementary and middle school teachers (21%) and/or the overall US workforce (21%; McLean et al., 2019).

In addition to low compensation, many other factors contribute to the *poor working conditions early childhood educators experience*. Teachers rarely have access to the types of supports that are routinely provided in most other occupations, including paid time *during work hours* to complete responsibilities associated with their job expectations (e.g., conducting observations, completing documentation and assessments, planning for curriculum and instruction, taking breaks, meeting and reflecting with supervisors and colleagues, completing paperwork). It is common for early educators to complete these responsibilities during their own unpaid time (evenings and weekends) or while simultaneously supervising children. Further, early educators have few if any opportunities to participate in professional learning opportunities and/or provide input and participate in decision-making regarding the policies and practices that directly impact them at the workplace (Whitebook, King, Philipp, & Sakai, 2016). In addition to the lack of support available, early childhood educators are offered inadequate incentives/rewards for increasing their education, professional learning and experience (e.g., Whitebook et al., 2016).

We know from research that *poor compensation and inadequate working conditions negatively impact early childhood educators' capacity to engage in the type of responsive, attuned, intentional interactions with children* that are most critical to support children's healthy brain development, to optimize children's learning capacity (McLean et al., 2019) and to buffer the stress and negative outcomes that result for children impacted by trauma (Nicholson et al., 2019; Perry, 2014). Poor compensation also makes it challenging to recruit and retain early educators in the field and leads to high turnover rates/low retention for staff who are in the field, factors that negatively impact program quality (McLean et al., 2019).

Juxtaposed with these realities, early childhood as a field is increasingly finding itself in the public spotlight, capturing the hearts and minds of a wider and more diverse group of stakeholders. Citizens and policymakers in the US have historically shared a collective hesitation to use public funds to invest in the first five years, preferring instead to position the responsibility on the backs of parents, as the care and education of young children has long been regarded as the private domain of the family (Beatty, 1995). However, it is now widely understood among policymakers and funders that 90% of children's brain development occurs by the age of five years (Casey, Tottenham, Liston, & Durston, 2005; Halfon, Shulman, & Hochstein, 2001), and investments in high-quality early learning programs result in the most significant return, unparalleled by educational interventions at any other period in a child's educational trajectory (Heckman, 2008; Heckman & Masterov, 2007; Heckman, Moon, Pinto, Savelyev, & Yavitz, 2010; Heckman, Stixrud, & Urzua, 2006). In response, *a wide range of state and federal policy initiatives in the United States are being directed at investing in early childhood, and with these investments come additional pressure, stakes and scrutiny, all of which directly impact the early childhood workforce.* Examples of these pressures are seen with the push for greater professionalization, expansion of Quality Rating and Improvement Systems (QRIS) and other efforts to improve the quality of early childhood programs through coaching, training, technical assistance and external program rating and evaluation.

## A Day in the Life of Early Childhood Educators

Early childhood educators have long days, juggle many responsibilities, endure significant stress and most are very passionate about what they do. Let's see the world through the eyes of a few of these dedicated professionals:

First is Natalia Suarez, a lead teacher in the two-year-old classroom at Bright Horizons, a corporate child care center in

California. She shares a peek into a typical day for her, navigating public transit with her child to get to and from work while also managing the impact of the high amount of teacher turnover at her center due to the low compensation and lack of benefits child care teachers receive:

> *I wake up at 5:30 in the morning every day. I make my two children's lunch boxes so they can go to school. My husband drives me to BART (public transit) and I take a train with my youngest son to the city. We get off at East Street, I drop him off at his school and then I get back on BART, come all the way to my center and then I work all day from 8:30 to 5:00pm. Then, when I leave work at five, I go pick up my son at school, we get back on BART, arrive at the station and then drive home. When I get home, I have to cook dinner, feed the kids, then feed myself, clean the kitchen. Sometimes I sleep with my son because I'm trying to put him to bed and while I'm reading to him, I fall asleep.*
>
> *Commuting on BART is very stressful. It's crowded, it never has a place to sit, even though it's kind of disgusting to sit anyway. It's crowded, there are a lot of people, people with no respect, people pushing each other. They try to put as many people inside the train as they can, even though it's so packed. It's very stressful. Especially, because I commute with my kid, it's even more stressful. And then at work it's stressful because we have a lack of teachers because the teachers don't get paid enough money so they leave their jobs. This means we don't have an opportunity for team building together and it starts to pile up more responsibilities on our remaining teachers. Then they start thinking about leaving too because they start to get very stressed and burned out. There are times when I have five kids crying at the same time. It's very hard. I just have two arms and then my coworker has two arms. We need more teachers . . . or I need to become an octopus. When the few*

*teachers we have start to all get burned out, at some point, they are all going to leave.*

Another example is with Mariana Reyes, a site supervisor working in a state-subsidized preschool program. Mariana works long hours taking care of children inside and outside of work. She is very committed to helping others and honest that she is not consistent about ensuring her own needs are met, especially stopping to eat throughout the day:

*My typical day, right now, I get up at 4:00 in the morning and because I live so far away from my workplace, and I need to commute, I leave for the gym at 5:00 in the morning. Then from the gym around seven, I take the bus and I come to work and start work at 7:30 in the morning. I work until 4:00 or 4:30pm. The day here is very busy . . . supervising the teachers, seeing the children, and when the teachers are not here, I cover for them. I also cover the teachers in the kitchen. . . . Sometimes I don't have time to take a break or to eat breakfast or lunch. The most important thing is to make sure the teachers are okay, give them the support that they need in the classrooms and to see that the children are happy and safe. That is the most important thing for me during the day. In the afternoon, I walk to the bus station, I take the bus and I get home around 6:00pm. Sometimes I don't eat dinner because I take care of my granddaughters. So, after they go to sleep, I go to sleep at 10:00pm. I wake up again at 4:00am and the day goes on. That is the routine that I have every day.*

These are only a few of the thousands of stories that represent the complex daily schedules of the dedication and passionate professionals working in early childhood. Rising early, public transit, long commutes, juggling multiple responsibilities, caring for others throughout the day and night. In these stories, there is stress and coping, exhaustion and generosity, tuning in to others' needs and sacrificing one's own.

**Reflection Questions**

- ◆ What does your average workday look like?
- ◆ Do you have any stressors like the previous examples that you experience with your daily schedule and routine?
- ◆ Do you ever feel like an "octopus", where you have to give to so many people from the minute you wake up until you go to bed?
- ◆ With all you have on your plate each day, are you able to carve out any "me" time? If so, what do you do for you in the middle of an "octopus day" where you are pulled in so many directions from sunrise to sunset?

## Stress and Trauma Early Educators Experience Inside and Outside of Work

> *Stress and self-care honestly go hand in hand. I think dealing with stress and finding proper ways to take self-care, it fine tunes with experience and wisdom. Like an aged wine.*
> *—Martín Fuentes, Family Advocate and Early Childhood Mental Health Specialist*

> *Even though I'm not a teacher, I work with teachers, home visitors and family child care providers. I feel their stress, and if I could go in and wave a magic wand, I would to take away the stress. There are so many levels of it.*
> *—Joyce Darbo, Head Start, Special Services Manager*

As reflected in the words of Martin Fuentes and Joyce Darbo, the early childhood workforce faces a wide range of stressors inside and outside of work, and these stressors impact early educators' professional work. Whitebook et al. (2016) explain,

> Children's well-being and learning are directly influenced by the emotional and physical well-being experienced by the adults primarily responsible for their education and care. . . [there is a] breadth of financial concerns affecting many teaching staff, including being able to feed their families or meet monthly expenses. The stress caused by low pay and inadequate benefits is often exacerbated by expectations to complete job tasks

during unpaid time or to work when ill, undependable breaks or schedules, and the absence of financial reward for professional advancement. The tenor of relationships among colleagues in a program is another important contributor to teacher well-being, influencing the ability of staff to work effectively as a team. . . . In a system dedicated first and foremost to the well-being of children . . . the emotional and physical well-being of its workforce is often neglected.

(p. 50)

An essential first step in a journey to embrace self-care is for educators to discover and acknowledge the main sources of stress that impact them personally and professionally (Lipsky, 2009). *Only after their sources of stress have been identified and named can educators begin to work on ways to manage and reduce the negative impact of these stressors on* their own health and well-being and their daily work with children, families and/or other adults.

---

### Low Compensation Is a Major Stressor for Early Childhood Educators

*The most stressful thing to me? There's day-to-day stress that I carry in my body. But then there's also this future stress of just the precarity of my work. I'm trying to save a little bit of money but it's nothing significant that will help. It's more like, "Okay, if I crashed my car I'll be able to fix it. But, I'm not going to be able to retire." I don't know what I'm going to do as I age and as my partner ages, but I want to keep doing what I love.*

*—Encian Pastel, Preschool Teacher*
*I'm stressed out about finances. I'm stressed out about retirement*
*—Joyce Darbo, Special Services Manager, Head Start*

*Working as a teacher in early childhood is one of the lowest-paid jobs in the nation.* "In 2017, median wages for early educators ranged from $10.72 per hour (or $22,290 full-time per year) to $13.94 per hour (or $28,990 full-time per year). These are quite literally poverty-level wages: the federal poverty threshold for a family of four in 2017 was $24,600" (McLean et al., 2019, p. 1).

Across the United States, early childhood educators "are in economic distress, and . . . this financial insecurity falls disproportionately on women of color, who comprise about 40 percent of this workforce" (Whitebook et al., 2018, p. 18).

The racial wage gap in early childhood disproportionately impacts early educators of color, primarily because they are more often working as teaching assistants as well as working with infants and toddlers (Whitebook et al., 2018). African American early educators working in center-based programs are more likely to earn less than $15 per hour than teachers from other racial/ethnic groups. Additionally, even with the same educational background, "African American workers earn lower wages than white workers ($0.78 less per hour, or $1,622.40 less per year, for a full-time, full-year worker). Women of color also hold fewer leadership positions in the field" (p. 27).

## Connecting Stress and Oppression

As the early childhood workforce is primarily women, a significant percentage are women of color and, as noted previously, almost half live in poverty and qualify for public subsidies, early childhood educators *experience many forms of oppression*. To oppress is to "hold down—to press—and deny" a group full access to resources in a society (DiAngelo, 2016, p. 61). Oppression is what happens when one group—the *dominant* (or sometimes called the "agent" group) has the power to enforce their prejudice and discrimination against another group, the *minoritized* (or the "target" group) throughout the society. Examples of oppression include racism, sexism, classism, ableism and ageism, among others.

## Examples of Different Minoritized and Dominant Groups

| Minoritized/Target Group | Dominant/Agent Group |
|---|---|
| People of Color | White (or in some cases light-skinned individuals) |
| Poor, Working-Class | Middle-Class, Wealthy |
| People with Disabilities | Able-Bodied |
| Elderly | Young, Middle-Aged |
| Women | Men |

*Source*: DiAngelo, 2016, p. 64

*How is a minoritized group "held down" by the dominant group?* Through policies, practices, traditions, norms, definitions, cultural stories and explanations (for events and/or circumstances) that use a deficit perspective to represent the minoritized group and give power and benefits solely to the dominant group (DiAngelo, 2016). A good example of this is seen within early childhood in the historical treatment of early educators. McLean et al. (2019) explain,

> It is no coincidence that a field that has been dominated by women—nearly half of whom are women of color—is also one of the lowest-paid occupations. Historic patterns of discrimination against women and people of color in the wider labor market have systematically pushed these groups into lower-paying jobs by discriminatory practices, such as limiting their access to education and higher-paying jobs or paying less for these jobs. Lower wages for women, in particular, were historically justified

based on the pervasive, but factually incorrect, idea that women were not responsible for supporting a family, and therefore, women's wages did not need to be as high as men's.

(p. 5)

---

**Prejudice:** "Pre-judgment about another person based on the social group to which that person belongs. Prejudice is based upon characteristics we *assume* others have due to their group memberships. . . . Prejudice consists of *thoughts, feelings, assumptions, beliefs, stereotypes, attitudes, and generalizations.* . . . All humans have learned prejudices . . . it is instantaneous and occurs at the pre-cognitive level (before I can consciously think about it or control it)" (DiAngelo, 2016, pp. 46–48).

**Discrimination:** "Unfair <u>action</u> toward a social group and its members that is based upon prejudice about that group. Discrimination occurs at the individual level; all humans discriminate. . . . Actions (based in discrimination) include ignoring, excluding, threatening, ridiculing, slandering and violence" (pp. 52–53).

**Prejudice + Discrimination + Power = Oppression** (p. 62)

*Caring for and teaching young children is often falsely and unjustly perceived as non-professional work, and the early childhood workforce is frequently perceived to be unskilled "babysitters" (prejudice); these attitudes/beliefs have led to historically low compensation and few or no incentives for professional advancement for early educators (discrimination), a cycle of oppression that is reinforced by excluding early childhood from many sources of federal and state funding (power).*

*A specific form of oppression experienced by many in the early childhood workforce is structural racism.* Structural racism is defined as systematic and disproportionate marginalization of People of Color across institutions of our society. Individuals participating in these systems often do not see themselves as being racist or as participating in practices that are racist. They might even be actively working against racism. However, structural racism does not occur at the interpersonal level (one-on-one interactions). Instead, structural racism represents the phenomenon that organizations and social institutions systematically, historically and unequivocally provide benefits to certain groups over others, resulting in racial inequalities in opportunities and experiences across many systems in our society. What are examples of these systems or societal structures? As pictured subsequently (see Figure 1.1), examples include our systems of education,

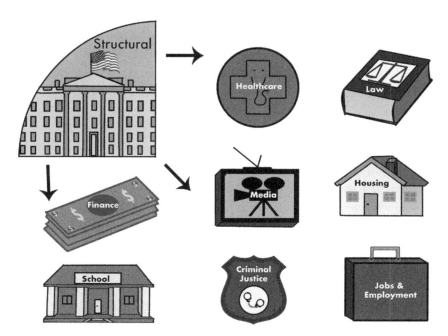

**FIGURE 1.1** Structural Racism: What Is Meant by Structural?

*Credit*: Alice Blecker

law/policies, finance/banking, employment/business, health care, housing, media, criminal justice and organized religion. People of Color face significant structural barriers in housing, health care, employment and education and within the criminal justice system that White individuals do not experience (see, for instance, Alexander, 2010; Bailey et al., 2017; Hanks, Solomon, & Weller, 2017). These systematic practices have consequences that are cumulative.

Teresa Fuller, a Latina director of an early childhood center, describes the stress she experiences from the impact of racism, especially given the current political context in the United States with an increase in hate crimes across the country (U.S. Department of Justice, n.d.) and people of color, especially Latinx immigrants, being targeted for deportation and violence (Sanchez, 2019). Dr. G. Cristina Mora, a sociologist at the University of California, Berkeley, who specializes in immigration and race politics, has documented how the current political context in the country is generating a deep sense of unease for Hispanic Americans like Teresa, no matter how long they or their families have lived in the country (Romero, Dickerson, Jordan, & Mazzei, 2019). Educator Teresa explains how she carries this stress with her as she goes about her daily business:

> A big stressor is just the political state of where our country is right now. The amount of disrespect, I just see it every day, it's just awful. People have been given permission to treat others horribly. I don't like to turn on the news. . . . I have to block out some things, because it becomes so overwhelming. I feel powerless about it. Absolutely powerless . . . recently, I went on a long trip to go meet a friend for a weekend. And as I'm driving through the desert, I thought, "Okay, if I were dressed differently, if I had a different accent, if I drove in a different car . . . if someone were to just approach me . . . my life could severely change just by how I look because I'm a Hispanic woman" . . . it's very painful.

*Self-care, as a practice and as a lifestyle, is an ongoing effort for women of color. To center ourselves, our needs and our goals often feels counter-intuitive . . . I still battle this idea in my mind that I should feel guilty . . . that prioritizing myself is somehow selfish or damaging. In reality, those harmful ideas are a part of us because we have internalized systems of oppression. Patriarchy, white supremacy and capitalism rely on us valuing paid and unpaid labor over ourselves and our happiness. What I want is for us to learn how to dismantle the negative feelings that we have attached to caring for ourselves. It is vital for us to learn how to be kind to ourselves, not necessarily for the benefit of others but for our own benefit. I want us to thrive. I want us to be well-rested, well-hydrated, moisturized, glowing and in love with ourselves, despite a world which tells us not to be. But what does that look like when you have kids, multiple jobs or when you're struggling with PTSD? I do not ask for help. I do not want to shatter the illusion of my strength. So I carry trauma on my shoulders until I break. I don't want to burden anyone with my needs because I don't want to be an inconvenience to anyone. Part of learning to love myself means shedding that sort of thinking. It takes time, but this piece is a step towards a positive direction.*

Lara Witt (2017a).
*Why decolonizing self-care fuels our resistance.*

*Oppression is held in place by CONNECTED SYSTEMS that overlap and reinforce one another.* Each form of oppression (e.g., racism, classism, ageism etc.) has distinctive characteristics and specific histories that distinguish it from other forms of oppression. However, the different forms of oppression in society interact with one another as connected systems that overlap and reinforce each other. For example, although racism and ableism are different systems of oppression, they also over-lap and reinforce one another in ways that have impacts at structural/institutional and individual/interpersonal levels. For example, a Black male with a disability would face the cumulative effects of oppression resulting from his membership in two minoritized groups based on his race and his disability (Bell, 2016, p. 13).

Drawing from Marilyn Frye (1983) and Robin DiAngelo (2016), we use a birdcage metaphor to describe the way that oppression is held in place by connected systems that overlap and reinforce each other.

**FIGURE 1.2** Birdcage Metaphor: Oppression Is Held in Place by Connected Systems

*Credit*: Alice Blecker

## The Birdcage Metaphor

Source: DiAngelo (2016, p. 71 adapted from Frye, 1983)

The metaphor of a birdcage has been used to explain the connected forces of oppression that overlap and mutually reinforce one another. The metaphor is explained in the following way:

If you were standing close to a birdcage and pressing your face against it, you would see the bird close up, but your awareness of the wires on the cage would be limited. Turning your face slightly so you could look closely at one of the wires of the cage would take away your ability to see the other wires. If you remained looking at just that one wire, you might wonder why the bird could not escape and fly away. This would be true if you continued walking around the cage to see the bird from different positions. As long as you continued pressing your face against the cage and limited your view to this close-up perspective, you might perceive that the bird had freedom to fly away. If you take a step back so you can see the entire birdcage, you would notice the different wires and how they lock together in a pattern, creating a strong barrier that holds the bird in place, placing significant restrictions on its opportunities and freedom.

The birdcage metaphor can help us understand why oppression is difficult for many people to see and recognize: We have a limited perspective and understanding of the world based on how we are positioned in society. Just as your understanding of the bird and its freedom (or lack thereof) would change based on where you stood in relation to the cage—and therefore how much of the cage you could see—the same is true for the oppressive forces in society. We are socialized to focus on our own experiences, our personal intentions and individual actions when thinking about injustice (e.g., an individual from the dominant group advocating for the rights of a minoritized group). However, focusing on single events or the actions of specific people does not allow us to acknowledge or "see" the existence and significant impact of the broader, interlocking patterns of oppression that exist across our society.

*For the early childhood workforce, the birdcage metaphor makes visible the connected forces that result from different forms of oppression—often racism, sexism and classism—that have a combined impact on educators' personal experiences with stress and trauma.*

**Reflection Questions**

◆ Oppression can be difficult to recognize. Reflect, write or discuss with someone else why this is the case.

◆ How might the birdcage metaphor help you to understand your personal experiences with stress, trauma and oppression?

◆ What's important to you about oppression and what do you still want to learn more about?

## Prevalence of Trauma in Adults Across the United States

The U.S. Department of Health and Human Services Substance Abuse and Mental Health Services Administration (SAMHSA, 2018) defines trauma in the following way, "Individual trauma results from an event, series of events, or set of circumstances experienced by an individual as physically or emotionally harmful or life-threatening with lasting adverse effects on the individual's functioning and mental, physical, social, emotional, or spiritual well-being". Trauma affects children and adults in every state, county and city in America. Trauma impacts people across all racial, ethnic, income and education levels, family constellations, geographic locations and community groups. Trauma has been described as our nation's single most important public health challenge (van der Kolk, 2014) that is too often silenced and unacknowledged for its significant prevalence and devastating impact in our public dialogue (Craig, 2016). Within the United States, 61% of men and 51% of women report exposure to at least one lifetime traumatic event (SAMHSA, n.d.)

To date, we do not have any empirical studies documenting adverse childhood experiences (ACEs) and/or experiences with trauma for the early childhood workforce. However, we do have research suggesting that early childhood teachers experience high levels of anxiety and depression (Whitebook et al., 2016). Additionally, as authors, our collective experiences working in the field for many years and leading trauma training for many early educators has made clear to us that ACEs and experiences of trauma are significant for many in the early childhood field. Not only do early educators work with trauma-impacted children and families, many are managing traumatic experiences in their families and lives outside of work.

Fawzia Saffi, a site director and teacher at a Head Start program, is an example of an early childhood educator who is managing her own trauma and loss while having to hear and be responsive to the stories she hears daily from the families at her center. We hear in Fawzia voice not only the hardships she faces but also her tremendous strength, the coping skills she has developed, her resilience and, most importantly, her commitment to the field and being attuned to the children, families and staff in her care:

> *I came as an immigrant to this country from Afghanistan. My first language is Farsi. Two years ago, I lost my husband. I grew up with him. I was 18 when I got engaged. He was a good man, my best friend, my husband, my family, everything because I don't have family here except my kids. So, he was everything for me. And then when I lost him, I had no clue what to do. I was lost . . . my family is out in Afghanistan*

*except two of my siblings. One is in Germany, one is in Canada. The year I lost my husband I also lost my mom at the same time, and then I lost my niece to a suicide bomb when she was only 28 years old. And then I lost my brother who had battled with cancer. He was very close to me. It was very hard for me to share with people, my pain. . . . And then last year I had a plan to go visit my dad . . . I found out he passed. These things are stressful. When I'm going to work, I leave whatever I have out the door . . . I don't want to take my stress out on them. This is my stress. It's a lot because I have nobody to talk to . . . sometimes, I'm sitting and suddenly I start crying. It's hard for me to deal with it. I have to take care of the families, teachers, children and staff . . . they are all my responsibility. . . . I want to give my job 100% or more than 100%. This makes me happy, if I do something right and I do my work on time, this makes me happy . . . that I did something in my life. Working with low income families . . . these families are going through a lot, single families, divorce . . . abuse, this kind of stuff is stressful but you have to listen to the families while they share their stories. You have to listen to them. And then you have to show you are here for them . . . these families are struggling just to bring food to the table, to feed their kids. This field is stressful, no matter what. I try my best and I want to be a role model for my own children. That's why we came to this country, for an opportunity. We had to survive. That is why I was a role model for my children in learning English and then I went to college and university and then I started my career as an early child educator.*

Fawzia recounts her personal and family experiences with refugee and war-related trauma, terrorism and traumatic loss, stressors that she has primarily had to process on her own without the support of immediate or extended family. Compounding her own traumatic stress is the stress she absorbs into her mind and body on a daily basis as she works with children and families who experience their own sources of trauma, including child maltreatment and abuse, domestic abuse, community violence and homelessness, among others. Fawzia is a survivor, and we see in her story her strength and will to cope and build resilience in the face of all she experiences. And it is this layering of stress for early childhood educators—their own and the influence of the stress and trauma brought into the workplace by children, families and other staff/colleagues that creates the conditions for secondary traumatic stress and the urgency to address self-care for the workforce. Educators like Fawzia are committed to the children and their well-being. They deserve to work in a field that is committed to *their* health and healing.

### Reflection Questions

- ◆ Have you experienced immigration to another country? Or moved from a place that was more familiar to you culturally or linguistically? What stressors did this cause for you? How did you cope, and what people, activities or places helped buffer your stress? What other things helped you cope?
- ◆ Have any of the children and families you work with recently immigrated to this country? Have you been able to hear their stories? How do you provide them with support?
- ◆ Fawzia talks about how to take multiple stressors and be consciously aware to intentionally not bring the stress to her interactions with the children. Do you face that same dilemma—specifically, holding your stress and not having it impact the children? How do you do that?
- ◆ Fawzia mentions that she finds herself sitting and sometimes the tears just start coming to her. Do you have someone to talk to or ways you cope when you become flooded with emotion (whether at home or work)?
- ◆ Fawzia mentions why she became an early childhood educator and how she wants to make a difference for

children and families. How did you decide to become an Early Childhood Education (ECE) provider?

*In addition to the impact of poor compensation, structural racism and other forms of trauma, early educators endure many other stressors in the context of their daily lives.* Following are some of the most common stressors early educators talk about impacting their daily lives and professional work:

Karen Tapia describes a persistent stressor she personally experiences and observes throughout the field of early childhood, the lack of funding and resources leading to under-staffing in organizations/programs and the *need to juggle multiple roles and responsibilities and manage a ceaseless workload*:

> *I find in the organizations that I've worked with that there's been a lot of red tape and a lot of chaos and confusion in the organization involving roles. I think there's often expectations of workloads that are way, way, way, way too large, and that has always caused me stress, and it causes me stress to see other people working harder than they need to be working and not having a work-life balance. The workload is a huge stressor.*

Connie Wright, who works with a state department of education, describes the stress she experiences by the continual *need to advocate for the importance of early childhood*:

> *I find it stressful that we're all in early childhood and we know how important it is but I feel like a big part of my job is convincing other people, just how important early childhood is. It's frustrating to me because I feel like, it should be known by now but we still have to argue that and push what we need done.*

It's very stressful to work so hard on a daily basis; to earn degrees and participate in professional development; to advance in skills, knowledge, dispositions and experience over time and to have genuine areas of expertise that are valued by parents, families and communities while continually being discredited by society, struggling to be given credibility or acknowledged as a profession, fighting for visibility among policy- and decision-makers. As DiAngelo (2016) explains, The process of oppression begins with misinformation, misrepresentation and/or invisibility of a minoritized group and their authentic lived experiences, "the group's history, interests, needs and perspectives—their voices—are minimized or absent" (p. 84) and the dominant culture does not represent any of the strengths or assets of the group.

> Instead of being recognized as a professional field that requires specific skills, knowledge and expertise, "*Care work is commonly seen as unskilled or something that women 'naturally' do, often for free.* Perversely, low wages for working in early care and education are also sometimes seen as justified in exchange for doing personally satisfying work—the idea that early educators are 'paid in love'. As a result, there exists a pay penalty for working in care-related fields" (McLean et al., 2019, p. 5)

Elsa Karlsson, an early childhood special education teacher, experiences stressors that many other early childhood teachers experience: *children with behavior that is challenging to manage* and burdensome *paperwork* demands:

> *We have a lot of children with very, very, very challenging behaviors. So we're hit and kicked and bit. That's one stress. But one thing is you never take it personally because it's not directed at you. It's just part of their disability. . . . If I model deep breathing, sometimes they'll start watching me. And I teach belly breathing to the kids to help them learn how*

*to calm down. . . . Sometimes when I get really upset with a child, I go to the "Peace Place" [a place in our classroom] to calm down and I say, "Ms. Elsa needs time in the Peace Place." I go there and I will deep breathe. If I'm stressed, it helps me calm down. The other thing that creates stress is the paperwork, the paperwork and the demands we have from our school district and the things that we have to do. That's really the hardest part of the job and there's nothing you can really do about that stress. You just keep working and working and try and get through all the paperwork. . . . The paperwork causes a lot of burnout in teachers. Some days you just want to scream and tear your hair out, but you just have to keep going through it to get it done.*

Although the early childhood workforce engages with many children and families who are highly impacted by trauma, they experience many stressors as adults and many report having experienced a high number of adverse childhood experiences, *very few learn about the neurobiology of stress and trauma*—for children and adults—in their coursework or professional development. On the contrary, early childhood professionals are communicating nationwide that they are not prepared with the skills, knowledge or strategies that they need to understand and work effectively with children and adults (including themselves) who have experienced trauma. This is no surprise, as the early childhood field has few resources on trauma-informed practices developed specifically for early childhood programs, which was the inspiration for our first book (Nicholson et al., 2019).

We need to address this critical gap and advocate for all teachers, providers, program leaders, specialists and staff and parents, guardians and family members to learn about the impact of stress and trauma across the lifespan and the essential factors that buffer short- and long-term negative impacts. It is important to remember that the most important protection children and adults can have from the negative consequences of trauma are positive relationships with caring and attuned adults who can buffer their stress and support them to develop coping skills and to build resiliency.

## Consequences of Stress and Trauma for Early Childhood Teachers

> *To put the world in order we must first put the nation in order; to put the nation in order; we must first put the family in order; to put the family in order, we must first cultivate our personal life; we must first set our hearts right.*
>
> —*Confucius*

Working in a demanding field with poverty-level wages, with many children and families who are impacted by trauma, in environments of scarcity with too few resources, high staff turnover and increasing expectations and pressure to increase quality and positive child outcomes takes a professional and personal toll on the lives of teachers, putting them at risk for burnout, compassion fatigue and/or secondary trauma (Perry, 2014). It is helpful for educators to build body awareness so they learn to identify signs of stress in their body. This awareness will help them interrupt the cycles of triggering their stress response systems and the circulation of dangerous neurochemicals throughout their brains and bodies, a cycle that, if continuous, can cause lifetime harm for adults' health, cognitive functioning and lifespan.

## Learning to Identify Physiological Responses to Stress: Fight, Flight, Freeze Reactions

When adults' fear activates their stress response system, their brains activate a *fight, flight or freeze* survival response based on the type and intensity of the threat (Balberni, 2001; Perry, Pollard, Blakley, Baker, & Vigilante, 1995; Schore, 2003; Stein & Kendall, 2004).

*Activating the stress response system is an automatic survival response from the adult's brain. This triggering response is involuntary*—it happens automatically and is not under an individual's control. It is driven by the lower brainstem for the sole purpose of self-preservation and survival (Porges, 2011). In a threatening condition, adults are unable to process information because their brainstem prevents the use of the pre-frontal cortex necessary for cognitive functioning. This means that adults who are in a fight, flight or freeze survival state are less able to engage in problem-solving, rational thought, focused attention, self-regulation of their emotions or behavior or to verbalize their experiences because the neural networks to their cortex are literally shut off in order to focus on survival. Only after the individual no longer perceives they are in danger, has calmed their central nervous system and returned to an optimal state of arousal can they begin to engage their cortex again (Nicholson et al., 2019). What are the consequences of this happening for early childhood educators?

## Signs for Adults That Their Stress Response Systems Are Activated

| Fight | Flight | Freeze |
| --- | --- | --- |
| Raises tone of voice | Calls in sick to work | Not able to stay up with work tasks |
| Directive and corrective | Walks away from children who have challenges | Shuts down emotionally and sometimes unable to think or speak |
| Physically redirecting child | Avoids problems with children, colleagues or supervisors | Goes through the motions of the day but is not tuned in to the children, others or themselves |
| Rushes over to protect other children and tells child to stop in stern tone | Makes excuses to leave a task or work | Cries alone or isolates self |

**Reflection Questions**

◆ It is human nature under stress to protect ourselves by defaulting to fight, flight or freeze. When we have too much stress not balanced by restorative activities, we can default more readily to our primitive fight, flight and freeze brain. Can you describe an example when you had so much stress that you were in your fight, flight and/or freeze (F, F, F) brain?

◆ When you were in your F, F or F brain, can you describe the following:

   ◆ What were the sensations in your body (i.e., heart racing, getting warm, headache, sweaty palms, numb, feeling nothing)?

   ◆ What were the feelings you had?

   ◆ What thoughts, if any, were going through your head (often it is hurting others, self or property)?

   ◆ What behaviors did you exhibit?

   ◆ Who was adversely impacted when you were in fight, flight or freeze?

---

### The Central Nervous System: The Command Center for the Stress Response System

Stress is a biological and psychological response that a person experiences when they are faced with social challenges and do not have the resources to cope. The hypothalamic-pituitary-adrenal (HPA) axis in the brain is in charge of the stress response. The HPA system works with the autonomic nervous system to release hormones that are vital to manage stress (Pally, 2000).

The *autonomic nervous system* is responsible for our survival and regulates our body's central unconscious processes (breathing, sleeping, hunger). It is divided into two systems, the sympathetic nervous system (SNS) and the parasympathetic nervous system (PNS), and both are involved in our neurobiological reaction to stress.

The *sympathetic nervous system* activates the fight or flight response and also maintains homeostasis (balance of the body's functions, including body temperature and balance of body fluids) in the body. Prolonged activation of the SNS can lead to the release of adrenaline in the body and is associated with increased arousal and increased activity. Moreover, the more often the SNS is activated, the more easily it is activated.

The *parasympathetic nervous system* is responsible for stimulation of several actions in the body, including salivation, urination/defecation, digestion and production of tears. Similarly to the SNS, the more often the PNS is activated, the more easily it is activated. Too much activation of the PNS increases the risk of developing psychiatric symptoms, including withdrawal, depression, helplessness and anxiety (Perry et al., 1995).

*Source*: Nicholson et al. (2019, p. 16)

## Neurochemicals Released by the Body When the Stress Response System Is Activated

*The stress level that's happening in early child education and then the lack of support that early child educators get is just incredible. . . . We need to do something because a lot of early childhood educators, they have weight problems, they have maybe high blood sugar, high blood pressure, and that can be taken care of. You really can take care of yourself.*
—Alexandra Morales, Coach and Trainer

*Adrenaline:* A neurochemical commonly referred to as the fight or flight hormone. It is produced by the body's adrenal glands after receiving a message from the amygdala that there is a potential threat or immediate danger. Adrenaline increases the body's heart rate, provides a surge of energy that helps us survive when we are in danger (e.g., helps us run away or move quickly) and helps to focus our attention (e.g., helps us scan our environment for signs of danger).

*Norepinephrine* (also called noradrenaline): A stress chemical similar to adrenaline released from the adrenal glands and from the brain that primarily increases arousal—responding to stress by increasing a person's ability to very quickly become more aware, awake, focused and responsive. Norepinephrine also creates the signal that leads blood to shift in ways that support survival (away from skin toward muscles to allow for "fleeing", away from limbs and toward organs to protect from injury).

*Cortisol:* Also a stress chemical released from the adrenal glands in a multi-step process: (a) The alarm center of the brain—the amygdala—perceives a threat and (b) signals the hypothalamus to release a hormone (corticotropin-releasing hormone), which then (c) signals the pituitary gland to release another hormone (adrenocorticotropic hormone), which then (d) tells the adrenal glands to produce cortisol. Cortisol is a helpful life-saving hormone when it is released in the body in moderate amounts. However, chronic stress elevates the production of cortisol in the body. When cortisol is continuously released in the body and the level of cortisol in the body is elevated on a persistent basis—as is the case with children and adults who experience toxic stress—it can cause tremendous damage to the brain and body, suppressing the immune system; increasing blood pressure and blood sugars; breaking down muscle, bone and connective tissue; contributing to obesity, leading to hypothyroid; and interfering with sleep, causing insomnia and night waking.

---

### What Is Allostatic Load?

Allostasis describes the process through which the body maintains stability through change (McEwen & Wingfield, 2003). When the brain perceives a stressor, allostasis mobilizes the biological systems in our bodies, including the release of neurochemicals and changes to our cardiovascular, gastrointestinal and immune systems in order to help our bodies prepare and adapt to a per-ceived incoming threat. The process of allostasis also helps to shut off the stress response system and to stabilize or return our internal systems to their normal functioning once the perceived threat is gone (McEwen & Wingfield, 2003; McEwen, 2006). Activating our body's biological stress response system is helpful and protective when we need to respond to an acute stressor. However, activation of the stress response system becomes harmful in cases of chronic stress, as returning to a state of rest is inhibited (McEwen, 2006). *Allostatic load* describes the accumulated "wear and tear" on our bodies from exposure to chronic stress (McEwen, 2000). High allostatic load is associated with the acceleration of disease and various negative physical and mental health outcomes, including:

◆ Emotional states of fatigue, anger, frustration and help-lessness (McEwen, 2006)

◆ Health-damaging behaviors, including overeating (Dall-man et al., 2003) smoking and binge drinking (Anda et al., 1990; Dube, Anda, Felitti, Edwards, & Croft, 2002)

◆ Suppression and dysregulation of immune system func-tion (Dhabhar, 2000), which can increase susceptibility to infection, delay the wound-healing process and decrease the body's response to immunization (Glaser, Sheridan, Malarkey, MacCallum, & Kiecolt-Glaser, 2000)

◆ Psychological disorders, including anxiety, depression, post-traumatic stress disorder and substance-use disor-ders (McEwen, 2006)

◆ Impacted cognitive functioning, such as memory and concentration impairment

◆ Increased risk of ill health, including sleep deprivation (Dallman et al., 2003), digestive problems, headaches, car-diovascular disease, obesity, diabetes and thyroid disor-ders (McEwen, 2006).

In addition to all of the negative health impacts that result from consistent exposure to stress chemicals, when *teachers are in a fight, flight or freeze survival state, they are less able to engage in problem-solving, rational thought, focused attention or self-regulation of their emotions or behavior* because the neural networks to their cortex are literally shut off in order to focus on survival. This can make it harder to maintain positive attuned responsive relationships with children *and* adults.

To interrupt this pattern, it is important for teachers to learn body awareness and to implement strategies to re-regulate when they internally perceive signs of stress, so they can work to remain calm and regulated and to manage their internal emotional state. Teachers can then use their calmness to attune to and co-regulate adults and children around them who are distressed. "Calmness" is contagious in our interactions with adults and children because of our mirror neurons.

> So when I get stressed in the classroom, when something happens in the classroom, the initial reaction is I want to have a very loud voice over the children, but I don't want to have a toxic environment because that's what I learned when I was a child. And so I just start singing. I just start singing and that is trying to calm me down. I sing children's songs and then the children sing with me and then it kinda calms us down and puts out the fires that are happening in the classroom.—Joanne Wilson, Family Child Care Provider

If you have done a body scan (e.g., pausing and paying attention to the sensations/signs of stress in your body) and notice stress physiologically in your body (i.e. increase in heart rate, sweating, becoming warm, shaking, head pounding, throat dry, feeling jittery, feeling numb), here are five things to try right away to regulate your central nervous system and remain calm or, in the case of a freeze stress response, to activate your arousal:

1. Take three deep belly breaths in through your nostrils and out through your mouth.
2. In advance, find a mantra or quote you can repeat to yourself over and over when you become triggered. For example, one teacher shared her quote that grounded her in stress, "Inner peace begins the moment you choose not to allow another person or event to control your emotions."—Pema Chodron.
3. Another teacher suggests pretending to put on a jet pack and mentally float above the situation as if looking down on it from the sky. He does this to help remove himself mentally and to gain perspective.
4. Think of a person, place or object that makes you feel safe and grounded. One teacher keeps a crystal rock in her pocket (safe object) that her mother (safe person) gave her. She holds it when she feels overwhelmed.
5. Seek out a ritual that can help you. Some teachers have said on their team they have a shared verbal clue or hand signal they need a two-minute break, and some get help by talking to another person (talking is like releasing steam from a tea kettle—releasing pent-up emotions can help calm). Others share that they pray to a higher power for inner strength.

## Preventing Burnout, Compassion Fatigue and Secondary Traumatic Stress: Restoring Your Energy

*Burnout* is described as a "reaction to job stress in which the focus is on the physical, emotional, and mental exhaustion caused by long-term involvement in situations that are emotionally demanding" (Pines & Aronson, 1988, p. 73) and a "psychological condition that involves a response to chronic stressors of the job" (Leiter & Maslach, 2004). Workplace conditions—workload, poor supervision, negative work environment, poor benefits or pay, difficulty with co-workers or excessive work demands and a lack of social support—have a cumulative effect and slowly develop into burnout over time (Gottlieb, Hennessy, & Squires, 2004; Maltzman, 2011). Burnout impacts individuals physically, emotionally, spiritually and/or mentally and results in emotional exhaustion and reduced feelings of personal effectiveness and accomplishment (Gottlieb et al., 2004; Maslach & Jackson, 1986).

---

### Cultural Differences in Burnout

How burnout may develop, be experienced and be visible may differ across cultures. Research on teachers and in other care-based fields such as nursing has found that burnout may impact some cultural groups differently or more than others (Aboagye, Qayyum, Antwi, Jababu, & Affum-Osei, 2018; Schaufeli & Janczur, 1994; Suñer-Soler et al., 2014). For example, researchers have found that health care professionals from Poland experienced higher burnout than those from the Netherlands, even when their work was similar (Schaufeli & Janczur, 1994). In another example, health care professionals in Spain experienced burnout very differently from their counterparts in Latin America (Suñer-Soler et al., 2014). These types of differences in stress and burnout across countries were rooted in cultural differences, such as types of social support systems or the role of religion (Pienaar & Van Wyk, 2006; Kaur & Noman, 2015). Therefore, even if working conditions may be similar for employees, these conditions may be experienced differently based on individuals' cultural background and experiences. This research reminds us that cultural differences may lead some employees to experience burnout more and/or differently than others.

---

*Burnout can be reduced or avoided if teachers learn to recognize the warning signs and if they actively plan for, and are supported to, engage in self-care practices.* When teachers buffer their stressors with self-care routines, their energy is restored and renewed. They have more reserves to pull from for maintaining a calm and regulated state and protecting themselves from the harmful impact of the continuous release of stress hormones in their bodies. Remaining calm also helps teachers to more successfully build and maintain caring and attuned relationships with children, families and their colleagues.

**Burnout can be avoided if:**
◆ Teachers learn to recognize the warning signs and symptoms of burnout.
◆ They actively plan for and engage in their own self-care.
◆ Supportive systems are present in the workplace.
◆ Cultural differences are understood, expressed and valued in the workplace.

---

*Burnout* impacts individuals physically, emotionally, spiritually and/or mentally and results in emotional exhaustion and reduced feelings of personal effectiveness and accomplishment.

**Warning signs of burnout include:**
◆ Feelings of negativity
◆ Feeling a lack of control
◆ A loss of purpose or energy
◆ An increased detachment from relationships and/or feeling estranged from others
◆ Feeling unappreciated
◆ Having difficulty sleeping
◆ Difficulty concentrating, continually feeling preoccupied
◆ Feeling trapped
◆ Difficulty separating personal life and work life.

Source: Gottlieb et al. (2004)

*I need to be a better advocate for myself and allow myself to take the time I need sometimes, and that doesn't come easily. I definitely divert to wanting to help others, and to being a person that says yes a lot, when sometimes I need to say no. And I think that when we further narrow that lens to professions that are really built around caring for others, whether that's nursing, or taking care of senior citizens, or any of those professions that are really based around how we support others in being healthy and being cared for, I think it's important for us to highlight why that might be a struggle for us to then to shut that off and to take care of ourselves. As much as I hear that saying, put your mask on before you put on someone else's that they talk about in an airplane, and as much I logically know and recognize that, it doesn't mean that it's easy to do.*
*—Grace Macmillan, Early Childhood Director,*
*Consultant and Trainer*

Burnout that is not addressed may turn into *compassion fatigue*. With prolonged stress and a lack of self-care activities in an adult's life to restore and buffer their stress, an individual may begin to suffer from compassion fatigue symptoms (O'Brien & Haaga, 2015). Compassion fatigue results when adults become overwhelmed by the suffering and pain of those for whom they are caring (Figley, 2002; Lipsky, 2009; Ray, Wong, White, & Heaslip, 2013). Individuals with high levels of empathy for others' pain or traumatic experiences are most at risk for compassion fatigue (Adams, Boscarino, & Figley, 2006; Figley, 2002).

Although compassion fatigue symptoms vary for each individual, there are common outcomes that occur when stressors are not mediated by self-care strategies. Compassion fatigue symptoms include but are not limited to feelings of depression, grief and anxiety; being short tempered; being more reactive emotionally; being socially withdrawn and angry; having nightmares and sleep challenges; having difficulty concentrating; loss of hope and irritability (Mathieu, 2007; O'Brien & Haaga, 2015). While compassion fatigue primarily impacts the individual providing the care, these symptoms can be transferred to the caring professional's family members and significant others (Mathieu, 2007; Ray et al., 2013). Some adults respond to compassion fatigue behaviorally with self-numbing strategies, including the excessive use of drugs, alcohol or overeating. Other adults direct their behavioral symptoms of compassion fatigue outward with aggression, irritability, short temper and/or reactivity toward others or even the environment (punch the wall, kick the furniture). The toll of compassion fatigue will be social, emotional, physical and/or spiritual. Research on compassion fatigue also relates this condition with poor decision making, crossing ethical boundaries and, at times, actions that result in hurting ourselves and others.

---

*Cultural Differences in Compassion Fatigue.* As with burnout, compassion fatigue may be experienced differently across cultures. There may be differences in what compassion means, what it looks like and how people are expected to demonstrate compassion (Papadopolous et al., 2016). For individuals, one educator may be more likely to experience compassion fatigue than another based on their own upbringing, beliefs and experiences. Compassion fatigue may also differ between schools or other types of organizations based on workplace culture. When the workplace encourages cooperation and collective values, this can support employees' abilities to demonstrate compassion toward themselves, their colleagues and those they work with and serve (Dutton, Kaltman, Centers for Disease Control and Prevention, & Atlanta, 2007).

---

When early childhood teachers are impacted by compassion fatigue, they are at risk of losing their ability to have empathy, compassion and desire to help the children and families they serve. Compassion fatigue can lead caring professionals to lose sight of the original reasons they entered into their work, to help others, and, in the case of early childhood teachers, to love, care for and support the development of young children and their families.

## Remaining Compassionate Is Difficult to Do When Stressed

Jacquelyn Ollison, Ed.D., is a committed educator with extensive education experience as a teacher and school site and district administrator. Her research examines compassion fatigue in urban public schools. Dr Ollison's dissertation explores whether compassion fatigue, including burnout and secondary trauma, is a factor in teacher attrition/turnover in urban schools. Using qualitative interviews and a survey called the Professional Quality of Life Scale (V5), Ollison gathered data with a group of 100 K–12 teachers across the state of California. Although her research was not completed in early childhood settings, her findings are compelling and likely relevant for our field.

### Key Findings

◆ Teachers working in high-poverty schools report experiencing less compassion satisfaction, higher burnout and higher secondary traumatic stress.

◆ Compassion satisfaction scores decline as a school's percentage of African American students increases and increase as the percentage of white students increases. This pattern persists even when controlling for poverty, indicating an effect of racial bias.

◆ Female teachers and teachers with less experience are the most likely to experience compassion fatigue.

◆ Teacher-student relationships are an intimate two-way affair in which students and teachers can compound each other's trauma.

◆ In a classroom setting, teachers are often unable to utilize the flight strategy, especially in conditions of understaffing, and therefore may be more apt to use a "fight" response. The consequences of teachers reacting in a "fight" or hyper-aroused state can be immensely detrimental, such as employing excessive disciplinary measures like suspensions and expulsions.

◆ Hyper-aroused states can cause burnout symptoms, including aggression, anxiety, irritability, callousness, pessimism and declining work performance.

◆ A compassionate approach to education that recognizes "teachers are, with students, the heart of the educational process" (Noddings, 2013, p. 197) is essential. Teachers should be supported so that compassion-centered education is possible without this coming at the expense of educators' own health.

◆ Not only students, but all members in the school system can impact the experience of secondary trauma for teachers, including parents, administrators and other teachers.

◆ Teachers often feel guilty when they are unable to do their job effectively. Struggling with the knowledge that it is easier to have compassion for students who are easier to handle than others can intensify this guilt.

◆ Dr. Ollison reinforces, "School climate and conditions matter. Teachers have concerns about how action taken by parents, students, other teachers and administrators affect their ability to create safe and academically challenging environments. Teacher morale is often affected by how students are treated and/or how students are treating them."

Dr. Ollison's dissertation can be found here: https://scholarly commons.pacific.edu/cgi/viewcontent.cgi?article=4599& context=uop_etds

---

**Warning Signs for Compassion Fatigue**

- Feeling helpless and hopeless
- Having a sense that one can never do enough
- Hypervigilance (heightened sensitivity to stimuli in the environment—lights, sounds, comments or actions of others, facial expressions)
- Decreased creativity
- Losing compassion and the ability to empathize
- Inability to embrace complexity
- Chronic exhaustion
- Inability to listen
- Dissociative moments
- Lack of efficacy in one's life
- Guilt
- Fear
- Anger
- Addictions
- Decreased sense of importance (impacting self-esteem and sense of value in the world).

Source: Lipsky, L. (2009). *Trauma Stewardship: An Everyday Guide for Caring for Self While Caring for Others.* San Francisco, CA: Berrett-Koehler Publishers.

---

*Secondary traumatic stress* refers to the effects of being exposed to another person's reaction to their traumatic experience. This type of stress can result from working with children or families who experience trauma and display trauma reactions. When teachers are working with others on a daily basis who have experienced trauma and display trauma triggers and behaviors, it is difficult not to absorb into your own mind and body the traumatic stress and the intensive feelings they are displaying in their communication with you. When teachers attune to another human being, they can easily be affected by the others' internal emotional state even when they are not directly experiencing any trauma. Over time, hundreds or thousands of these experiences can profoundly affect us and put us at risk for several outcomes:

◆ *Feeling overwhelmed and stressed out.* It is not uncommon for those in the caring professions—like early childhood educators—to internalize the stress and trauma from the young children and families they are working with to a level that leaves them feeling totally overwhelmed and incapacitated by their own stress. The result may be an impact on your personal and professional life, including a decreased ability to manage your daily tasks and focus on your job or impact on relationships or the ability to attend to the needs of others in a consistent and trauma-sensitive way. In the absence of awareness, an early childhood educator may be impacted by these experiences rather than taking charge of their own well-being and self-care to prevent burnout or compassion fatigue.

◆ *Becoming numb or harmful in our interactions with ourselves, others and/or the children and families we serve.* Becoming numb is a survival response many professionals who work closely with individuals and communities that are strongly trauma impacted have when they observe and witness trauma stories on a daily basis. This survival response may look from the outside like the caring professional is losing compassion and the ability to "respond", which may look like shutting down emotionally, calling in sick frequently, avoiding children or families or giving up on a child or family (perhaps because of the feeling that every strategy you have tried is not working). A lack of response, a dissociation from the present moment, shutting down and ignoring can cause additional harm to the children and families that need our support healing from trauma. It can also be confused with or disguised as staying calm when one is actually shut down and disconnected. Jamil Zaki, a professor of psychology at Stanford University and the director of the Stanford Social Neuroscience Lab, explains that this feeling of "numbness" is named "defensive humanization" in the research literature. He explains:

> There is a double-edged sword of empathy for people in caring professions. On the one hand, many of these people are driven to their work by a preternatural care for others, but on the other hand, that same care can cause them to lose themselves. . . . [when they are] chronically surrounded by other people's deep suffering. And as a result, oftentimes I think people in caring professions feel like they're stuck in a double bind between caring for other people adequately but potentially grinding themselves down or turning themselves off. This is something that is called in the medical profession **defensive dehumanization** . . . they feel like they sometimes have to turn off their empathy and stop seeing [others] as people just so they can go on being people.
>
> (Zaki, J., 2019)

◆ *Becoming short-tempered and reactionary in our interactions with ourselves, others and/or the children and families we serve.* Becoming on edge, short of temper or reactionary is another survival response educators may have as a sign of the impact of secondary traumatic stress. Behaviors such as blaming, being short-tempered, yelling, being critical (of self or others) or being punitive (punishing children instead of regulating, supporting or teaching) become the very behaviors that can cause more harm to the very individuals that seek our help and healing.

Joyce Darbo is a special services manager for a Head Start program. Joyce explains how she always thought secondary traumatic stress was only a risk for the teachers who work directly with young children who are trauma impacted and that she was protected. However, she realized that the stress teachers' experience in their work with children *does* directly impact her, as the teachers bring their stress into their interactions with Joyce, which she has discovered does have somewhat of a contagious effect:

> *I think about that secondary trauma stuff. I always thought, 'well, teachers probably have it, but I don't.' But I do. I get the stress of the teachers on me. They unload it on me and then I feel the stress from the kids in the classroom . . . and then, when I hear the parent's story about their kids and the family, it's a lot. You can't help but feel for them. . . . It's a big ball of emotions that I didn't really realize* <u>really affects me</u>*. It does. I think about it a lot and I'm trying to sort it out and figure out the best way to approach it or where to put it, you know?*

---

### Stress Is Contagious

Human beings are relational, and therefore we absorb the emotions of those around us. Our capacity to instinctively and immediately understand what another is feeling or experiencing is due to our mirror neurons. In this way, the mirror neuron system is the neurological foundation that supports humans' ability to empathize, socialize and communicate our emotions to others.

Mirror neurons are activated when an individual observes someone else taking an action (e.g., walking toward them, gesturing that they need help etc.) or when they observe someone experiencing an emotion (e.g., fear, anger, happiness, surprise), as they help us to perceive other people's intentions (Acharya & Shukla, 2012; Conkbayier, 2017). That is, one person's emotional state is "mirrored" by the neuronal system of another as the mirror system of one person alters their emotional and physical state to match the emotional and physical state of the person they are interacting with. An example of this is when we see someone crying and feel sad knowing that they are hurting, or we sense someone is stressed and this creates our own feeling of internal distress. This process of taking in another's emotional state happens at a subconscious level, which means individuals are neither aware of this process nor in control of it.

The process by which stress is "contagious" begins with one neuronal system that mirrors another's neuronal system. In the case of a teacher working with a child in a traumatic stress response (e.g., a "fight" response where a child is kicking, hitting and screaming), it is critical that the teacher remain calm. Children's mirror neurons will imitate internally what they see, hear and feel modeled by their caregivers (Levine & Kline, 2007). As a child's mirror neurons help them to subconsciously decipher an adult's intentions and emotions (through the adult's facial expressions and body language), adult caregivers must communicate to young children—especially when they are triggered and in distress—that they are cared for and loved and that the adult will work hard to help them feel safe and protected. Many children who have experienced trauma have not experienced attuned relationships with adults who will remain calm and relationally connected to them when they display stress behaviors, which is the number-one experience they need to have over and over in order to heal. This is why it is so essential for adults to engage in their own self-care. Only by developing strategies to attend to the personal stress responses they experience when children express challenging behaviors can adults "mirror" for children emotional and physical states associated with love, care, empathy, understanding, support and safety. (Nicholson, Perez, & Kurtz, 2019).

*Many research studies have demonstrated that stress is "contagious" among humans, nonhuman primates, rodents and other species* (Carnevali et al., 2017; de Waal & Preston, 2017). Specifically, the stress of those around us may affect our physiology (physical health) and our behavior. Research with humans has documented that stress is contagious not only when we directly observe another person under stress (Buchanan, Bagley, Stansfield, & Preston, 2012; Engert, Plessow, Miller, Kirschbaum, & Singer, 2014) *but also when we are in the presence of an individual in the aftermath of their stressful experience* (Waters, West, & Mendes, 2014). One study that examined this phenomenon subjected human mothers to a social stressor in a separate room from their babies. The mothers were then reunited with their babies, who showed increased heart rates and increased social avoidance compared to babies in a control condition. Research with humans and animals highlights "the power of stress to impact those around us across space and time" (Buchanan & Preston, 2017, p. 175).

**Reflection Questions**
  ◆ Have you ever been around someone who was anxious or stressed, and you started to feel stress yourself?
  ◆ Have you ever been around someone who was calm, and you started to feel calm too?
  ◆ Do you notice how your internal emotional state is contagious with your colleagues? Children? Family? Friends?
  ◆ How can you connect this research with Joyce Darbo's description of the stories she hears at work "really affecting" her?

Without intentional self-care strategies and an ongoing routine of restorative activities, the risk to teachers' own self-suffering, burnout, compassion fatigue and secondary traumatic stress increases. This may lead to negative outcomes for themselves, young children and/or families and other adults they interact with at work. *For this reason, self-care is not just a nice thing to do, it is critically important for the holistic health, quality of relationships and protective factors that buffer stress for all in the early childhood workforce.*

**Spotlight on Practice**

Fatima Ahmad is an administrator serving children ages 18 months to five years of age in an Early Head Start/Head Start program that is part of a community homeless shelter. Fatima works with many children impacted by trauma, and the majority are experiencing homelessness. She is very aware of the need to care for herself to prevent burnout and compassion fatigue. Fatima uses a variety of strategies to de-escalate her own and her staff members' stress at work so they can remain calm and self regulated, which is essential for the children and families in her program to feel a sense of safety and to prevent further traumatizing them.

*We have a lot of children that come with trauma histories. Not all people are geared to work with them as some teachers get overwhelmed so easily working in this program. Sometimes some possess the knowledge, but that doesn't necessarily mean that they have the patience or the experience to be able to help the children. It's so hard to find the right staffing when you have the most vulnerable population. We have families who are constantly exposed to trauma, really a lot of stressful situations, and sometimes the families are so absorbed by their own problems that they forget—they don't see the whole picture. They live in the trauma and they cannot really break out of the cycle. So in order to reach them, we have to have a really solid team who are really willing to take the time and the strength and the effort to develop a positive relationship with the families. Build the trust and equality. In our facility, it's not about, "I am wrong or you are right" it's about partnership. And the partnership, when it's there and it's solid, it benefits the family and it benefits the children and the teaching team.*

*So, for example, a family that is experiencing homelessness, and at the same time they are in the Child Protective Services system and they experienced domestic violence and they are fighting over custody of their children . . . this is an*

*example of a typical family we serve. How would these ex-
periences affect their parenting style and the time they are
available to give to their children? It's not an easy thing to
go through one of these difficulties or hardships so imagine
if they are having to deal with these all at once and then they
have to look for housing at the same time and to struggle
with basic needs. We are not talking about extravagant needs
like trips or fancy stuff, I am just talking about basics like finding a roof over their heads and finding food for their table.
So it's hard. I actually have been attending a lot of trauma
informed practice workshops and trainings to learn how to
manage the stress. And one thing for sure that I learned was
when you feel stressed, it doesn't help you and it doesn't help
anybody around you. So imagine for example, if you have
an angry parent and if you match his energy, it's a lose-lose
situation, right? But if you calm down, and you keep quiet, it's
called mirroring (using your mirror neurons), when you are
calm, you reflect this calmness on the person in front of you.
So if you keep calm and the parent is irritated, he will calm
down. Another strategy I use is to let this parent get his feelings out, and at the same time I am protecting myself by imagining I am in a safe spot. You can imagine wherever a safe
spot was or a safe memory from your past or from your childhood memories, from your current surroundings, anything
that you like and it can just shield you in the moment.*

*Another practice that I like to do whenever I feel that I am
beginning to get irritated or overwhelmed, I have a special
code with my team, we have a special word "Code Blue", and
if we say it, that means we have reached our limit or we are
close to our limit and we need to switch places with someone and step out for a couple of minutes and then come back
fresh. So we use this. If I say "Code Blue" it might be regarding
a child so the other teacher knows to switch with me or to
switch with somebody else so she can handle the situation.*

*One more thing that is helping me at work is they are providing a lot of resources for us in terms of mental health help. So we have a mental health consultant on site almost every week and I can just to talk with him about anything. It can be personal, it can be work related, but it is just somewhere where I can vent. It helps me. It helps all of us. The same way I vent to the mental health person, I try to be actively listening to others like the families or my staff. Even if I am not offering solutions, after I actively listen to them, I see relief in their eyes. . . "someone is hearing me". When you foster this emotional security and safety, you see wonders. And that's the same for an adult or for a child. When you make your team feel safe, they are productive. When you make yourself feel safe, you are productive. When you make your families feel safe and lead them to feel that they are trusted, they will be successful. The only thing I am trying my best to stay far away from are toxic people, people who always think negatively. Because it's contagious and it really affects everybody's mood and productivity. So when you can give hope you get hope back and that's how you survive your stressors. And you don't get absorbed by all the trauma you see. Hope, for me, hope is the key.*

### Reflection Questions

◆ Fatima talks about the importance of mirror neurons and that those around us (children, families and co-teachers) absorb our internal emotional state. How do you notice how your internal emotional state ripples through the classroom and impacts those you interact with? Do you notice the difference when you are calm? When your emotions escalate?

◆ Fatima also talks about using a special signal to tell her teaching team she needs help and is overwhelmed. Their word is "Code Blue". Do you have a special communication strategy with your team that you use to signal you need help? If you don't work with a team, how do you signal to yourself and what strategy/strategies do you use to help yourself during times when you feel overwhelmed?

◆ Fatima mentions the importance of the trauma-sensitive strategy of "feeling safe". How do you help yourself feel safe? Children feel safe? Families feel safe?

## Dangers That Impact the Health of the Butterfly

*There are many factors that threaten the survival and well-being of the butterfly.* Whether loss of their habitat, change in climate, human or non-human (birds, wasps, spiders, insects) predators, pesticides, herbicides or other factors, the health of butterflies

*Credit*: Alice Blecker

is significantly impacted by the conditions they experience in their environment.

As this chapter highlights, *early educators also face a range of environmental factors that threaten their health and well-being and increase the field's high turnover rates.* The quality and conditions of the environment significantly influence educators' experience of stress, a topic highlighted in the next section.

## Attending to the Program/Organizational Climate to Address Teachers' Stress

Early educators' success in practicing self-care is significantly impacted by the culture, emotional climate and conditions within the centers, programs, schools, organizations and systems they are working within. As a field, we need to strive to integrate knowledge of the importance of culturally responsive self-care across every level of the early childhood field. *Our collective goal must be to create workplace cultures, policies, services and daily practices that are healthy, emotionally supportive, inclusive and healing for everyone who engages with them, certainly the children and families served, but also, and importantly, all of the early childhood educators working in these environments.*

Self-care is not effective if teachers are working within programs or larger systems that are unhealthy and trauma inducing, as the conditions of their work environments can and do put them at risk for burnout or more serious negative mental and physical health outcomes even if they are attentive to their own self-care routines and practices. To be truly effective in their work—especially given how demanding the work is for early childhood educators today—self-care needs to become intentionally integrated into the policies and practices within early childhood centers, schools, programs, organizations and systems. And the value of self-care has to be acknowledged and practiced up and down the organizational charts and hierarchies of our organizations. In essence, self-care needs to be considered in the framework of a concept integrated across our field.

## Parallel Process

*I don't think you realize how important self-care is until you take the time out to do it. I know for me at least, I was taking care of everybody else first. I'm going to take care of everybody else, I'm okay. But I think when I started making that effort to make sure I was taking care of myself also, I was a much happier person. And then I think I was able to be even more help to other people because I was happy. Sometimes I think I've gotten lost in making sure I was taking care of everybody else and not necessarily taking care of me. And then I came to realize I really wasn't taking care of them as well as I thought I was because I wasn't happy, because I was putting all my energy to them and not investing in myself. And when you don't invest in yourself, you run low on fuel. So even though you think you're going strong, you're not.*

*—Leslie Collins, Preschool Teacher*

The concept of the "parallel process" (Stroud, 2010) represents the belief that the quality of relationships, including communication and shared experiences between early childhood professionals (e.g. supervisor and supervisee), can significantly affect the way they interact with others, including children, families and co-workers, and, similarly, the manner in which educators interact with a child, family member or another colleague can influence parents' and families' interactions and relationship development with their own children (Heffron & Murch, 2010, p. 9). As Stroud (2010) explains, parallel process is rooted in reflection:

Providers who remain aware of their personal triggers and internal stressors, and who actively use self-care techniques, are more emotionally available to support families . . . parents with a deeper understanding of their stress responses, personal triggers and parenting history can be less reactive and more emotionally available to their child . . . and supervisors also need to reflect on their internal processes and develop self-understanding . . . as knowing oneself is vital in the relationships one develops.

(pp. 47–48)

The goal of parallel process is for early childhood professionals to have supportive spaces where they feel "emotionally held"—for example, in the context of mental health consultation, coaching or reflective supervision, where they are safe to explore their feelings and where they feel supported in revealing where they are along a professional developmental path, so that they are more likely to create similar spaces for children and families to feel respected and supported in their evolving developmental journey in parenting (Stroud, 2010, p. 48).

This concept of creating a supportive workplace is a framework that applies to all aspects of early childhood educators' workplace environments. As we have discussed in this book, our emotional states influence others around us. The theory of parallel process and research on mirror neurons and the contagion of stress suggest that when we are on the receiving end of kindness, we are in a better space to be kind and caring with the adults and children we interact with on a daily basis. And similarly, when we are on the receiving end of negativity, we will be more likely to act in more reactive or punitive and punishing ways with others.

**Remember:**

♦ When you are present in the moment listening to another adult, tuning in to their emotions and story, it is regulating and calming to them. Adults being supportive to each other when they are under stress is a calming and regulating strategy.

◆ The right part of your brain houses the emotions and wants to tell the story and be heard in order to regulate and then allow for the left brain to be ready to map a plan/solution to a problem (Siegel & Bryson, 2012).

◆ When someone has shared their story (how they feel and what happened) and they feel regulated, calm and like themselves again, it will be easier for them to engage in attuned and responsive interactions with other adults and children.

◆ The way you are with other adults should be influenced by the way in which you want them to be with other adults in the workplace and the children and families being served by the program. Additionally, as educators, we also need to be continually open to others' cultural perspectives and experiences.

*Supervisors and program leaders have a critical role in providing ongoing support to their staff and reducing the negative effects of burnout and compassion fatigue.* When educators feel supported, validated and valued by supervisors, they find it easier to manage the stress and demands associated with their jobs. The quality of relationships and communication between a supervisor and her staff can significantly affect educators' experiences of stress in the workplace and the manner in which they interact with children, families and their adult colleagues. If supervisors are critical, controlling and punitive with their staff, educators may react to the stress by repeating these patterns in their interactions with others. In contrast, if supervisors build caring, attuned and supportive relationships with staff, they are modeling the types of behaviors that are optimal for teachers to use in their interactions with others at work and creating the conditions for a positive emotional environment. Similarly, if supervisors emphasize educators' strengths and resiliencies, their staff will learn to do the same. Parallel process reminds us that the climate supervisors create in their interactions with the staff they supervise has a direct and important impact on everyone in the program. And this directly relates to self-care. If staff see their supervisors participating in self-care, publicly acknowledging the importance of self-care *and* working hard to integrate self-care directly into the program's policies and "best" practices, they will have support and incentives to engage in their own self-care. This builds momentum in creating a positive cycle where educators engage in self-care, which reduces their risk for burnout, compassion fatigue and secondary traumatic stress and creates greater stability and possibility for increasing quality within programs.

Staff in every role should be encouraged and supported to engage in ongoing self-care, and program leaders need to create structures that support and make self-care accessible. The field of early childhood needs to do the same—intentionally embracing self-care, trauma-informed practice and wellness as important elements of large-scale efforts to create high-quality early childhood systems.

Trauma Transformed created a continuum that is a useful tool for program leaders from early childhood homes, centers, programs, schools, organizations and systems to use to identify their current strengths and gaps related to self-care and wellness (see Figure 1.3). On one end of the continuum are environments that are stress and trauma inducing, where self-care practices are not supported and the workplace environment is actually harmful for the physical and emotional health of the staff. On the opposite end of the continuum are environments that value self-care and wellness and explicitly integrate caring for the workforce into policies and practices in order to buffer stress for staff and support their health, healing and well-being so they can do their jobs effectively while also taking care of themselves.

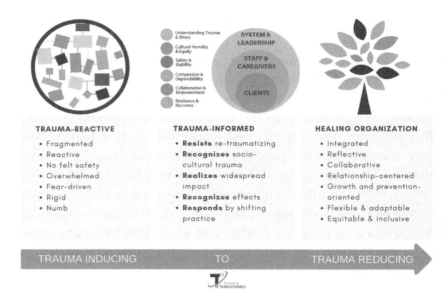

**FIGURE 1.3** From Trauma-Inducing to Healing Organizations

*Source*: Trauma Transformed (www.traumatransformed.org)

## Trauma-Organized Programs

People working within trauma-organized settings or impacted by their services do not feel an inherent sense of safety. Relationships are lacking trust or frequently disrupted before trust can be adequately built. Information, communication and work feel fragmented, people and systems/processes are overwhelmed, leadership and the climate are fear driven and rules are rigid; that is, they leave no room for local variation or flexibility. As a result, staff do not feel a sense of agency to influence the conditions that impact them, leading to feelings of numbness and hopelessness.

### Self-care in trauma-organized environments:

♦ Self-care practices are not supported within the program.
♦ Many barriers exist that make it difficult for educators to practice self-care at work.

◆ There is a lack of trauma-informed practices in place to support trauma-impacted children, families and the workforce. As a result, the environment increases stress for those spending time in it. The program/environment can be trauma-inducing, re-traumatizing and/or triggering.

◆ Staff do not feel valued or understood due to cultural differences. They often feel at odds with the leadership and/or the norms of the environment.

## Trauma-Informed and Resilience-Focused Programs

Trauma-informed and resilience-focused programs are environments where staff have an understanding of the neurobiology of stress and trauma and the impact they have on individuals (children and adults) as well as programs/organizations. All staff share a common language to talk about stress and trauma, and this knowledge is used to inform policies and practices in efforts to improve the workplace culture and reduce stress for employees and the children and families they serve.

### Self-care in trauma-informed and resilience-focused environments:

◆ The importance of culturally responsive self-care is understood and acknowledged and is intentionally integrated into and supported by the program to different degrees (this is often an area "in progress" for trauma-informed programs). For example, staff may receive training on the neurobiology of stress and trauma and the importance of culturally diverse and responsive forms of self-care, staff may develop a shared vocabulary for discussing the impact of stress and trauma on children and adults (e.g., fight/flight/freeze behaviors, triggers, self-regulation etc.) and learn diverse strategies that buffer stress and build resilience that pay attention to cultural differences.

◆ Teachers may be supported and encouraged to build body awareness and pay close attention to their body's reactions to stress and to learn techniques (e.g., breathing, swapping with a colleague when they need a break etc.) to support their ability to remain self regulated in their work with others.

---

### Words Aren't Enough

Matthew Davis, a preschool teacher who works for a large corporate child care center, explains how self-care is a language that his agency has taken hold of and is really emphasizing in communication with employees *while at the same* reinforcing messages about the importance of employees' "performance" at work. This sends contradictory messages to Matthew and his colleagues. Simultaneously, teachers are receiving messages from their supervisors and the corporate office leadership about the importance of their self-care while their agency is creating the very conditions that undermine it for the employees. Matthew explains:

> *Coming from our corporate world, there has been a lot of talk about self-care. I have had to navigate actually taking care of myself, the literal self-care, and how my program's ideology and language are being offered to the workers, that is really sort of, "Yes we care about you, but also, we want your productivity, we want you to be at work." For me it's complicated. "What does it mean to care for myself?" and "What does it mean to ensure that I'm in a system that is supporting and taking care of me and people taking care of each other?" How do I navigate these messages from the agency like, "Take deep breaths." It's true, breathing can be helpful, but it's also not the end of caring for yourself. Sometimes we're in situations where we are stressed because <u>they've</u> created the stress.*
>
> *I think a classic example of that was with a survey they sent out to us where we are asked to give feedback to the*

---

*agency about the climate of our workplace. The feedback from the teachers was that we are really stressed. And so they hired someone to come in and teach us Tapping Mindfulness Techniques so we wouldn't feel stressed anymore, right? It's not that Tapping Mindfulness Techniques aren't useful things to know about, but the message to the teachers was, "You'll be fine if you just do these things . . . your stress is your fault because you're not thinking enough about your loved ones, it's not our fault for creating a situation where you feel you can't be with your loved ones because you're taking care of somebody else's children for such long hours."*

*There's an ongoing tension at my workplace for reward-ing excellence, paying people for performance, paying people more if they seem to have done more. And then we all have to navigate within this system, how much am I willing to give up to "perform" to do "more" to be "rewarded"? You can imagine what that message creates between the teachers/ people who are in a really collaborative relationship-focused organization. Where things don't get done if we are not help-ing each other yet, we get messages from the agency that position us as competing against one another. There's always an underlying message, "If you do more, you might get paid more." And rent is really expensive . . .*

*As a staff, we are moving into valuing connection over accomplishment. And so there's always going to be a tension between navigating what the agency wants from us and what we want for ourselves . . . this affects everything from our pay to our quality of life. We need companies that actually do listen to the teachers.*

Matthew's story creates a warning for all program leaders and policymakers. Trauma-informed and healing-oriented orga-nizations do not appropriate the language of self-care while continuing on with business as usual. Instead, they change and align policies and practices throughout the program/organization so all staff are not only encouraged to engage in self-care, they are supported to do so in every aspect of their job.

**Reflection Questions for Organizational System Leaders**
- Before rolling out new policies and procedures, do you seek input from a diversity of employees?
- Does employee input drive change, policy and/or practices?
- How do you promote self-care? If you do, have you sought input from employees on what is of value to them or do you roll out new initiatives without any input?
- Are there systems in place to train leaders on reflective practice supervision and the use of inquiry versus command, direct and control?
- What ways does your organization listen to input from all levels?
- Are there efforts to understand, connect with and value cultural diversity in backgrounds, experiences and beliefs?

## Healing-Oriented Programs

Healing-oriented programs move past being trauma informed and focus on becoming healing environments. What are the characteristics of a healing environment? A healing environment is a space where adults work collaboratively together and honesty and authenticity are valued; this means that people can be honest and share narratives about their lived experiences and identities and know that they will not be shamed or punished for doing so (e.g., educators experiencing homelessness do not have to hide this reality from their supervisor; immigrants on staff feel a sense of trust in sharing with their supervisor their concerns about the increased number of raids and deportations happening in their neighborhood, making it stressful for them to travel to work).

Healing-oriented programs create intentional spaces and time to pause and to reflect to make meaning of and learn from difficult experiences (e.g., teachers working with trauma-impacted children can find safe spaces to process the range of feelings and concerns they have for the children and their families). There is a value for human connection, for taking care of oneself and for taking care of others: an ethic of care for others, and collaboration is encouraged and supported in the workplace. Individuals work together to contribute toward a greater good, which is articulated in a program mission and a set of values or principles that guide everyone's work. There is an explicit focus on learning and growth, and optimism and progress/success are acknowledged and celebrated across the program with a primary focus on the results of collaborative efforts (instead of individual call-outs and competition). Joy, creativity and innovation are valued and supported.

**Self-care in healing-oriented environments:**
- ◆ Self-care is intentionally integrated into policies and practices for the entire program, school or agency.
- ◆ Individuals in every role are not only encouraged to engage in ongoing self-care, the structures of the program provide supports and opportunities to make self-care accessible, and they allow self-care to be individualized and culturally relevant (they do not mandate everyone engage in a specific activity, and activities intentionally reflect a diversity of practices and techniques). Examples of the sources provided in healing organizations to support self-care, healing and wellness might include access to mental health consultation, reflective supervision, coaching, mindfulness, yoga and/or meditation practices,

spiritual services, affinity groups, an employee assistance program, sufficient lunch breaks and various professional learning opportunities, including meetings off site.

◆ Educators have regular, ongoing opportunities to check in and express their needs in a supportive environment where their needs are followed up with actions to address them.

◆ Culturally responsive practice is valued and supported in policies and practices, including but not limited to self-care.

### Reflection Questions

◆ Where would your program fall across this continuum? What aspects of your program or school are stress/ trauma inducing? Trauma informed? Healing oriented?

◆ Given where your program falls on the continuum, how do the overall climate and support (or lack thereof) for self-care impact you and the others on the staff? The children and families you serve? The different cultures and communities represented?

---

### Healing-Centered Engagement

Dr. Shawn Ginwright, the author of *Hope and Healing in Urban Education. How Activists Are Reclaiming Matters of the Heart and the Future of Healing: Shifting From Trauma Informed Care to Healing Centered Engagement* (2018), explains that although the term *trauma-informed care* is important, he believes it is incomplete. He introduces the concept of *healing-centered engagement* for several reasons:

◆ Trauma-informed care correctly highlights the specific needs for individuals who have exposure to trauma but incorrectly assumes that all trauma is an individual experience rather than a collective one.

◆ Our current focus on trauma-informed care does not address the root causes of trauma in neighborhoods, families and schools. And because trauma is a collective experience in many cases, we need to disrupt the environmental contexts (the toxic systems, policies and practices) that caused the harm in the first place.

◆ Trauma-informed care emphasizes treatment of the trauma rather than fostering healing and strengthening the roots of well-being.

Dr. Ginwright promotes an approach to trauma that is *healing centered* and involves culture, spirituality, civic action and collective healing. A healing-centered approach does not describe trauma as an individual isolated experience but instead sees trauma and healing as experienced collectively. He further proposes the term *healing-centered engagement* to represent a more holistic approach to health and a wider range of healing-centered options—inspired by the fields of positive psychology and community psychology—for responding to trauma and fostering well-being. This approach shifts the focus from a treatment-based model that views trauma and harm as an isolated experience to an engagement model that is strengths based, emphasizes a collective view of healing and re-centers culture as a central aspect of well-being. Additionally, a healing-centered approach acknowledges that well-being comes from participating in transforming the underlying causes of harm within our societal structures and institutions.

Dr. Ginwright (2018) describes four key elements of healing-centered engagement that both align with and are distinctive from current discussions of trauma-informed practice:

1. *Healing-centered engagement is explicitly political, rather than clinical.* "Healing centered engagement views trauma and well-being as a function of the environments where people live, work and play. When people advocate for policies and

opportunities that address causes of trauma, such as a lack of access to mental health, these activities contribute to a sense of purpose, power and control over life situations. All of these are ingredients necessary to restore well-being and healing."

2. *Healing-centered engagement is culturally grounded and views healing as the restoration of identity.* "Healing centered engagement is the result of building a healthy identity and a sense of belonging. . . . Healing centered engagement embraces a holistic view of well-being that includes spiritual domains of health. This goes beyond viewing healing only from the lens of mental health, and incorporates culturally grounded rituals, and activities to restore well-being (Martinez, 2001). Some examples of healing centered engagement can be found in healing circles rooted in Indigenous culture where young people share their stories about healing and learn about their connection to their ancestors and traditions, or drumming circles rooted in African cultural principles."

3. *Healing-centered engagement is asset driven and focuses on well-being rather than trauma symptoms.* "Healing centered engagement offers an important departure from solely viewing young people through the lens of harm and focuses on asset driven strategies that highlight possibilities for well-being. An asset driven strategy acknowledges that young people are much more than the worst thing that happened to them, and builds upon their experiences, knowledge, skills and curiosity as positive traits to be enhanced."

4. *Healing-centered engagement supports adults with their own healing.* Adults need to heal from trauma just like children. Healing-centered engagement emphasizes the supports that adults need to sustain their own personal healing and well-being. "Healing centered engagement has an explicit focus on restoring and sustaining the adults who attempt to heal [others]—a healing the healers approach."

Central tenets for healing-centered engagement include com-mitments to *build empathy* with those who experience trauma. Also, having the ability to *acknowledge the trauma and its impact, but not be defined by it*. Dreaming and imagining a positive future where one is resilient, optimistic and hopeful are elements of a healing-engaged approach. This shift recognizes that the lived experiences of *healing and well-being are fundamentally political, not clinical*, requiring a critical examination of the policies, prac-tices and political decisions in our programs, organizations and systems that harm children and adults. Part of the healing process is developing an awareness and ability to *critique the practices and policies that contributed to the experience of trauma*, which acts to prevent individuals from internalizing and blaming themselves for the traumatic experiences in their lives. Learning to engage in this type of critique supports individuals to examine and consider differ-ent cognitive and spiritual responses they can have in response to trauma. Finally, individuals can learn to work collectively to respond to the political decisions, policies and practices that contribute to their trauma. By *taking loving and collective actions*, individuals can strengthen a sense of power and control over their lives.

*Let's look inside an early childhood program and see the difference between a trauma-inducing environment and a trauma-informed and healing-oriented approach* by examining interactions between a teacher/early childhood director and her supervisor, the execu-tive director of the non-profit agency that employs her. The first example reflects a trauma-inducing program with a negative climate based in fear, a lack of trust and punitive actions against staff. The second example describes the same scenario within a trauma-informed and healing-oriented program where the focus is on listening, attunement, staff agency, collaborative inquiry and problem-solving and intentional actions to build and main-tain trusting relationships.

## Scenario #1: Trauma-Inducing Interaction

*Today I was walking through the halls to a meeting and the executive director of our school, Dr. Ellie Patel, yelled at me across the building to come and talk to her. I ran over to see her and she was escalated in her facial expression and tone of voice. She started yelling at me and saying that the early childhood program was under-enrolled and we were losing money. She said that she would have to close my program and that I would lose my job if I did not recruit more families.*

—Colleen, Head Teacher and Early Childhood Director,
Paraiso Child Development, Inc.

This is trauma inducing because the executive director called Colleen to talk about a critical issue without any advance scheduling or notice and interrupted a meeting Colleen was on her way to attend. She also did not give any advance notice to Colleen about the topic she wanted to discuss so Colleen could prepare herself for an appropriate response. Dr. Patel yelled at Colleen instead of taking an inquiry stance and wondering how the problem occurred or could be solved. Threats were made to close the program and/ or Colleen would be at risk of losing her job. Using threats to motivate and the use of scare tactics can be stress/trauma inducing.

## Scenario #2: A Trauma-Informed and Healing Approach

*The executive director, Dr. Ellie Patel, emailed me asking to set up a meeting to discuss enrollment for our program. She asked me to bring to the meeting any data on the past year's enrollment numbers by month, our enrollment strategies to date and any thoughts I had about why our early childhood enrollment is low. In the email, she asked for ideas and solutions to help increase our enrollment. She offered three choices of dates to meet but asked me to suggest an alternative if none of the dates worked for me. When I arrived at the meeting, she spent some time asking about my family and my recent vacation. She remembered that I had three children and asked specifically how they were doing and how my vacation was. We laughed and chatted a bit and then moved on to the agenda. Together, we looked at the data, considered the potential factors causing the problem and discussed a range of possible solutions. We set three measurable and reasonable goals to achieve in the next 60 days, and we scheduled another meeting together to check in. Dr. Patel asked if I needed additional support to achieve these goals and if there were any barriers to achieving them. I felt she listened to me, trusted my assessment of the situation and supported my ideas. She seemed to care how I felt and wanted our program to be successful. I did not feel alone and I left her office wanting to be successful. I felt motivated to help reach the goals we had set together for my program and the school.*

In the second scenario, we see evidence of a trauma-informed approach. In this scenario, Dr. Patel used her understanding of the neurobiology of stress to take intentional actions that reduced stress for Colleen and provided her with opportunities to have some agency in their interactions together. Colleen received advance notice of the meeting and the topics they would be discussing (reducing her experience of uncertainty). Colleen was also asked for her input (giving her a sense of control and agency), and she had an opportunity to prepare her thoughts and suggestions in advance (acknowledging her strengths and value within the program). Dr. Patel took time to attune to Colleen when she arrived at the meeting and to strengthen their relationship and trust with one another. In doing so, she was checking in with Colleen and creating a supportive environment where they could work collaboratively to explore the problem and construct solutions together, actions that served to reduce the risk that the meeting would become a stressful and triggering event for Colleen.

## The Butterfly in the Ecosystem

*The well-being and survival of a butterfly are entirely dependent upon the health of the ecosystem around it.* Butterflies are highly sensitive to changes in climate and the conditions of their habitat.

Credit: Alice Blecker

The presence of butterflies is a signal to scientists that an ecosystem is healthy. Given the diversity in types of butterflies, there are also a range of environments that support them to thrive. Although butterflies live in environments with nectar-producing flowers around the world (with the exception of the arctic), certain environments may be healthy to one type of butterfly and inhospitable to others; some species thrive in the harsh conditions of a desert environment, others can only live in dense rainforests and still others are healthiest in the ecosystems of prairie lands, marshes or meadows. It is easy to apply this metaphor when considering the self-care of educators.

*Like butterflies, educators' ability to thrive or to suffer is significantly impacted by the ecosystem around them.* Additionally, the diversities observed in the 17,500 species of butterflies in the world—represented in differing size, colors, wing patterns, shape of antennae and habitats where they are found—is also symbolic of the individual early childhood educators who each have their own professional roles, relationships, responsibilities, interests, strengths, backgrounds, learning edges and vulnerabilities that inform their personal experiences of stress and the specific approaches to self-care that are meaningful to them and help them to energize.

> *Humans? Some of us are surviving, following, flocking—but some of us are trying to imagine where we are going as we fly. That is radical imagination.*
>
> (Brown, 2017, p. 21)

*The previous picture provides a visual image of the butterfly in the context of healthy ecosystem,* symbolizing *safe, supportive and engaging workplace environments for early childhood educators* where the conditions are in place to support them to work effectively, to grow and learn as professionals, to care for themselves and others (children, families and co-workers). In this image, we include a large oak tree, as oak trees are one of the most beloved trees throughout the world and have powerful symbolism. Oak trees, oak leaves and acorns symbolize humble beginnings, patience, faith, strength and power, morale (confidence and enthusiasm of an individual/group), endurance, resistance, longevity and knowledge. This image highlights the need for the butterfly to live in a healthy environment in order to thrive, just as educators need to work within centers, homes, programs, schools and organizations/systems that support their health and well-being.

Looking at this image, we are reminded that it is not effective or equitable to place the responsibility for self-care on teachers' shoulders alone. Just as butterflies need a habitat filled with flowers to pollinate, leaves to lay their eggs and food to eat, teachers need to work within programs that invest time and effort in building trusting, respectful and strength-based relationships between children, families and educators and safe, predictable and culturally responsive environments: environments that value self-care, health and healing engagement and that create policies to align with these values, where people are collaboratively working to create a positive emotional climate and where adequate funding, resources and leadership are in place to guide the implementation of self-care and wellness policies into practice. We look at this image and are reminded that the butterflies will not survive without a healthy habitat, just as early childhood educators' individual self-care efforts will not be effective if the environments they work within are stress and trauma inducing. Let's look at the specific elements of the ecosystem in more detail:

*The Sun: "Continuous investment required to build and sustain high-quality early childhood programs"*. The sun symbolizes the need for continuous system-level investments (e.g., workforce compensation, safe and appropriate facilities and other program resources etc.) that are critical for high-quality early childhood programs to be sustainable and effective. Many of the elements of the sun are not yet in place and the focus of historical and current efforts at system reform and advocacy for workers' rights, for example, the Worthy Wage Campaign and the unified framework and call for greater investments documented in the National Research Council and Institute of Medicine's (2015) *Transforming the Workforce for Children Birth-Age 8* Report.

*The sun represents the foundational and critical investments that are crucial for early childhood as a field—elements that are required for the health and survival of the butterfly.*

*The Rain/Access to Water: "Ongoing investment in professional learning".* The water represents access to opportunities for professional learning and growth. This requires access to the structures that support adults' learning (e.g., paid time and space where educators can dialogue, reflect and learn with their colleagues through ongoing collaborative inquiry and reflective processes in staff meetings, communities of practice, individual or group coaching, interactive training experiences, technical assistance, reflective supervision, higher education coursework, reflective supervision, mental health consultation etc.) *and* the conditions within the workplace that create feelings of trust, safety and support that are necessary foundations for learning to take place. For example, mindful listening is used to build trust, understanding and empathy in communication; experimentation with new behaviors and practices is encouraged and mistakes are perceived as opportunities to learn; progress and efforts are acknowledged; all staff learn about body awareness and de-escalation/calming techniques; educators' own questions guide their professional learning and continuous improvement; creativity, curiosity and innovation are supported and a value for culturally responsive self-care is built into all professional learning opportunities and structures.

> *Without the water—access to opportunities for professional learning and growth and the structures and conditions to support adults' well-being, the ecosystem could not survive; the water is essential for the butterfly's health and well-being, as without the water, the ecosystem would not continue to grow.*

*The Soil and Roots: "History and current context of the program and community".* The soil represents the *many assets, capacities* (funds of knowledge, aspects of community cultural wealth), *coping strategies, forms of resilience and creative solutions that are found among the children, families and staff* working in or attending the program and/or within the wider community, resources that inform culturally responsive approaches to self-care for the individuals working in that context.

*The roots represent the vulnerabilities, stressors and historical as well as current sources of trauma and oppression that impact the children, families and staff at the program and the community where it is located.* These historical roots impact educators' experiences of stress and the strategies/resources they have available to them for self-care. For example, educators working in communities that are significantly impacted by poverty, community violence and structural racism are likely to experience higher levels of toxic stress and trauma and be at greater risk for compassion fatigue and secondary traumatic stress.

Having healthy soil in the ecosystem is an important foundation for creating a healthy, butterfly-friendly landscape. Roots are significantly influenced by the soil in which they live and become indicators of soil quality. If the soil is low in nutrients or water, is tainted by pathogens or is compromised by other problems, plants and trees in the ecosystem will not grow well. Yet plants and trees also influence the soil in which they grow; thus, the butterflies' health and well-being is directly impacted by the dynamic and interdependent relationships between the soil and the plants/trees/flowers and their roots.

*Acorns: "Early Childhood Educators' Individual and Collective Hope for Change".* Creating high-quality trauma-informed and healing-engaged environments in the field of early childhood must be driven by an individual and collective sense of hope that conditions for early childhood teachers can and *will* be changed for the better over time. Along with hope, the characteristics of strength, resilience, perseverance and determination/agency are acknowledged as essential for disrupting the inequitable conditions that exist and creating opportunities for all early childhood educators to have the healthy workplace conditions they deserve. We use *acorns* to *represent potential for change, new growth and imagining possibilities for the future of the early childhood field—* mighty oaks from little acorns grow. Looking at a small acorn, it can be hard to imagine how it could grow into a large and stable oak tree—equitable conditions for the early childhood workforce to thrive—that could live for hundreds of years. An acorn's growth is impacted by the conditions of the soil and other factors in its environment—an acorn needs nutrient-rich soil, sunlight and rainfall to thrive and to grow a taproot that pushes deep into the ground, securing it for sustained growth. Seedling trees are exposed to many dangers—e.g., fires, insects, wildlife, humans. Despite the different factors that threaten their viability and life, many saplings live on and grow into small oak trees within five years that flower and produce their own acorns, completing and re-generating a cycle of growth and transformation.

*The rebirth symbolized by the acorns represents our individual and collective hope that over time, we will make progress on disrupting the inequities and experiences of stress, trauma and injustice that early childhood educators across the United States and internationally give voice to throughout this book.*

## Summary

*I'm a teacher and also a mom and I'm also a single mom, so self-care is usually the last thing I get to work on because of everyone else that needs taking care of. But I'm learning how important that self-care is. I'm learning that I have to do self-care because if I don't, my stress just eats me up and then I'm not as effective at my job. Our jobs are so important, but if we don't take care of ourselves, then we won't be there to do our job. And teachers are so undervalued already, that I think we need to value ourselves.*
—Elsa Karlsson, Early Childhood Special Education Teacher

Early educators face many stressors inside and outside of work, and some endure different types of trauma. As evidenced in the narratives throughout this chapter, the conditions of early educators' jobs—including poor compensation and lack of benefits that lead to financial instability, the pressure to increase quality and the increasing number of children and families who are impacted by trauma—are major factors contributing to their stress. The climate of the program or school plays a very significant role in either buffering educators' stress or contributing to and exacerbating it. Throughout this book, we spotlight the innovative ways that educators are responding to and coping with the inequities in our field. It is essential to acknowledge educators' strengths and many forms of resilience while also making visible the difficult and honest truths about the unjust and oppressive conditions they experience working in early childhood. Only by making these complexities visible will efforts to fight for equity in the profession come to fruition.

*My parents are old school Catholics and the church is very central to their upbringing. I grew up spending about a month out of the year in Mexico in a very small town in Nayarit. During the fiestas, which run for a couple of weeks in January, is when we celebrate Jesus of Nazareth. And we would see Jesus of Nazareth everywhere. And that was the image all around my dad's room when he was ill too. And I remember my sister just being tired of so much Jesus of Nazareth everywhere and at one point just asserted—"Enough! Enough with the sacrifice. Enough already! Hasn't he suffered enough? Can we see some joy, something beautiful*

*and peaceful?!" And I think she just felt not only sick of the suffering but the idolizing of suffering, the focus on suffering constantly almost as a necessity—as an accompaniment to anything and everything—martyrdom. And while I can appreciate that this image was also synonymous with their hometown, it also exemplified what we had come to accept—that the pain and sacrifice is what we must accept.*

*Religion, Catholicism in particular, ultimately influenced my family's feelings about self-care and their own value and self worth. Just the need to sacrifice, which is also really a part of their journey and surely what prepared them for the life we now have the luxury of living today. Part of it is also just having very few resources. My mom was raised on a ranch and it was a lot of work and so there wasn't really a lot of time for self, it's more about your contribution, your role in the household, and my mom sewed and embroidered, in addition to the day to day work of maintaining the home and ranch. I think it wasn't until I saw her really as an adult, when I became an adult, that I saw how much her work was—even though I saw it as her suffering in some ways, it was really her self-care too. Sewing is what brings her joy and what brings her peace and I see now how that was woven into all she created. Even the process itself, while requiring skill, focus, precision, and countless hours, back pain, injuries, and stress, she makes beautiful pieces that make her proud and brings so many people joy; her upholstery is a beautiful craft, an art, that becomes a part of family memories that permeate all the senses—touch and smell. The forever backdrop to all our celebrations and rosaries, chairs, cushions, curtains, pillows, couches, and details make the picture. Her sister, my Tia shared one day, as we visited her on her birthday, while my uncle was hospitalized (she has been his primary caregiver for years), we encouraged her to seek some help so that she could take a break and we asked her, "Well, what do you want to do? You know, you need a break". And she was like, "¡Cuando trabajo, siento que estoy volando!" (I just want to go work. When I work, I'm flying!) In that moment I felt as though a window opened up, reminding me of how at peace my mom would be at work when I'd go with her as a child. It made me think of how proud she felt of her work, her sense of independence and accomplishment that came from that . . . and that it meant she could also support her family, and visit her family in Mexico at least annually. Being with her family is everything, where she can just be.*

*I think self-care used to always sound like it was not for me and it sounded like everything I don't like, like massages from strangers. I do like bubble baths, but I guess I just didn't think of it as self-care. I just thought of it as like, "This is what I feel like doing." I think this past year self-care has become much more important and apparent to me. Looking back at some of the patterns in my life I have discovered my own way to take care of myself. I'll give you an example. When my father passed earlier this year, it was really important for me to honor how I felt. My father was very traditional. When he lost his brother, that was really the one time I saw my father crying and hurt. He mourned by wearing black for a year, no music for a year, no parties for a year. It was ritual. I realize now how much certain things that are kind of ritualistic have been helpful for me and so I decided to honor him the way he would have. Wearing black was easy and in tune with how I've felt. And for months, I didn't want to hear any music either. But a point came about three months later that I found myself tightening up, not finding my words, and feeling like a dark cloud over my daughter, who was used to me streaming music everywhere, with impromptu dance parties in the kitchen, and singing in the car. It was our jam. It was what I treasured during our moments together. On Easter after my father's passing, I began to hear some songs that reminded me of my father. I forgave myself a bit for doing so and felt him close, knowing that without the music, I was tightening the corset . . . without dance, my body was locking me in in ways that were all too familiar.*

### Reflection Questions

♦ How does your current definition of self-care differ from that of your parents/adult caregivers? Why might these differences exist?

♦ Do you remember reflecting on your ideas of self-care compared to others or compared to your own past notions?

♦ How, like Doménica, do you honor your feelings around sadness or loss?

♦ Doménica used rituals as a form of self-care. Do you have any rituals that you use that make you feel safe and secure or contribute to your personal self-care plan? Where do these rituals come from? Why do you feel they work for you?

# 2

# Foundations of Culturally Responsive Self-Care

*How can early childhood educators identify and draw from their own backgrounds, experiences and values in self-care practices?*

**Key Topics Covered**

- ♦ Defining Culture and Cultural Conceptions of the Self in Self-Care
- ♦ Cultural Neuroscience of Stress and Culturally Informed Beliefs About Healing
- ♦ Decolonizing Self-Care, Critical Race Theory, Culturally Sustaining Practice
- ♦ Intersectionality/the Multiple Layers of Influence on Conceptions of the "Self" in Self-Care
- ♦ Culturally Responsive Self-Care as a Lifelong Journey of Discovery

*Early Educators Across the* United States *and Internationally Shared What the Concept of Self-Care Means to Them. . . .*

## When you hear the words 'self-care' what do you think of?

Big part of being human
Investing in myself  Letting off steam  Community
Separating work and home  Self regulation
Refilling my cup  Replenishing mind, body & spirit
Supporting myself  Balance  Finding peace
Taking a break  Wellness  Being aware of what I need  Rest
Grounding  Slowing down
Meeting my own needs  Quietness  Relaxation  Not selfish
Letting yourself grow  Hitting pause  Putting myself on the schedule
Decompressing  Nurturing ourselves  Recharging  Solitude
Taking care of my mental health  Figuring yourself out
Being compassionate with myself  Ensuring I'm in a supportive system
A Lifelong process  Attunement to inner self  Saying no when necessary
Unwinding  Listening to my body  Seeking Support
Caring for physical health  Taking time for myself
Being in tune with myself  Letting go  Breathing
Caring for me  Fighting others' expectations of me
Nurturing my spirit
Acknowledging our pain and hardships

# What Does Self-Care Mean to You? Culturally Responsive Definitions of Self-Care

Our discussion of culturally responsive self-care begins a need to define "culture" and our beliefs about the influence of cultural beliefs on educators' experiences of stress and trauma; their diverse conceptions of the "self" in self-care and the wide range of resources, supports and practices they use to buffer their stress and care for themselves. Adding "culturally responsive" to discussions of self-care acknowledges how privilege and structural oppression impact early childhood educators' identities and lived experiences both inside and outside of the workplace. Culturally responsive self-care highlights the need to expand our understanding of the diverse pathways educators take in learning to cope, build resilience, heal and support their health and well-being. In essence, promoting culturally responsive self-care is an intentional act to reclaim and reconceptualize the concept to be more equitable, accessible and meaningful for our diverse early childhood workforce.

## What Is Culture?

Culture is a broad concept that refers to deep-rooted customs, values, beliefs, languages, social norms and practices shared among a group of people that may be transmitted across generations (Rogoff, 2003, 2011). According to the cultural psychologist Barbara Rogoff, our lives can be considered coherent constellations of cultural practices that may dynamically change over time, over social and environmental settings and across generations (Rogoff & Angelillo, 2002; Rogoff, 2003, 2011). This idea of considering culture an interrelated set of factors, including racial and ethnic identity, social class, language/s spoken, income, gender, family roles, rituals and communication styles can be contrasted with definitions of culture that treat factors such as income, race, schooling, ethnicity or nationality as static, independent attributes (Rogoff, Najafi, & Mejía-Arauz, 2014).

Even without our conscious awareness, culture influences how we think, believe and behave, which affects how we teach and learn (California Department of Education, 2018; Gay, 2010; Hill, McBride-Murry, & Anderson, 2005; Milner IV, 2017). Different cultural groups differ in ways of thinking, behaving and engaging with the world (Henrich, Heine, & Norenzayan, 2010), and these ways of thinking and being are often transmitted across generations as a type of shared "information system" that shapes the uniqueness of cultures and leads to the development of meaningful practices around life events (Matsumoto & Juang, 2013).

These cultural practices and values, such as how we mark and celebrate life events, may change over time. Those who are part of the same social groups but of different generations, such as our parents and grandparents, may share some values but also differ in important ways in their beliefs and practices (Rogoff, 2011, 2017).

It is essential that we learn about diverse cultural perspectives and challenge any beliefs we have that there is one "right" way. Being a culturally responsive educator—and considering what it means to support and participate in culturally responsive self-care practices—requires that educators suspend their own assumptions to gain greater understanding of the multiple ways of being, learning, communicating, relating and healing in the world (Rogoff, 2003; Rogoff et al., 2017).

## Iceberg Model of Culture (Hall, 1976)

Edward T. Hall (1976) introduced the iceberg model of culture, explaining that there are layers to culture that must be understood and that, too often, we only focus on the surface elements of culture that we can more easily understand and identify (see Figure 2.1: Iceberg Model of Culture). Hall's model describes three levels of culture:

◆ *Surface culture (observable):* Elements of culture that are easily seen, identified and accessed. Surface culture is what people often think of when they consider the concept of culture. These include food, dress, music, art, crafts, dance, literature, language, celebrations, games, religion and more. Institutional efforts to encourage culturally responsive self-care may reflect surface culture by including culturally diverse music or foods during meetings or celebrations.

◆ *Deep and unconscious culture (not observable, below the water line):* These represent a culture's core values, attitudes, preferences and ways of interpreting experiences. Different cultural groups can share a core value (respect, love of family), but the way these values are interpreted and acted upon can be very diverse. This includes learned beliefs about what is good, right, desirable and acceptable and what is perceived as bad, wrong, undesirable and unacceptable. Aspects of deep and unconscious culture impact how individuals interpret concepts of time, space, humor, the meaning of facial expressions, body language, eye contact and touching and perspectives and concepts of leadership, modesty, marriage and family, child-rearing, attitudes toward elders, kinship, gender, class, decision-making and problem-solving and many more factors. A workplace environment that encourages discussion of contrastive practices across cultures without focusing on defining a single "best practice" may increase cultural awareness and encourage collaboration and understanding within a team.

Aspects of surface culture may be a reflection of the deeper and less visible layers of culture.

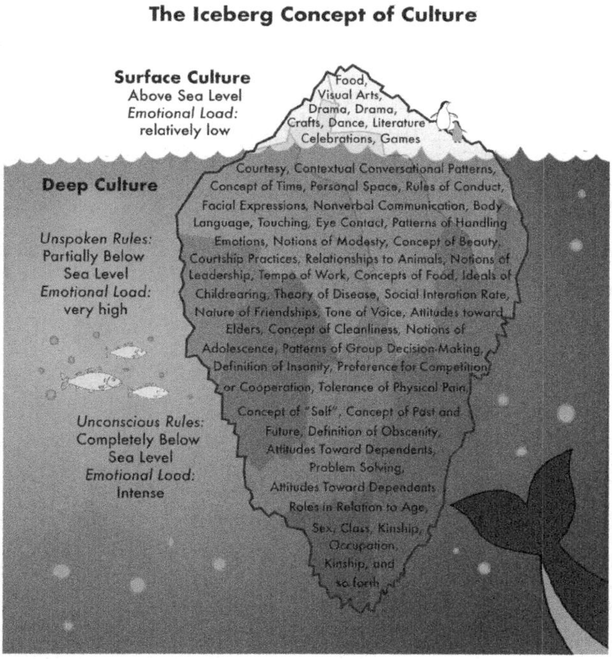

**The Iceberg Concept of Culture**

**FIGURE 2.1** Iceberg Model of Culture

*Source:* Adapted from the Indiana Department of Education, Office of English Language Learning and Migrant Education, www.doe.in.gov/englishlanguagelearning

*Credit:* Alice Blecker

**Reflection Questions: Make Your Cultural Assumptions Visible**

Review the iceberg model of culture and then choose a few of the following questions to reflect upon by yourself or in conversation with others with a goal that you surface some of the cultural beliefs and practices and life experiences that influence your identity, your beliefs and assumptions about self-care and your professional practice.

◆ Did extended family live with or close to you? What role did they play in your upbringing?

◆ What sorts of spaces or events brought your family or cultural community together? What foods, music or spiritual practices did you engage in? How did your family identify ethnically or racially?

◆ What languages were you expected to learn or not learn—and why?

◆ Where did you live—urban, suburban or rural community?

◆ What role did education play in your family? What types of knowledge/skills are valued?

◆ What family folklore or stories did you regularly hear growing up? What messages did they communicate about core values?

◆ Who were the heroes celebrated in your family and/or community? Why? Who were the antiheroes?

◆ To what extent were celebrations or family events intergenerational affairs, inclusive of parents, grandparents and children?

◆ Review primary messages from your upbringing: What did your parents, neighbors and other authority figures tell you respect looked like? Disrespect?

◆ How did your family respond to different emotional displays—crying, anger, happiness?

◆ What physical, social or cultural attributes were praised in your community?

◆ How were you expected to interact with authority figures? Who was defined as an authority figure?

◆ Who did you define as "family?" How did you greet family?

◆ Were children typically present in adult spaces, or were there separate spaces for children?

◆ To what extent was extended family involved in your upbringing?

◆ What image comes to mind when you think about a young child learning? Is the child silent and listening or active and talkative? Is the child sitting, standing, moving? Is the child alone or with others? What do you think influenced you to associate learning with these images and beliefs?

Source for Questions: Hammond, 2015, p. 57

## Cultural Conceptions of the Self

Many discussions of self-care in early childhood focus on teachers caring for themselves so they are more attuned with young children. However, focusing on self-care simply as a practice to improve the quality of educators' work with children and their workplace effectiveness leaves out an essential consideration: the value that self-care provides for educators themselves. We, therefore, begin our consideration self-care by asking, "What role does the 'self' play in culturally informed discussions of self-care?" In this book, we consider the self as a culturally informed concept and acknowledge that cultures differ in their understandings and conceptualizations of the self.

Conceptions of the "self" in self-care have traditionally been aligned with Western/European American (dominant) perspectives. Western dominant beliefs about self-care emphasize the "self" as an individual. European American cultures typically value individual achievement, reward competition and focus on self-reliance. Many aspects of Western culture are rooted in an individualistic mindset. In Western, individualistic cultures, "the self" tends to be considered an independent, autonomous entity. Discussions of self-care with this orientation emphasize private internal aspects of the self (i.e., thoughts, emotions), aim for individuals to be unique and to develop internal values and beliefs and describe the importance of setting personal goals.

In contrast, some groups/communities have "collectivist" cultural orientations and think of the "self in relation to others". Collectivist cultural beliefs focus on the well-being of the group versus the individual, discourage competition and focus on caretaking of others, such as family and community. Non-Western cultures tend to perceive the self as an interdependent entity that emphasizes external, public aspects (such as social roles, relationships) and social harmony (Markus & Kitayama, 2010). A conception of "self" as an individual, independent from others, may, therefore, not be culturally relevant or appropriate within a culture that focuses more on interdependence. Indigenous cultures of the Americas, Eastern cultures and several other groups tend to take a collectivist perspective in conceptions of the self and in ways of being.

### Indigenous and Collective Practices

Cultures differ in the ways children learn from their environments and from other people. These differences are important to understand in the field of early care and education, as teachers' own values or the values of schools or other institutions may contrast with each other or with those of children, families and communities. Understanding and valuing various practices that are not typically reflected in dominant Western institutional culture may help alleviate stress or conflict when these differences arise.

In Indigenous communities of the Americas, as well as within other more collectivist cultures, children are often raised in multi-generational contexts, and they learn to observe the world around them without being explicitly taught. The social organization of these activities focus on collaborative engagement and flexible leadership (Rogoff et al., 2017). This may differ from dominant, individualist Western classroom practices in which the teacher may be the authority and may expect children to work independently. Collectivist practices may be passed down across generations, so that families with intergenerational, cultural ties to Indigenous cultures may be more likely to engage with or use these practices, even if these families do not consider themselves Indigenous.

Individuals who have more experience with Indigenous practices may demonstrate adaptive behaviors such as being able to attend to and learn from multiple surrounding activities, collaborating and helping others and using nonverbal alongside verbal communication behaviors, compared to those who have much less experience with Indigenous community practices (Silva, Correa-Chávez, & Rogoff, 2010). In some communities where there is more experience with Indigenous practices, children are able to focus on activities that do not involve them and can take initiative to learn from observing these activities, even when they are not being spoken to (Silva, Shimpi, & Rogoff, 2015).

Our ongoing engagement with cultural values and practices can influence our understanding of our self and others (Kitayama & Uskul, 2011). As a result, in order to critically engage in self-care or to encourage self-care in the workplace, it is essential to understand cultural variations in notions of the self.

Cultural differences in how we define and understand the self can even influence how we experience the world. These differences can impact the functions of our brain, including how we experience emotional well-being or remember emotional or life events such as weddings or birthdays (Liddell & Jobson, 2016). Cultural differences in how we form and retrieve our autobiographical memories and how we understand ourselves (our self-representation) can also relate to our perceptions of our own stress and trauma (e.g., Cacioppo & Berntson, 1992; Kitayama & Uskul, 2011).

## Cultural Neuroscience of Stress

Cultural differences in our beliefs, practices and values may impact how our brains function and can influence the ways in which we think, see, experience, feel and behave. (Han et al., 2013; Kitayama & Uskul, 2011; Liddell & Jobson, 2016; Markus & Kitayama, 2010). The field of *cultural neuroscience* studies the relations between our brain and behavior across cultures. Researchers in this field have found that culture wires our brain (Park & Huang, 2010). The way we experience and process information is influenced by our cultural views of our selves (Oyserman, Novin, Flinkenflögel, & Krabbendam, 2014). Culture influences the structures in our brains along with the physiological processes involved in our fight, flight and freeze reactions. This, in turn, influences the development and experience of stress and PTSD (Jack, Blais, Scheepers, Schyns, & Caldara, 2009; Martínez, Franco-Chaves, Milad, & Quirk, 2014).

When we experience trauma, our cultural experiences may influence how our emotional states may be impacted, and there may be differences in our perceptions of threats, our emotional or memory load, our physiological arousal levels and even our recovery times after the stressful situation has passed (Liddell & Jobson, 2016; Park & Huang, 2010). There are even cultural differences in PTSD in terms of how individuals store and retrieve trauma-related memories (Jobson, 2009).

Research has also shown that individuals who are from a more collectivist compared to individualist cultural background show differences in their brains when perceiving others' distress (Cheon et al., 2013). This may relate to how connected individuals may feel to each other across cultures. Though research has shown neural differences in stress and trauma across cultures, there is a clear need to conduct more research in the field of cultural neuroscience. Most studies looking at trauma have traditionally focused on majority rather than minoritized populations.

Finally, the role of the types of supports or care strategies may have different impacts on people from different cultures. For example, the effectiveness of stress-relief strategies differs across cultures. For those from individualist types of cultures, more direct forms of social support are associated with a decrease in stress, but for those from more collectivist cultures, this may have the opposite effect (Sue, 2005). Therefore, it is important to understand that techniques for self-care or other-care may work for some but not for others. Self-care cannot be seen as a one-size-fits-all model.

## Culturally Informed Beliefs About Healing

Dominant Western approaches to care, healing and self-care tend to focus on medicinal models, in which "curing" of separate health issues or diagnoses is a goal; however, many Indigenous, Eastern and non-dominant cultural approaches focus on more holistic health of a person rather than the individual symptoms (Sue, 2005). In Western medicine, there tend to be several assumptions about reality; for example, that it is based on directly observable elements, such as time and space. These are assumed to be experienced and measured in the same way across cultures. However, Indigenous groups often disagree and see these sorts of universal assumptions about reality as causing illnesses (Sue, 2005; Sue & Sue, 2013).

Dominant Western mental health models and practices focus on treating the individual (Sue, 2005). In contrast, people from collectivist-oriented or Indigenous cultures often use practices involving the community or group rather than focusing on treating the individual alone. According to Sue and Sue (2013), non-Western and Indigenous healing prioritizes group harmony and interconnectedness. Illness or suffering is seen as related to a larger imbalance in the relation between a person and others (including living and non-living), as well as within the person, in terms of spiritual well-being (Sue & Sue, 2013).

We need to recognize, understand and value these differences between collectivist and individualistic cultural orientations of the self and of conceptions of what self-care means, yet we should also take care not to oversimplify and identify individuals or groups as being solely categorized as *either* collectivist *or* individualist (Markus & Kitayama, 2010; Rogoff et al., 2017). Constructs like "self" or "self-concept" are complex, dynamically evolving and influenced by a wide range of factors (Harb & Smith, 2008). As a result, we need to expand our definition of "self-care" to be inclusive of models that are both focused on Western individualist and independent ideas as well as those that are more collectivist and interdependent.

Karen Tapia draws from her roots as a citizen of the Cree and Cherokee nations and her Native American spirituality to illustrate a worldview in which the individual is not necessarily at the core of the understanding of "self" but instead in which her existence and purpose are built from connections in an interdependent way. Karen's connection-based interdependent views have also blended with notions of uniqueness and self-knowledge, reflecting her various cultural experiences with Indigenous as well as dominant Western viewpoints.

*We are all related, we are interconnected in the universe, that's what we believe from my Native American roots. So everything we do has an impact on everything else. It has an impact on the earth, it has an impact on the air, it has an impact on the water, it has an impact on animals and plants and other human beings. Really, there's an intentionality to life in Native American spirituality that is very, very critical. There is also an idea that we are co-creators with our Creator, whether you believe in a higher power or not. We walk this earth and walk in a good way with actual love and care and concern for every single piece of the universe. It's not just about us . . . the essence of our teaching is that you are a uniquely created human being. There's no one else like you in this whole universe. That's true for everything, every waterway, every piece of land, every bird, every animal. They're unique, and they have a unique purpose, and so it's really important to understand what your purpose is and that your purpose is not just about what you do out there, but it's also about what you know about yourself inside, and how that impacts who you are out there. Beyond that we know that collectively we pray together because there is power in collective prayer and we are strengthened in our purpose by others also holding our vision and purpose with us. There is strong intention in ceremony, ritual, prayer and celebration to keep the community and the individual strong and focused and supported.*

—*Karen Tapia*

As illustrated by Karen's story, the notion of the "self" may differ across cultures, and these differences are critical to understanding and implementing practices toward care and well-being of educators, children and families.

## Frameworks to Strengthen Our Understanding of Culturally Responsive Self-Care

We introduce several frameworks to deepen our understanding of culturally responsive self-care. These different frames expand our knowledge of the wide range of beliefs and practices related to self-care across diverse cultural contexts. They also bring into our view the need to relate educators' experiences of privilege and oppression with their complex identities and experiences working in early childhood and their different conceptions of and orientation to self-care.

## Colonization and Loss of Self and Cultural Connection

Many minoritized groups have lost their cultural connections due to colonization, and this dispossession can be devastating and deeply traumatic. When groups and communities are colonized, their land, languages, food, music, spiritual connections, belief systems and social organizations are claimed, destroyed, seized, forbidden or lost and replaced with those dictated by the oppressive and colonizing group. Hassel, Tamang, Foushee, and Bad Heart Bull (2019) explain how diverse ways of knowing and being are replaced with Eurocentric perspectives that are positioned as "best" for all despite their lack of meaning or authenticity for communities impacted by colonization. They state, "We are commonly driven by norms, values, schedules, and deadlines that are characterized by Euro-Western worldview orientations. We are often left with the presumption that perspectives of good professional practice are universal and will (or should) work regardless of context" (p. 8).

---

*Colonization* "extend[s] beyond dispossession of land to include ways in which one culture imposes itself upon another. This includes not only a peoples' food system, but also their ways of knowing and understanding the world" (Hassel et al., 2019, p.8)

*Decolonization* is the process of fighting oppression by re-claiming and re-establishing cultural ways of knowing and being (intellectual, spiritual, behavioral, political, economic) and detaching from the beliefs and practices imposed by the colonizer. Witt (2017b) explains:

*Putting ourselves first is decolonizing. Think about it. Black women have always had to take care of others before considering themselves—this dates back to American slavery. . . . To declare that we will put ourselves first (that does not mean we lose the capacity to care for others, but to remember ourselves) is revolutionary and is a part of this decolonizing work. It's being honest and embracing every facet of who you are—that means your skin, your hair, your voice, your sexuality, how you walk, how you communicate, how you feel, everything and being una-pologetic.*

Manaal Farooqi (2018) describes the problems in the current way that self-care is being discussed in the United States and the need to expand our conceptions of self-care to be more inclusive of the wide range of practices diverse individuals and groups have always used. She highlights the need to decolonize self-care and reclaim its boundaries and contours to acknowledge the culturally informed self-care practices created and used by marginalized communities to cope, heal and resist in the wake of various forms of oppression they navigate. Manaal Farooqi explains:

> Our understanding of self-care needs to be widened to make the practice more relevant to and accessible for marginalized people . . . self-care has become . . . synonymous with bubble baths, wine, alone-time, coloring books and more. It's often seen as a movement that was both discovered and invented in the recent past. However, just as it was conceived, it has also been catered towards a specific audience: white people . . . we need to decolonize self-care so that it's accessible to all people— particularly Black, Indigenous and people of color (BIPOC), because marginalized people are told repeatedly not to center their own self-care.

## Decolonizing Self-Care

Many individuals and groups—especially those who are most impacted by oppression and historical trauma—have identified the need to reconceptualize self-care to be more accessible, culturally responsive and aligned with their lived experiences. Artreach Toronto, a community organization in Canada, is one example of a group advocating for the need to widen our understanding of self-care to become a more inclusive set of practices. They explain how self-care can be woven into many *traditional and cultural practices for Black, Indigenous and People of Color as tools of healing, remembering or even resistance:*

◆ "For refugees or those from diaspora, food can be a means of connecting to their homes even when they cannot go or be there themselves" . . . it can connect people to fond memories and their own traditions. Through this reconnection, decolonizing one's diet and reconnecting with the rituals of preparation, serving/sharing and eating the foods of your culture can be a healing act as well as an act of restoration.

◆ "As self-care can be meant to be grounding and rooting, it could include engaging in activities that you grew up engaging in, observing, or hearing about. When looking at the movement from this perspective, it allows those looking to access self-care as something that isn't confined to particular (majority) practices."

◆ "Simple things such as going for walks, spending time with family or friends, and reading . . . accessible activities like cooking, cleaning, attending a religious service or just binge-watching your new favorite show . . . whatever makes you calm . . . bring you joy and that are easily accessible, such as going for a run."

◆ "For Black, Indigenous and people of color, the popular culture references of self-care may not feel relatable. . . . Traditional knowledge isn't always accounted for or acknowledged as a valid form of self-care, which means our views on the practice are often limited. Generally speaking, when asking someone what traditions, foods, or art they find comforting **that come from their cultural background**, the topics they speak of are integral to their conception of self. Without recognizing that traditional knowledge can form a huge part of self-care, the movement is limited and not truly accessible to everyone."

Decolonizing self-care reclaims this concept and set of practices to be more accessible, equitable and inclusive of everyone, especially individuals and groups most impacted by colonization and structural oppression in society. This process begins when we open up honest conversations about *"what self-care is and who it's for"*. By critically examining whom self-care is for and reclaiming self-care to be understood as accessible and culturally responsive and culturally sustainable practices, self-care can become a decolonizing set of actions . . . offering what Linda Tuhiwai Smith (2012) describes as "a language of possibility, a way out of colonialism . . . reimagining the world, a way into theorizing the reasons why the world we experience is unjust, and posing alternatives to such a world from within our own world views" (pp. 41, 204).

Source: Manaal Farooqi (Sep. 25, 2018). *We Need to Decolonize the Self-Care Movement. Here's Why*

Teresa Fuller's story of loss is an example of the impact of colonization. She experienced intergenerational heritage language loss in her family and has endured multiple sources of oppression (e.g., xenophobia, racism and pressures to assimilate to the dominant language and culture). The ties between her identity as Hispanic, connections with her family and a lack of access to her parents' language have given her a sense of cultural loss. In response, Teresa is able to reflect on the importance of preserving families' cultural heritage languages and takes a strong advocacy role with families in her program who may be struggling with pressures to assimilate to the majority language and culture.

*I think for me the awareness of being Hispanic, growing up in California during the time from my parents, when maintaining their native language was not encouraged at all, when they were punished. I kind of like what's happening now in our society where the more you could fit in and assimilate, the greater odds you would be accepted. So to lose that language for me meant I lost the connection with my grandparents. So, we have little ones coming in, whether they're from China, Korea, Chile, Japan, Italy, when we're speaking English to them all the time, and the parents show the pressure that their child, that they have to only speak to them in English. I try to reassure them that it's so important to maintain that, their native language, that it's okay and that we will help them to learn English. But it's okay for them to keep that language at home because that's a part of who they are, that's a part of their family, that's part of their culture, that's a part of just being. And to lose that, I kind of transfer my own pain and my own sadness of what I've lost in that whole process.*

—Teresa Fuller

## Critical Race Theory and Counter-Stories

Critical race theory (CRT) provides an important lens with which to support the examination of culture, especially the pervasive impact of racial inequalities in the ideologies, narratives, institutions and structures of society (Ladson-Billings & Tate, 1995). CRT assumes that racism can be both a conscious and unconscious act and it is endemic to, and a permanent aspect of, American society. Although race is recognized to be a social construct, the impact of race and racism are acknowledged as real and unjust (Bell, 1995). CRT asserts that the *experiential knowledge of people of color is essential for understanding the ways of knowing and naming racism and other forms of oppression in society* (Delgado, Stefancic, & Liendo, 2012; Fernández, 2002). Further, CRT can help us further understand and extend the findings from cultural neuroscience (Liddell & Jobson, 2016). Trauma due to racism can impact experiences of stress and stress responses in individuals from oppressed cultural groups.

*Counter-storytelling*, a foundational element of CRT, positions people of color as the experts of their own experiences. As Ladson-Billings and Tate (1995) claim, the "the voice of people of color is required for a complete analysis of the educational system" (p. 58). CRT has identified several ways in which racial inequities are perpetuated in educational systems: (a) the use of *deficit-thinking* (Valencia, 2010) to position individuals as lacking and deficient; (b) acts of *racial microaggressions* (Kohli & Solórzano, 2012) defined as, "brief and commonplace daily verbal, behavioral, or environmental indignities, whether intentional or unintentional, that communicate hostile, derogatory, or negative . . . slights and insults" (Suárez-Orozco et al., 2015; Sue et al., 2007, p. 271); (c) positions of *color-blind racism* or a refusal to acknowledge the impact of structural racism in society and blaming people of color as solely responsible for the social problems and inequities they experience (Bonilla-Silva, 2013) and (d) *internalized racism*, resulting from the daily impact of racism on one's identity and belief system, leading people of color to reinforce White superiority by privileging the beliefs, values, cultural routines and practices of the dominant culture while positioning their own heritage and cultural communities as inferior (Kohli, 2013).

Many of the educators' narratives throughout this book reflect the tenets of CRT—the racial inequities perpetuated in educational systems, including the early childhood field—and the consequences this has for individuals and communities. *Through the educators' counter-stories, we learn of their stress and experiences with trauma **and** the many innovative and meaningful ways they are caring for themselves in very difficult and inequitable circumstances.* Through their stories, we witness strengths, persistence, hope, love and passion. By centering their voices, we have a more complete understanding of the early childhood systems they are working within.

Using a CRT framework allows us to identify racial inequities that are daily realities for many of the women of color who constitute a large percentage of the early childhood workforce. Counter-storytelling positions educators as experts of their own experiences. CRT and counter-storytelling highlight minoritized groups' strengths, funds of knowledge, community cultural wealth and assets, self-determination and agency, creativity and forms of resistance in their efforts to heal, build resilience and strengthen their empowerment and liberation in the face of stress, trauma and oppression.

*Culturally Sustaining Pedagogy (CSP).* Culturally sustaining pedagogy (Paris, 2012; Paris & Alim, 2017) is a framework that seeks to perpetuate and foster—to sustain and extend—the cultural practices and ways of knowing that may be marginalized by systemic inequalities based on race, ethnicity and language among other factors. CSP rejects the idea of "cultural" universal practices (including self-care practices). Instead, CSP highlights the importance of sustaining historical cultural and language-based routines and practices while also acknowledging that cultural practices are always dynamically evolving within diverse communities. We use CSP to expand traditional discussions of self-care by listening to practitioners working in many roles within the field representing a wide range of diversities (race, gender, ethnicity, heritage language, country of birth, religion, ability, education, income etc.). Through educators' stories, we learn about the cultural approaches that are genuine and helpful for them in "caring for the self"—some of these represent heritage practices (that sustain rituals, routines, prayers etc. from their ancestors or family, tribal or ancestral communities), and others are reflections of their own contemporary cultural frames and ways of knowing that represent the dynamic and evolving nature of cultural routines, values and practices. We draw upon the importance of *sustaining* cultural and linguistic practices within the CSP framework to spotlight how culturally responsive self-care practices are not only a way to ensure that self-care is meaningful and accessible to all educators but also a lever for strengthening equity by sustaining cultural and linguistic diversity in society.

Fatima Ahmad, an administrator serving children ages 18 months to five years of age in an early Head Start program, is working intentionally to sustain the cultural and language practices of the children and families she works with in a subsidized program for low-income families that is part of a community shelter. Most of her children come with a trauma history, and the majority of the children are experiencing homelessness. Fatima draws from her cultural values of care for extended family systems and her status as a polyglot as strengths with which she can connect to the children and families she works with.

Even though her culture and language differ from the children she works with, she notes that overlapping cultural values shared between Middle Eastern and Hispanic families help her connect in a deep, meaningful way. Her intentional and consistent reflection on the intersection of language, culture and thought helps her sensitively build relationships with her ECE team and to support them to sustain their family language and cultural practices:

*I speak multiple languages. I speak Arabic, English and French which helped me a lot to absorb Spanish. I learn a lot from the children here, I am absorbing more Spanish from them so I can understand most of what lots of the families are saying. I'm still processing and I'm hoping one day I can respond back. But at least I understand what they're saying. Culture wise, the Hispanic culture is so similar to the Middle Eastern culture. Like, for example, they appreciate so much that extended families and they have these forms of different family members supporting each other. Even shared housing together. Which commonly happens in Middle Eastern countries. You see that people supporting each other, a lot of people sharing housing, they don't have to be homeless to do it it's just part of the culture.*

*So it helped me a lot to understand how to respond to different cultural situations without offending anybody. I have different ethnicities in the program. I have Middle Eastern, Spanish speaking populations, African American and Pacific Islanders, I have a combination of multiple cultures in one program, older and younger generations, I also have foster care children too and Native American. I feel my background has helped, even with my team members because sometimes when your first language is not English, when you respond, most of the time you have to process as a question in your own language and then respond to it in English. Sometimes when you do this, it's more of your language coming out or your heritage coming out, more than the English language itself that is coming out. So you have to really be careful and be culturally sensitive so you don't offend the people that you are helping.*

## Intersectionality

Intersectionality represents, "the critical insight that race, class, gender, sexuality, ethnicity, nation, ability, and age operate not as unitary, mutually exclusive entities, but as reciprocally constructing phenomena that in turn shape complex social inequalities" (Hill Collins, 2015, p. 2). Specifically:

- ◆ Race, class, gender, sexuality, age, ability, nation, ethnicity and similar categories of analysis are best understood in relational terms rather than in isolation from one another.
- ◆ These mutually constructing categories influence systems of power and oppression in society (e.g., racism and sexism are interrelated).
- ◆ Individuals and groups who are impacted differently by these systems of power (privileged and/or marginalized) have different points of view about their own and others' experiences, especially in relationship to inequality (Hill Collins, 2015).

Identity has been a focal area for scholars using an intersectionality approach, especially examination of the manner in which intersecting identities lead to diverse social experiences for individuals and social groups (Crenshaw, 1991). Intersectionality research examining identities often analyzes how individuals experience both privilege and marginalization in accordance with their various social identity categories (e.g., race/ethnicity, immigration status, citizenship, income, language(s) spoken [Anthias, 1998, 2013; Bonilla-Silva, 2013; Cho, Crenshaw, & McCall, 2013]) and how marginalization is perpetuated by power dynamics.

*Identity* is defined by the individual as well as the external society in which the individual lives. Identity involves the questions of "Who are you?" and what the elements are that make up your values, practices, relationships, career and the groups with which you affiliate. Identity includes elements that are chosen by the individual (affiliations) as well as those defined by social strata, such as social roles (e.g., mother) or social group (e.g., religion in which you were brought up) (Rogoff et al., 2017).

Intersectionality as a framework allows us to describe the diverse factors that influence early educators' identities and lived experiences, their different exposure to stress and trauma and the variations in cultural beliefs and practices that inform their strengths, coping skills and approaches to health and healing. The framework of intersectionality makes visible why self-care practices need to be culturally informed and personal to be authentic and effective.

*Given the diversity of the early childhood workforce, it is clear that more attention needs to be paid to expanding cultural perspectives of the "self" in self-care.* Figure 2.2 represents an intersectional conception of "self" in self-care.

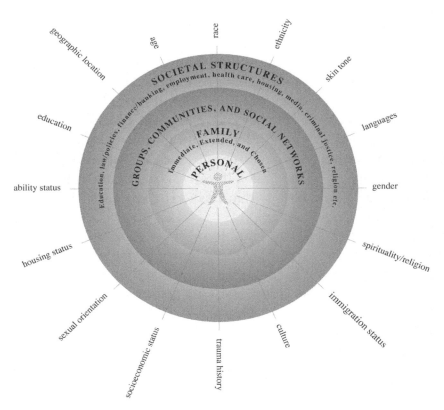

**FIGURE 2.2** Multiple Intersectional Layers of Influence on the Self

*Credit*: Julia Hennock, Hannah Shack

The conception of the "self" in culturally responsive self-care is one that is dynamically influenced by many co-occurring or intersecting personal, sociocultural, historical and political factors, as shown in Figure 2.2.

*The "Personal" circle* includes the various (and dynamically evolving) factors that make up the social categories one claims for their identity (e.g., age, race, gender identity, language, socioeconomic status, religion or spirituality etc.). For some early educators, this innermost circle would include the self as an individual (reflecting a Western individualist worldview), surrounded by their *"Family" circle* representing their closest "family-like" relationships (biological, extended and chosen family) and then the *"Community/Group Circle"* that includes all their addition social connections and the groups/communities in which they participate (e.g., work colleagues, neighbors, places of worship, sports leagues, community choir group etc.).

For educators whose cultural perspectives are more aligned with Indigenous or collectivist-oriented worldviews, the "individual" self may be de-centered and instead their personal, family and community/group circles would be integrated. The self would be understood not as a separate "individual" but instead as existing *in relation to* other people (e.g., family, friends, community members, ancestors) and, for some, the relation would extend beyond people to include the land/environment/universe around them (as reflected in many Indigenous Peoples' cultural ways of knowing).

*The "Societal Structures" circle* represents the historical and structural systems (e.g., systems of education, law and policies, finance /banking systems, employment opportunities, health care system, housing, media, criminal justice and organized religion) and the prevailing social norms and dominant cultural beliefs that influence educators' exposure to privilege/opportunities and stress/trauma and oppression (e.g., access to housing, health care, stable employment). These structural and historical systems of power influence how educators experience their different social categories of identity (e.g., positioning them with opportunities and privilege and/or preventing or limiting their access to resources and experiences and perpetuating cycles of marginalization and oppression). Figure 2.2 indicates these relationships with educators' social categories of identity as lines that extend across all of the circles.

### Reflection Questions

♦ How would you draw this model to reflect your conception of self? Would your "self" be at the center? What changes would you make?

- ◆ How might your conceptualization of your "self" align or differ from those of your ancestors, colleagues or family?
- ◆ Reflect on the interrelated and dynamic attributes, experiences and beliefs you may have. What might you consider to be intersectional?
- ◆ Consider the social structures you may experience. Describe the power relations between these structures and how these have influenced your intrapersonal conceptions of self as well as your interpersonal relations with others.

## Self-Care Aligned With Early Childhood Educators' Complex Intersectional Identities

*Early childhood educators describe many ways in which their intersectional identities influence their work, including why they entered the field, their exposure to stress and the decisions they make about self-care.* Their stories reflect on how their teaching and caring practices are influenced by culture, race, gender, ability, age and other factors. In addition, they describe how their individual experiences of stress and self-care are deeply influenced by the social categories of their identity—both identity categories that they claim and some that others identify with them that they *don't* claim as their own. There is often an active negotiation between the values and image of the self they grew up with and how they are currently experiencing, reflecting and expressing their understanding of self and intersectional identities.

Martin Fuentes speaks of how his cultural background (beliefs, experiences, language) is a source of knowledge and strength and leads him to make a positive impact on the diverse groups of children and families he works with:

> *I grew up having two parents who were employed and I was a dual language learner with Spanish being my primary language and English secondary. My parents didn't know about*

*the services that were out there and available to support us. My main background is mental health, working with children zero to five, or teenagers in the juvenile probation department, system of care history, at risk youth. My role now is being a bridge, for parents to know about the services available to them and supporting them to get those services for their child. For example, making sure that the kids have their vaccinations, their yearly checkups, physical checkups, dentals. And that the parents follow through with any kind of community resources, referrals that they have been given. My background, my culture and language really contributes to what I do because of the population that I work is similar to my background, which is of Hispanic, predominantly immigrant parents from Mexico or Latin America. Having the knowledge I do, knowing about the services, and being able to provide that information to the families really helps. Also, being a male in this field also really influences my work in a positive way . . . for example, when I deal with dads and they see a male counterpart in the field, they're like, "There's a male who is of Hispanic descent and speaks my language, maybe I should hear him out." And I think that that really opens the family to really explore these opportunities and have these services provided to them, like the importance of getting the child's physical evaluations, getting dental care every six months, exploring alternatives to their children's behaviors—exploring why they are behaving a certain way and not blaming their significant other or the teachers or anything else, but rather exploring developmentally and learning about the challenges that their child is encountering. So, yah, my background helps a lot.*

Linda Jones reflects on her values and intersectional identity. The way she looks, the language she speaks and her family-rooted values make it challenging for her to be easily categorized by the majority culture. These challenges are also her strengths, which have further been shaped by her family's work ethic, as part of their story of building a life in a new country for her to grow up in, her ability to speak Spanish and her awareness of the legal and cultural and employment challenges immigrants face. She explains:

*I am an immigrant and so I find that I relate a lot to the families knowing that a lot of our families come from a different country, a different culture. . . . My parents made a choice to come to this country for a better life for us and they had to struggle, they had to do a lot of things that probably some other parents might feel is beneath them or too much. And so I can relate to that. I saw my parents always work and that was not easy. So to me that always showed me that hard work is not a bad thing, but honorable work is good and that's what you aspire to, be productive, and I would say doing things that don't get you in trouble. So being mindful of the legal system, right and wrong and all that is something that you need to be mindful of. Because I speak Spanish I do have a connection to families in our agencies and the staff, and so that's always a good way to break the ice and I think be accepted because I don't look like the typical Spanish speaking person, but I speak Spanish. Sometimes that has made my life hard because people don't know how to figure it out, how to place me. You're not Black but you're not Hispanic, you know. Those kinds of questions, "What are you?" and those kinds of things.*

---

### Spotlight on Practice

Charles Harris, site principal in an early childhood department within a large urban school district, shares how aspects of his intersectional identity influence his work and self-care practices.

*My inspiration for entering the field of early childhood. I did my student teaching in Jackson, Mississippi at a school with a population that was 95% African-American. What I noticed throughout the* school was that there were no men in early childhood education, and specifically, there were no men of color. And so that's what really drew me to this field.

The impact being a man of color has for the children and families in our community. It makes a big impact because I look like them. I'm a man of color, and we serve a community of color. And so I think that makes a huge impact. And I also think that there's a lack of men in the children's homes. There are a lot of single-parent homes according to the data that we see in my district. The children don't see a lot of men, not just role models, but a lot of men, not only in their homes but in the community. I remember when I was teaching one of my students asked me, "Mr. Harris, why did you come to work dressed like you're going to church?" And so that right there told me that they, in the community where I was teaching, never saw men dressed to go to work. When the men got dressed up, they were usually going to church. My students didn't usually see men as full professionals going to work. So my background as an African-American man in early childhood has a huge impact on the work I do.

The benefits and limitations of my work ethic. I'm a perfectionist and I have very high expectations not just for my staff, but also for myself. I believe that a lot of the stress that I bring upon myself at work, has a lot to do with me. I think this is a model that has carried me a very long way . . . that failure is not an option. Right? I know that the children are dependent on us. So, my stress level is brought on by my expectations.

Managing my stress: Self-care strategies that work for me. I learned early in my practice being an administrator that it's not good to make decisions when I'm under stress. It's just not a good practice because you're probably making emotional decisions which are not the best decisions. A lot of times when I am stressed, I usually close my door. Music really helps, it gets me through the day. I listen alone in my office with the door closed. I love jazz and R&B. It puts me in that very happy place because it reminds me of my partner and he puts me in a happy place.

*Another thing that has gotten me through a lot of stress is knowing, "I can't be everything to everybody". It's so easy for me to tell others to take care of themselves, to take advantage of self-care but do I actually do it too? I've learned to make sure that I practice what I preach: Taking care of myself. For me that means making sure my family is first and knowing my mind has to rest. And making sure that I'm surrounded with people who hold similar values to me and who understand when I say I'm tired. Understanding this is really, really, really important to me. It's important that my friends and partner understand what my work is like and respect that when I say I'm tired, I'm actually tired and not trying to ignore them.*

*All my friends and my partner are equally busy as we all are professionals. We all have very, very long schedules and my friends have children so that takes a lot of their time. We can all get so caught up in work, we tend to lose focus. What brings me back is to at times, step away from work, and just really surround myself with family, friends and enjoy life. We always try to just put things on the calendar and make sure that we are holding up to our commitments to one another.*

Elsa Karlsson, early childhood special education teacher, lives in Anchorage, Alaska. Elsa describes how her upbringing shaped her notions of herself growing up. As an adult, she has taken these ideas and revised them based on her current beliefs. She now uses her currently evolved perspective in her work with children with special needs.

*When I was growing up, kids were not given a voice. You were seen and not heard. And I always hated that because I think it was important to be able to say how we're feeling. Like in my family we are not allowed to express our feelings or anything, especially anger. So all that had to be kept to the side. And so I think that has always come through is I think kids are important. Where I was growing up, we didn't feel important at all. Only the adults were important. But I think children are very important and that they should have a voice, because they are our future and we need to give them a voice now so they learn how to express their feelings and what they need so that they become better human beings down the road. I think that even with my special education kids who are, so many of them are cognitively impaired, they still have a voice. And I think it's important that we hear it because then we can help meet their needs and help them grow into becoming more independent or just to grow in themselves as a better human being.*

Jennifer Andrews reflects on her development of identity based on her family background growing up with parents in the 60s whom she described as "hippies" and the time she spent in nature with a lot of freedom and adults around her who were playful and fun but little exposure to rules and protocols: a family life that left her feeling disconnected from the cultural norms of her schooling. She finds herself drawn to early childhood because of its connection to playfulness and joy and reflective practice as a context that provides freedom to explore and learn about oneself and about professional practice within the context of a structured process . . . a mirror of what she describes as a lifelong desire to find a balance between the "bigger reality of life" and "being rules based and following protocols":

*My background, I grew up in the 60s and my parents were hippies and so we would often take vacations at the beach and I spent a lot of time in nature. So my brothers and I typically were climbing trees and our parents believed that we should run free and they were trying to follow our lead and be supportive to who we were becoming as human beings. And the other side of that is that I didn't get a lot of explanations about protocols and etiquette and rules about life and then they sent me to regular school and the schools that I went to had a lot of rules. And so there was often a cultural disconnect for me between my home life and school life. And so I always was trying to catch up and try to figure out how the world worked outside of my home environment. The other side of that is I grew up with a lot of adults around me who were playful and funny and fun to be with so as I was growing up, my picture of adulthood was I think shaped by these adults who approach life with a lot of enjoyment and appreciation and playfulness. And so as an adult I tend to gravitate in that direction of wanting to be a playful adult who enjoys life.*

In another example, Monique Lee's upbringing illustrates an example of interconnectedness across generations in her family. As a result of a more collectivist background, her worldview has an expanded notion of family and care beyond her household. Monique brings this to her work with families and children.

*I'm Filipino. So I have a family, well this is true with a lot of families but in the Filipino culture, you know, family closeness. I had my Grandpa living with me and my Aunts lived with me within the household when they first came from the Philippines, my parents' home, that's where my Grandpa was at. And my Aunts would come every weekend. So I believe with that, having that background, I really feel that connection to the family members that are our community at school here, that I try to build on that and try to actually get their culture into my classroom as well. But that affects me as my—that influences my job is I want to be close to my families and I want my parents to know me and I want to know them, not just seeing them as their children.*

## Butterflies Have Diverse Colors and Wing Patterns

The different colors and patterns on the butterfly wings represent the diversity of early educators. This includes their different intersectional identities and their specific program and community contexts, cultural backgrounds, personal interests, strengths, learning edges and range of experiences with privilege and oppression. These factors and more influence their self-concept and the forms of self-care they find genuine and replenishing for their energy reserves and healing.

## Self-Care as a Lifelong Journey

The stories throughout this book illustrate the complex and diverse and transformative learning journeys educators take in expanding their self-awareness and embrace of self-care practices. These journeys involve a constant negotiation of identity and values as they navigate across diverse cultural settings over time. Encian's story is one example of the complex intersections that exist between educators' identities, their lived experiences and discoveries they make about meaningful and genuine forms of self-care.

*I feel like self-care is a really loaded word. When I was a teenager, I was getting into joining collective efforts for social change in various ways, including going to mass demonstrations but also doing local organizing, working in the city where I grew up. I had this supervisor at a movie theater where I worked, who was older, I don't know, maybe she was in her 30s but she seemed really old to me . . . I really looked up to her and it turned out she knew all these people that I was doing organizing with, but she had really strong feelings about them, and was like, "They are trying to do all these things for other people but their own lives are totally messy and they need to work through some things." And so she was kind of against the mass organizing that was happening. But it was just like this "A-ha" moment for me because I thought those activists that I was organizing with were really just so cool and knew everything. And I didn't think of them as just messy people . . . I've always remembered that moment and when I reflect on it now, I think, "Oh . . . self-care isn't about necessarily taking yourself out of the struggle so that you can do nice things for yourself and pamper yourself and treat yourself. It's about really being intentional about, 'okay, if I'm going to be contributing to these movements and I'm going to be trying to help people get free . . . that's not going to work and it's going to be counterproductive if I'm bringing my own mess into that.' That's going to create more work for whatever collective I'm participating in" Self-care's about figuring yourself out and working on healing your own wounds so that when you come in to these group endeavors, you're able to hold your own and contribute . . . respecting other people's space and encouraging other people's leadership in a way where it's a symbiotic whole. You're part of this thing, and you're not taking it over with your drama or with your own needs that are unfulfilled.*

*And so self-care's about doing all of the self-work . . . I guess the good thing about the term is it's reminding us that self-work doesn't have to be a struggle, this grueling thing where we're forcing ourselves to do mindfulness exercises or whatever. It is about care. It's about how are we nurturing ourselves and letting ourselves grow all the time. We never stop growing. One of the wonderful things about the early childhood field, I think, is that we're in this mindset of nurturing growth across all these different domains and seeing the child as a whole person. This practice puts us caregivers in a great position to also think about ourselves as whole people, and ask, "Well, how do we grow ourselves creatively, spiritually, physically, as well?" I think different people have different starting points of what self-care means . . . it's healing. It includes de-stressing, but what Aikido practice has taught me, is it's not just like you build up all this stress and then you escape to the woods for a week and then you're on a clean slate, because then the stress just builds up again. It's finding ways to deal with stress in the moment where you're not taking it into your body. You're trying to ground yourself, find alignment, hold your space and be in the stressful situation and respond to it without absorbing it, into yourself. And that doesn't mean I can do that perfectly. It's a lifelong process. But the fact of thinking about it that way and of course, practicing it with my body has shifted things for me and hopefully is making me a more effective participant in the groups I'm a part of.*

Through Encian's story, we see how his ideas of self-care evolve over time to center more on his own experiences and needs. In the beginning, he expressed the idea that self-care was a way to escape and pamper one's self. However, Encian came to realize that, at least for him, self-care was more about how to gain the ability to responsibly participate in liberation movements. Encian's practice of Aikido helped ground him so he was prepared for his role in activism. Instead of being an isolated process, self-care became integrated into Encian's life as a process that was worthy of his attention and nurturing because he redefined it to be meaningful to him—his identity, his life experiences and the most meaningful ways of caring for himself. Self-care became a cornerstone reflecting his very personal transformative learning journey.

## Summary

Early childhood educators can take a strengths-based approach to understand how their cultural backgrounds and experiences relate to their experiences of stress and self-care. Conceptions of the self and what self-care means may differ greatly across cultures, with Indigenous-oriented models tending to focus more on the self as interrelated compared to more Western-based individualized notions. Cultural neuroscience helps us understand how these cultural differences relate to how stress may be experienced, stored and retrieved differently across groups and how these cultural experiences shape our brain's physiological and neural structures. Further, culture impacts how we may respond to certain types of healing strategies.

Through reflecting on and understanding the role of your own culture and your intersectional identities, and by seeking to learn about and value those of the people you work with, you can decolonize self-care, going beyond one-size-fits-all models to create culturally sustaining practices that are reflective of the diversity of values, lenses and belief systems of the communities in which you are engaged. Finally, the counterstories presented in this chapter position educators as experts of their own experiences: diverse professionals with agency and options to support their healing, resiliency and empowerment despite the marginalization and oppression they endure working in the field of early childhood. This journey toward defining self-concept and self-care is dynamic and ever changing across the lifespan.

*Last September I was in a really uncomfortable space, not wanting to be somewhere. And I didn't realize until the next day when I was in pain all the way from my toes up through my shoulders and my neck. I was just in total pain. My doctor couldn't help me at all. It was useless. And then my therapist connected just how tense I had been, not only on that day, but likely the build up, the anxiety of preparing to be around certain people and the feeling of being stuck, trapped, paralyzed, and silenced; and that day just threw me over. And so I think I started to feel that again, when I wanted to hear some music. I've slowly tried to read my body, recognizing that sometimes it's the only way I hear my feelings, as if I'm retracing my steps. And as my body began to lock up again, and my words stopped falling out of my mouth, I played a couple songs that brought me back to my father. I cried loudly. I screamed. I sang. I drove . . . I drove and screamed and sang loudly. And I finally danced in the kitchen. And in the shower. Not on the dancefloor still, because I'm not quite there yet in my grief, but I know, finally, that I can listen to my body, and trace it back to my heart, and everything else will follow.*

*I've realized that hearing music and singing was really what I always did for self-care and not having that was really hard for me. While the silence and prayer continue to serve its purpose, I needed the music. Without it, I'd lost my words and became stuck. I grew up with music everywhere; competing music through our windows, from our neighbors' kitchens to the cars that would thump down the street, it was just constant. And sometimes now that I hear some of the music that my mom would play over and over, it was really painful, sorrowful, sad music that now I love and I get nostalgic about. I'm sure many people are like, I don't want to hear this. It is so terrible, it's too sad. But it's . . . you know, it's home. And so it's comforting. It gives my pain a voice, when I run out of words. It relieves my body, when I've forgotten to listen to how much I'm locking in. And it helps me completely feel and share my joy. Music is something that I brought back for myself and something I needed.*

*I also realized that even prayer is really therapeutic for me. It is very meditative. This is something that I have recently really appreciated. My grandmother used to make us pray the rosary every night. And my mother used to make my siblings do the rosary every night too. I was born 15 years after them and it wasn't something my mom continued with me. But, I realize now how the rosary was really her time where everybody had to shut up and be still and she commanded the room and it was, I think her peace. I was talking with my Tia about it recently because I have been trying to learn the rosary. After my dad passed, I hosted most of the Novenarios, which is nine nights of rosary and lots of food, lots and lots of food and wine (in our case, at least), and I always feared how we could lose this tradition with the coming generations, when it's been such a critical part of our healing throughout my life and generations of our family. And so I was trying to learn it, I could not figure it out—the intervals or variation based on day of the week or* event. I was even listening to it on Spotify. I could not memorize it, but I'd follow along, and count the same beads from my grandmother's rosary that she left me the last time she visited the states when I was a child. And when we did one of them at her house, she had us do it like twice back to back cause she does one for her children every night as well. And as she held me before I left, feeling frustrated and utterly hollowed out in grief, she told me, "Just pray you don't have to think about the words, just say it, just let it flow." And so I have . . . and slowly it brings me back to myself, back to my father, back to my peace.

I've just been really grateful for it for as much as I feel like I pushed religion away so much, I now feel like it's what I've been gripping on to. I'm still not going to totally participate in a lot of the components that I don't agree with, but it's like I went to my old church where I grew up just because I felt like I needed to go home in some way and I did not connect that it was going to be a special Father's Day ceremony and they'd bring all these fathers to the stage. I went so that I could sit where my father usually sat. And I did. I must've sobbed for like an hour pretty much during the mass and afterwards. While I've been told at times that I need to "Go to church to get the devil out of you" and to have faith, for me it's about that community and the space, the place, the rituals, the songs, and the patterns that were grounding for me. Where I knew that every Saturday night, we'd go to mass and dinner afterwards; it was one of my few routines. And even though once I started college, I didn't want to go back, when I would go, I would go when it was empty. I'd go and I'd light a candle and pray alone. I didn't want to sit in mass. I didn't want to go to confession and didn't want to participate in everything. But I think now it's really been something to fall back on for myself—whichever part I choose to pick up and embrace, I just go with it.

**Reflection Questions**

In Doménica's initial quest for healing, in what ways was her environment not a good "fit" for her to thrive?

- ◆ What aspects of her intersectional multicultural identity were not being adequately nurtured?
- ◆ Why do you think Doménica had lost parts of her cultural connection?
- ◆ Why do you think it is important to acknowledge culture in self-care?

Doménica's search for a cure for her pain was unsuccessful until she reconnected with the music and religion of her family.

- ◆ What activities link you to your parents, grandparents and/ or children?
- ◆ Why are these types of intergenerational connections healing?

In what ways were Doménica's individual experiences reflective of larger collectivist constructs?

- ◆ How did Doménica both center and de-center herself in her healing?

As we grow, we may move across different social contexts or away from home. In doing so, we might either adopt new practices and/or reject old ones. Can you reflect on any practices that were important to your family and/or community growing up but that you no longer keep? Are there any you have or would like to re-engage with?

# 3

# Building a Culturally Responsive Self-Care Toolbox

*What are specific strategies early educators can use to take care of themselves in culturally responsive and meaningful ways?*

**Key Topics Covered**

- ♦ Culturally Situated Self-Care Practices
- ♦ Strategies for Self-Care That Focus on "Tuning INward"
- ♦ Strategies for Self-Care That Focus on "Tuning OUTward"
- ♦ Health and Wellness Toolkit

*Early Educators Across the* United States *and Internationally Shared Their Strategies for Taking Care of Themselves . . .*

In this chapter, our aim is to present a diversity of strategies that early childhood educators have reported to be helpful to reduce their stress and care for themselves. As we mentioned in the Introduction and Chapter 1, the way stress and burnout are experienced and addressed differ across individuals and groups.

**What are the different ways you reduce your stress and take care of yourself?**

Speaking to a counselor Hot Bath Mindfulness
Laughing Swimming Gardening Venting to friends and family
Exercise Glass of wine Acupuncture Fishing Reflection
Sleeping Essential oils Taking a break Self-affirmations
Reading
Spending time alone Unplugging Zoning out Connecting with community
Watching TV Petting dogs Eating comfort food Snuggling with pets
Breathing Yoga Dancing
Visualization Imagining a safe space
Listening to music Looking at photos Hiking Going to church
Going to the beach Asking for help Running Aikido Calling friends
Working on my car
Spending time with friends Massage Playing with grandchildren
Walking Singing Home improvement Journaling
Hula hooping Meditation Painting
Eating healthy Recognizing personal limits Being in nature Manicures
Praying Therapy
Screaming alone in the car Spending time with family

*The self-care practices you find meaningful and decide to integrate into your life will be personal to you and likely influenced by your specific background, culture, comfort and where you are in the process of practicing self-care.*

The variety of options described in this chapter are organized into two broad categories:

◆ *Strategies that emphasize "tuning inward".* These strategies involve a focus inward, on oneself. They include strategies that strengthen self-awareness, self-reflection, the use of inquiry, mindfulness and self-compassion. By 'tuning inward', educators learn to manage the emotional intensity and complexity of their work. By learning to pause and develop self-awareness about their personal triggers and internal stressors, educators learn to prevent and/ or interrupt their stress response systems from triggering and the stress chemicals being released throughout their bodies. Tuning inward also supports educators to respond with more empathy and attunement to themselves and in communication with others. *As stated previously, tuning inward may not be culturally relevant for some educators.*

◆ *Strategies that focus on "tuning outward".* These strategies emphasize a look outward—connecting with other people, with community and/or animals to restore energy reserves, to create buffers to toxic stress and to heal minds and bodies.

## Mirrors, Windows and Sliding Doors

Sorting the various self-care strategies and approaches into these two categories was done simply to organize the information in a manner that readers could review quickly and efficiently. In reality, the way that individuals authentically integrate self-care into their lives dynamically blends different strategies from both categories, as readers will see in the narratives subsequently. As you read through this chapter, we hope the various ideas and personal narratives offer what Rudine Sims Bishop (1990) describes as *mirrors, windows and sliding doors*. She explains:

> Books are sometimes windows, offering views of worlds that may be real or imagined, familiar or strange. These windows are also sliding glass doors, and readers have only to walk through in imagination to become part of whatever world has been created or recreated by the author. When lighting conditions are just right, however, a window can also be a mirror. Literature transforms human experience and reflects it back to us, and in that reflection, we can see our own lives and experiences as part of the larger human experience. Reading, then,

becomes a means of self-affirmation, and readers often seek their mirrors in books.

(p. 1)

Our goal is that all of our readers see *mirrors* that reflect ideas for self-care that they already engage in and/or feel familiar and comfortable: stories that validate their experiences and ways of knowing and being. And windows and sliding doors that validate the diverse experiences of others, although unfamiliar, can offer novel provocations and invitations to take a risk, open your heart and mind and try a new form of caring for yourself. As you read through this chapter, ask yourself:

◆ Which self-care strategies are my mirrors that reflect the self-care I am already using and/or familiar with?
◆ Which self-care strategies are windows and doors that offer me inspiration for new ways to care for myself?

## Bite-Sized Actions

With so many strategies throughout this book, readers might feel overwhelmed and not know where to begin or worry that they don't have time or energy to add more to their plate, leaving them wondering if making a small change will really create a meaningful difference. These feelings and concerns are understandable and likely shared by most educators reading this book. Drawing on Zaretta Hammond's (2015) wise advice, we recommend that readers *take bite-sized action*. Choose one or two strategies to begin working on. Don't try to take on too much all at once. Learning to prioritize your self-care is long-term work. The most important commitment educators can make is to continually be working at it, one step at a time. As you read through this chapter, ask yourself:

- ◆ What should I acknowledge that I am already doing to care for myself—strategies that I enjoy, that work for me or that I should be doing more often?
- ◆ What is one bite-sized action I can take to expand my personal self-care toolbox?

## Strategies for Self-Care That Focus on "Tuning INward"

*For me, self-care has to do with attending to my sense of self. Throughout the course of the day, I tend to attune strongly to other people and try to be supportive and helpful to others. And I think that's a tendency that I have to want to attend to others and try to help them, to be a support to others. And so,* **self-care for me is bringing the attunement back to my inner self and my inner world and listen to myself inwardly.** *I think that's an area where when we are growing up, we're not taught how to do that. And so I've had to teach myself how to do that through meditation and journaling and other kinds of modalities to come back to my sense of self and experiences, a sense of strength and empowerment about myself. To visualize myself as someone who has value and someone who has a lot to offer to the world. So, when I do self-care I do a lot of visualization, meditation, self-reflection.*

—*Jennifer Andrews, Early Learning Specialist, State Department of Education*

*Credit*: Alice Blecker

*My devotion time is really important to me, and also I'm involved in my church. I'm on the women's board and I help with the youth group. For me, that's just my serene space is my devotion. I think that really helps me do a lot of calming and just relaxing. I have to relax in my home with God. You have to have that time with him. I get up now at 5:00 am, so I can pray first before I read, and it has to be really quiet. I do all my family, and friends, and then I do the devotion part.*

—Rhonda Pitts, Preschool Teacher

## Building Self-Awareness

*Self-awareness* is the ability to know yourself. The more you know yourself, the better you function in your professional and personal relationships. Awareness of yourself can include the following:

◆ Your strengths
◆ Your areas of growth and development
◆ Knowing what you feel in a particular moment and the intensity of your emotions. Learning whether you react based on your emotional state or pause and wait until you can regulate and then think through solutions
◆ Knowing what frustrates or triggers you
◆ Knowing what brings you joy, calm and/or happiness
◆ Knowing what energizes and restores you and what drains your energy
◆ Knowing your values and beliefs and how they impact your behaviors, interactions and professional practice.

Self-awareness is cultivated with intentional tuning inward. This includes awareness of your body, mind and spirit. This can also be phrased as physical/sensory (body), intellectual (mind) and emotional (spiritual, psychological) awareness. We present two example strategies you can use to develop self-awareness. The first is a temperature check. The second is a body scan.

*Emotional Temperature Check* (Source: Julie Kurtz, LMFT). Educators can use this in many ways. They can check in with themselves each morning before they leave for work, in the middle of the day on a break, after they arrive home and before bed. Becoming aware of the emotions and emotional intensity they are experiencing in the moment can help them develop insight as to whether they need more self-care or self-regulation strategies to restore themselves back to the Green, 0–3 or Calm/Optimal State of Regulation. Educators also have the choice in the far-right column to list some things that may be impacting that state of emotion. Emotional self-awareness is an important foundation not only to learn about how you are feeling in the moment and the intensity of your feelings, but it is the precursor to knowing when to use tools for self-regulation support.

| Emotion Check-In Using Colors | Scale of Emotional Intensity Using Numbers | Intensity of Emotions Using Words | Name Each Feeling List if the Feeling is Small, Medium or Large (S, M or L) List/Track What Person, Place, Event, Activity Led to This Feeling |
|---|---|---|---|
| **Red** (Triggered) | 7–10 | Intense | |
| **Orange** (Early trigger signals) | 4–6 | Moderate and increasing | |
| **Green** (Calm, optimal state of regulation) | 0–3 | Calm and regulated | |

*Body Scan.* Pausing and paying attention to how the sensations in your body feel is an important way to promote self-care. In our busyness, we forget to pay attention to the clues our body gives us that we are becoming too stressed out. Our body is often the first to send a physiological signal that we have stress. Each person exhibits stress symptoms in different parts of their body. You can check in with yourself throughout the day by putting an X where you feel stress in your body in the following silhouette. The X symbolizes where you feel stress—your head, neck, jaws, hands, feet, hips, lower or upper back, neck, eyes, mouth, ears, stomach or heart. You can place more than one X if there is tension or physical stress being communicated in more than one place in your body. This pause can help you develop self-awareness about your physical body.

Following is a sample from a professional development self-care training conducted by Julie Kurtz where she asked teachers to draw a body scan on a flip chart. They indicated where in their body they experience stress sensations. Notice how they indicated their physical stress. You can draw your own daily body scan to increase your self-awareness about your level of stress. Body stress can be described with words (stomach pain) or sensations (feels like a volcano erupting in my stomach or a hammer pounding in my head) or simply by placing in X where in the body you might be feeling discomfort.

In the following image, teachers described the following body sensations that were cues to their own stress: Stomach pain and digestive issues, heartburn, shoulder pain, grinding of teeth, hip tightness, head and neck pain.

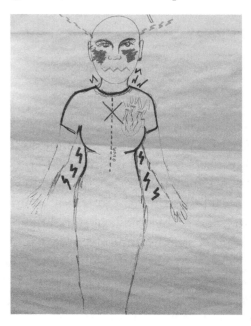

## Completed Body Scan

When you pay attention and tune in to your body, you can notice your clues to stress, such as your breath, heartbeat, temperature, muscles, belly, hands, head or feet.

Reflect on yourself for a moment: When you are in the green, orange or red zone, what does your energy look like and how does it differ from color zone to color zone (green, orange or red)? Do you become listless, frozen, disconnected or numb; do you try to escape or run from the situation, or does your energy increase and you become more aggressive physically, emotionally or mentally? Can you pay attention and intervene before it escalates too far into the zone of dys-regulation (red)?

*Identify Your Emotional Triggers.* It is helpful for educators to learn to identify their emotional triggers. These are those things that push their emotional buttons and activate the harmful stress chemicals to circulate throughout their bodies, lead them to have strong emotional reactions that can frighten and harm children and/or create conflict with the adults they are interacting with and disrupt a positive emotional climate at their workplace. Ideally, educators will identify the specific behaviors or environmental conditions that cause them to have strong emotional triggers. Once educators have discovered their personal triggers, they are better equipped to learn to use strategies to effectively manage their emotions and prevent future triggering events from happening.

Following is a tool developed by the Oakland Starting Smart and Strong Resilient Oakland Community and Kids (ROCK) Initiative (www.oaklandsmartandstrong.org/rock.html) and used by Head Start and preschool teachers working in state-subsidized early childhood programs in Oakland, California. Lawanda Wesley, Oakland Unified School District's Director of Quality Enhancement and Professional

Development of Early Education, describes how they use the tool with teachers:

> *The Trigger Tool was introduced during our first ROCK Professional Learning Community (PLC) convening as a way to introspectively reflect on how the teachers are feeling in the moment when children are having a trauma response. We explained that teachers bring their whole selves as educators to their work and there are moments where children's trigger responses (because of our mirror neurons) impact educators; times teachers' ability to co-regulate children is essential to be responsive and supportive. The Trigger Response Tool was then reviewed by the teachers and later completed during the third or fourth sessions of the PLC. We referred back to it during our PLC discussions to help the teachers maintain awareness about their stressors and to think about self-care responses they could use to help calm themselves and be available to attune to the children.*

*Use This Tool to Identify Your Personal Triggers That Impact Your Teaching Practice*

*Please read each item and answer honestly. Rate each item from 1–5.*

Now that you have finished rating these items, *identify your biggest triggers*. These are items that you scored a "5" (or perhaps a "4"). Be as specific as you can. For example, if certain noises make you want to "explode", describe the specific noise that makes you feel this way and why you think that is. Then, reflect on the following questions in relation to each of these triggers:

♦ What are your beliefs about this behavior (e.g., your cultural values and beliefs associated with this behavior)?
♦ How does it make you feel? Where in your body do you feel the reaction?

**TABLE 3.1 IDENTIFYING PERSONAL TRIGGERS**

| 1 | 2 | 3 | 4 | 5 |
|---|---|---|---|---|
| Does not bother me at all | Makes me feel a little uncomfortable | Makes me feel stressed | This upsets me | I'm going to explode! |

*Please indicate your level of agreement with each of the following statements.*

| I am triggered . . . | 1 | 2 | 3 | 4 | 5 |
|---|---|---|---|---|---|
| By loud noises. | 1 | 2 | 3 | 4 | 5 |
| When I have to wait for something. | 1 | 2 | 3 | 4 | 5 |
| When my daily routine is changed. | 1 | 2 | 3 | 4 | 5 |
| When someone whines. | 1 | 2 | 3 | 4 | 5 |
| When other people are talking near me. | 1 | 2 | 3 | 4 | 5 |
| When I don't understand what someone is saying to me. | 1 | 2 | 3 | 4 | 5 |
| When someone starts to talk with me unexpectedly. | 1 | 2 | 3 | 4 | 5 |
| When someone asks me for help. | 1 | 2 | 3 | 4 | 5 |
| A colleague gives me feedback/constructive criticism. | 1 | 2 | 3 | 4 | 5 |
| When I'm exhausted. | 1 | 2 | 3 | 4 | 5 |
| Someone tells me to correct a mistake. | 1 | 2 | 3 | 4 | 5 |
| When someone disagrees with me. | 1 | 2 | 3 | 4 | 5 |
| Arriving to work on time. | 1 | 2 | 3 | 4 | 5 |
| Working with a coach. | 1 | 2 | 3 | 4 | 5 |
| When someone points out a mistake I made. | 1 | 2 | 3 | 4 | 5 |
| Talking with families. | 1 | 2 | 3 | 4 | 5 |
| Being observed. | 1 | 2 | 3 | 4 | 5 |
| When I see students are having a conflict. | 1 | 2 | 3 | 4 | 5 |
| When I disagree with a colleague/supervisor. | 1 | 2 | 3 | 4 | 5 |
| Deadlines, time pressures. | 1 | 2 | 3 | 4 | 5 |
| When I have to do something new or different. | 1 | 2 | 3 | 4 | 5 |
| When others touch me (i.e., handshake, pat on the back). | 1 | 2 | 3 | 4 | 5 |
| When I don't understand a certain idea or concept. | 1 | 2 | 3 | 4 | 5 |
| Teasing by others. | 1 | 2 | 3 | 4 | 5 |
| When I don't finish something on time. | 1 | 2 | 3 | 4 | 5 |

*(Continued)*

**TABLE 3.1** (Continued)

| | | | | | |
|---|---|---|---|---|---|
| Asking for help. | 1 | 2 | 3 | 4 | 5 |
| When I am confused about a task/activity. | 1 | 2 | 3 | 4 | 5 |
| When I have to follow specific instructions. | 1 | 2 | 3 | 4 | 5 |
| Violence in the school community. | 1 | 2 | 3 | 4 | 5 |
| My supervisor gives me feedback. | 1 | 2 | 3 | 4 | 5 |
| When my students are hungry. | 1 | 2 | 3 | 4 | 5 |
| Fears of deportation for my students and their families. | 1 | 2 | 3 | 4 | 5 |
| When my students are homeless or housing insecure. | 1 | 2 | 3 | 4 | 5 |
| Being rated by an evaluator. | 1 | 2 | 3 | 4 | 5 |
| When language barriers prevent me from communicating with students' families. | 1 | 2 | 3 | 4 | 5 |
| Not having time to reflect and talk with my colleagues about my teaching practice. | 1 | 2 | 3 | 4 | 5 |
| Working with a mental health consultant. | 1 | 2 | 3 | 4 | 5 |
| My supervisor gives me constructive criticism. | 1 | 2 | 3 | 4 | 5 |
| When I feel different than everyone around me because of my race. | 1 | 2 | 3 | 4 | 5 |
| When I feel different than everyone around me because of my gender. | 1 | 2 | 3 | 4 | 5 |
| When I feel different than everyone around me because of the language I speak. | 1 | 2 | 3 | 4 | 5 |
| Not having adequate staff coverage. | 1 | 2 | 3 | 4 | 5 |
| When someone doesn't think I am smart.* | 1 | 2 | 3 | 4 | 5 |
| When someone makes fun of my abilities.* | 1 | 2 | 3 | 4 | 5 |
| When I am reminded of my special education label or diagnosis. | 1 | 2 | 3 | 4 | 5 |
| When someone changes the meeting time without notice. | 1 | 2 | 3 | 4 | 5 |
| When someone doesn't keep their promises or the group's agreements.* | 1 | 2 | 3 | 4 | 5 |
| Other: | 1 | 2 | 3 | 4 | 5 |

◆ How do you typically respond to this behavior? Do you pause and wait until you can regulate and think through solutions? Do you consider the behavior as a way someone communicates? Do you consider how your response can increase or decrease the stress responses of the child or adult you are communicating with?

Engaging in this process can help teachers to build self-awareness of the specific behaviors that trigger strong emotional reactions in them and why this is the case. With this knowledge, teachers can use their increased self-awareness to develop strategies for self-care and for adjusting the environment to reduce their exposure to triggers, allowing them to be more attuned, self-regulated and responsive in their work with adults and children.

*Journaling to Increase Self-Awareness and to Promote Healing.* Expressive writing is a route to healing—emotionally, physically and psychologically. Dr. James Pennebaker, author of *Writing to Heal* (2004), has seen improved immune function in participants of writing exercises. Stress often comes from emotional blockages and overthinking hypotheticals. He suggests that when we translate our experiences into language, we make them more "graspable". And in doing so, you free yourself from mentally being tangled in traumas. Other benefits to consider from putting pen to paper:

1. Journaling helps create a pause button and prevents impulsive reactions.
2. Increases empathy for yourself and others.
3. Helps increase self-awareness (sensations, emotions, thoughts and behaviors).
4. Helps you see all the characters in the movie, not just yourself.
   ◆ *First make your own journal or purchase one that you feel most reflects your spirit. Some adults go to the bookstore or online and/or Google search for journals. Some choose those with recycled plain paper and others with fancy designs and again some prefer one with a lock. In some instances, there are apps that can safely secure your journal entries.*
   ◆ *Decide what your journaling practice will be the first 3–6 months.* Developing a habit takes practice that is consistent. Your new practice can be daily or a

few times per week. After 3–6 months, re-evaluate if you can increase or if you should reduce the number of days in your routine.

*Body Scan Journal Entry.* Describe with a body scan, a visual symbol or an X how you feel in your body. Examples may include pounding like a hammer, nervous like butterflies in your stomach, rocky like a rocking chair, heavy like a rock, empty like a container, exploding like a volcano, hot like the sun, racing like a roller coaster, buzzing like bumble bees, tight like a rubber band, icy like ice cubes, angry like a T-Rex dinosaur. There are many visuals that can describe how your body feels, and you can draw that image or simply an X mark where your body may be feeling stress. Alternatively, there is an app called Stop, Breathe & Think that promotes the mindful act of naming emotions and sensations to help you put them in perspective and create a greater sense of calm.

*Positive Strength and Asset Journal Entry.* Noticing your strengths can promote a more balanced mental mindset. When we are stressed, we tend to focus on the things we don't do well or don't like about ourselves. We can get caught in a cycle of negativity and habits of self-talk that are self-deprecating and negative (I hate myself, I am not good at anything, no one likes me etc.).

*Today I notice one of my strengths. I am very good at helping others, especially the infants in my classroom. I know exactly how to calm each one and I am good at it. Babies love me and they easily stop crying because when I hold them or rock them they calm down easily in my care.*

*Self-Regulation Journal Entry.* After you check in with your emotional temperature, do a body scan and determine how you are physically, mentally and emotionally. What will you do if you find you have intense levels of emotion? What if you are dysregulated and feel reactive and even drained emotionally? If your emotional state is in the red or on the scale of 7–10, you can use or develop a toolbox of self-regulation strategies. With increased self-awareness, you will learn that emotions are only a temporary state, always changing. If you react when your emotions are in the red color zone or in the 7–10 zone of the scale, you may act in ways that hurt others, yourself or property. It is better to get in the habit of stepping away and taking a tool from your self-regulation toolkit. Through journal writing, one question to explore is self-regulation tools you use or could use to calm your regulatory system. What tools do you use right now that help you calm down, regulate or come back to that optimal zone of regulation? One way to start with self-regulation is to reflect in your journal entry with the following inquiry questions:

- What healthy strategies do I already use to bring me calm and self-regulation?
- What are five strategies that bring me calm and regulation that I use at home? Five at work? Five outdoors or in the community? Other?
- Which strategies do I use that are not calming but that cause me more dysregulation?
- Are there any tools I already use daily? Weekly? Occasionally?
- Are my self-regulation strategies healthy (do not harm me, others or property)?

You can complete this table in your journal. Bellow is a sample one that is already completed.

| Sample Self-Regulation Strategy | Is My Strategy Healthy for Myself and Others? | Where Do I Use This Strategy? |
| --- | --- | --- |
| Going for a walk | Yes | Park |
| Talking to a trusted friend | Yes | Going out on the weekend |

*(Continued)*

| Sample Self-Regulation Strategy | Is My Strategy Healthy for Myself and Others? | Where Do I Use This Strategy? |
| --- | --- | --- |
| Time with family | Yes | At home or on the weekends |
| Breathing | Yes | Anywhere |
| Listening to music | Yes | Car or on a break from work |
| Reading a book | Yes | Break at work or home before bed |
| Having a cup of coffee or tea | Yes | Work or home |
| Walking a pet or loved animal | Yes | Home in the evening |
| Taking a bath or shower | Yes | Home |
| Playing a game | Yes | With family at home |
| Eating a box of cookies | No | At home |
| Yelling at my kids | No | At home |
| Participating in community events/ seeing my neighbors | Yes | At home |
| Phone call with friend | Yes | Anytime |
| Gardening | Yes | By myself in my yard or at the community garden |

## Using Inquiry: Asking Questions to Strengthen Self-Awareness

When educators engage in *inquiry*, they learn to ask questions about their daily practice in order to become more responsive and attuned to themselves and to others (Cochran-Smith & Lytle, 2009). Asking questions allows educators to create a "pause" and to purposely slow down; strengthen their self-awareness and think about, instead of act upon, their internal thoughts, feelings and reactions. Through pausing, they learn to ask questions instead of making assumptions or coming to premature conclusions about a situation.

Using inquiry, early educators develop a habit to stop and wonder, *"What is this a case of?"* and ***"Why am I reacting/feeling the way I do?"*** in order to explore the meaning of their emotions and/or behaviors so they can begin to consider what someone is communicating to them about what they need and how they feel. A teacher noticing a child beginning to scream across the room might pause for a moment and ask herself, "What is Adam's screaming and kicking communicating to me about how he is feeling and what he needs from me right now? How is his screaming making me feel inside? What do I need to do to remain emotionally available to support him and guide him back to self-regulated behavior?" Or, a coach might observe a family child care provider and ask herself, "I notice that Kim is not responding when Aaron asks for help. I wonder why she is responding to his request to participate in this way. I will share my observation with her and listen to what she shares with me."

*The Power of Inquiry: Creating a momentary pause to ask a question can help teachers to:*

**Gain self-awareness:** Learning to notice how they are feeling in a moment. After a preschool teacher observes one child kicking down another child's block structure, she "tunes in" to ask a question about how she is feeling (What do I notice in my body right now?) while she begins to walk over to the block area. She acknowledges her feelings and thinks to herself, "I notice that my heart is beating fast and I am feeling very angry and ready to explode and yell across the room. Why am I having such a strong reaction?"

**Interrupt reactive behavior and maintain self-regulation:** Learning to acknowledge how they are feeling without acting out those feelings. The preschool teacher notices that she is really angry (her face is hot and her heart is racing) and wants to yell. While she acknowledges this feeling, she does not act on it. Instead, she asks herself, "What can

I do to calm myself down at this moment?" She decides to take five deep breaths to calm her stress response system.

**Increase empathy for self and others:** Learning to understand that all behavior has meaning and the behavior is communicating a story of what is happening internally inside of another child and/or adult. Pausing and asking questions can help educators learn to observe others (both children and adults) more carefully and try to understand the stories they are communicating—through their words, gestures, behavior, play, art and other forms of expression. Inquiry supports them to challenge their deficit assumptions or premature judgments about interactions, experiences or the intentions of others.

Joyce Darbo, a special services manager for Head Start, describes how she is learning to insert a pause and to use inquiry to interrupt her stress response when working with her colleagues. Creating a pause allows her to ask questions about how she is behaving and whether her behavior is productive or counter-productive. Through pausing, checking in with herself and asking questions, she is learning to be more attuned and have empathy for others' perspectives and experiences. She is also learning to focus less on advocating solely for her position (being "right") and more on the shared goals that she and her colleagues are trying to accomplish together in their work with children and families.

Joyce has a demanding job with many responsibilities. She oversees many programs, including services for children with disabilities and mental health referrals for children in 17 school districts. She also leads the county's program for social emotional competence and provides on-site consultation to early childhood programs to build the capacity of program staff to respond effectively to children with special needs or challenging behaviors, and she teaches at a private university. Joyce talks about how increasing her self-awareness allows her to remain kind and attuned to others and also to focus on the shared goals she and her colleagues have instead of the differences that create stress for her. She explains what happens when she is at work and in a moment of "feeling stress" and how she is learning to manage stress at work in new ways:

> At work when I'm in the moment, I tend to be quiet and so I try to be self-aware. Like why is it triggering me? What is it about the situation that is doing that to me? So I kind of stop and I just start thinking about it. I'm wondering why am I taking it like that? And I think I get defensive at first, but it's not a loud defensiveness. I'll get defensive and kind of curl up. Like wait a second, wait a minute. And then I will think more . . . well how did _I_ sound? How did _I_ come across? Like what could _I_ have done better? So I really do think about how I come across, how I can support the person, how I can better understand their positions. I've been really working on it. It doesn't come easy. But before I started to develop self-awareness, I think I would overreact. I would talk too much. I would dominate the conversation. I would be dismissive, I'd be irritated, I'd kind of ghost a little. I would just do all this horrible stuff and it would never get anywhere. So now, I really do work hard to stop and think about, "What would be better for this whole situation? Is this helpful? Is this helping what needs to get done right here?" So I really do stop and think and I try not to over-speak or react. I'm still doing some of that horrible stuff I mentioned, but I think that I realized that it's not productive. I spend a lot of time in meetings and I spend a lot of time interacting with teachers. I have been thinking, I have to keep working with them and it's not helpful for me to be that way. . . . I just realized that it doesn't leave me with a good feeling. I don't like that feeling. I want to be supportive and I know that me being that way was not supportive. I have learned that it's about being self-aware and knowing that there's a goal . . . it's not about me and it's not

*about them, it's about the child. It really is about the kid and the family. I think I just got to that point where I just need to realize, this isn't about me.*

*This act of pausing and questioning for Joyce was a micro-moment* that allowed her to cultivate responsiveness and develop more awareness and attunement with her colleagues by monitoring her tone of voice, the words she used and the non-verbal behavior she was displaying. By strengthening her self-awareness, interrupting her quick reactions and using questions, Joyce is creating benefits for her own physical and mental health (she is interrupting her stress response system from being triggered) and also contributing to a more collaborative, respectful and emotionally supportive work climate for all of her colleagues.

♦ How do you pause yourself so that you don't become reactive? What strategies do you use in the moment?

♦ Joyce has a growth mindset. She seeks to use self-awareness to cultivate an open and flexible state where she can continue to grow rather than stay stagnant. Her honesty with herself allows her to move forward and upward on a personal growth journey. Have you had moments where you looked at your own patterns and realized the impact they were having—whether positively or adversely—on those around you?

## Mindfulness, Meditation and Prayer

Mindfulness is the continuous awareness (self-reflection) and non-judgmental respect for our emotions, thoughts and bodies (Siegel, 2007). Mindfulness does not control the mind but rather **transforms the mind to be more present and clear.**

*Mindfulness* is generally believed to be a learned skill that enhances attention and self-regulation (Baer, 2003; Siegel, 2007). In the early education field, mindful practice and concentrated attention are central. When teachers are mindful, they are present to what is going on in the classroom and can attend more closely to the children's needs. Mindfulness allows one to be present in the moment and just notice, not judge. When we are mindful, we allow whatever feeling, sensation, situation to come up and trust "this too will pass". We take a curious stance and notice and allow the world to ebb and flow around us but not to control us. When we perseverate on thoughts about what is coming in the future, we can feel anxiety. Conversely, when we are stuck in focusing on the past, we can become immobile or depressed.

When educators make time to relax through mindful practices, they give their bodies and minds time to restore and heal from the day-to-day stressors they experience. An activity like taking deep breaths in and out is one example of a tool educators can use to slow down a racing body and mind and bring them back into the present moment. When they can focus their attention on the present moment rather than worrying about the past or future, they can slow down their racing, worried minds. Mindfulness approaches may help build a protective buffer for educators who face many daily stressors in their jobs.

*Meditation* can promote gratitude as a "quality of mindfulness" (Emmons & Stern, 2013, p. 852). Monique Lee, preschool teacher and director, talks about how for her, finding gratitude in small things every day is an important strategy for her self-care. She tries to find things around her that inspire feelings of joy and wonder. And, inspired by the children, she has learned to reinsert play into her adult life:

> *I think it's important to find gratitude in your day because there's always something that happened that's good, even just a little thing. . . . I'm looking outside my window right now, and I see the leaves blowing. . . . I'm thinking, "You know, that's just nice that there's a nice breeze out today." I'm grateful for that, grateful that I can go and see that. I also think you have to find joy and wonder in things . . . to stop and take a*

*break and find the things around you that create a sense of joy and wonder. Especially when you work with children, to see wonder and to enter into their play and observe how they are playing. As an adult, to have some fun and play . . . I think that's what keeps me young . . . building with kids in the block area and maybe playing with Play-doh, coloring. You know, they have adult coloring books now! So, finding an outlet where you can find joy and wonder and play in something even as an adult is important.*

*Meditation.* The National Center for Complementary and Integrative Health defines meditation as a mind-body prac-tice that aims to promote calmness, relaxation, balance, overall health and well-being. While there are many forms of medi-tation, most practices center around the focusing of attention and being mindful of one's thoughts, feelings and sensations (NCCIH, 2016). *Meditation can be effective even if the duration is as short as five minutes each day.* Meditation is associated with many health benefits and can:

◆ Generate feelings of calm, peacefulness and control to start off your day
◆ Lead to increased feelings of emotional well-being and energy (because of the endorphins released)
◆ Strengthen focus and attention and body awareness.

---

### Mindfulness Meditation

**Research on Mindfulness Meditation has documented its many benefits. Evidence suggests that it can:**

◆ Improve immune system functioning (Davidson et al., 2003)
◆ Change brain structure in areas that influence learn-ing and memory processes, emotional regulation and

perspective taking (Holzel et al., 2011; Shapiro, Jazaieri, & de Sousa, 2016)

♦ Alter stress reactivity by fostering faster biological adaptation to stressors (Goleman & Schwartz, 1976; Shapiro et al., 2016), as well as lowering average cortisol levels during periods of both rest and stress (MacLean et al., 1997)

♦ Increase one's capacity for creative problem solving (Ostafin & Kassman, 2012)

♦ Increase psychological flexibility and improve executive functioning (Ochsner & Gross, 2008)

♦ Improve clarity in information processing and allocate one's attention more effectively (Shapiro et al., 2016)

♦ Enhance happiness, empathy, creativity (Shapiro et al., 2016) and optimism (Gootjes & Rassin, 2014)

♦ Reduce anxiety, hostility, depression and illness symptoms (Beauchamp-Turner & Levinson, 1992; Shapiro et al., 2016)

♦ Improve working memory capacity and lessen mind wandering (Mrazek, Franklin, Phillips, Baird, & Schooler, 2013)

♦ Strengthen self-compassion, which is predictive of other positive outcomes, including wisdom, personal initiative, curiosity, exploration, happiness, optimism and positive affect (Neff, Kirkpatrick, & Rude, 2007).

Karen Tapia, the director for a state early childhood mentor program implemented at 104 community colleges, starts her mornings with a quiet meditation, a practice she started in her childhood inspired by her family's cultural practices as citizens of the Cree and Cherokee nations. During this time, Karen smudges to cleanse the atmosphere, says prayers, expresses gratitude. She also adds to this readings of inspirational texts and voices affirmations, all part of her daily self-care practices:

*I usually get up about 5:30 or 6:00 and the first thing that I do, and this is has been a practice since I was 14 years old, is I have some quiet time for meditation. In that quiet time, that probably lasts about a half an hour to an hour in the morning, I start by smudging, reading some inspirational spiritual-type writings. I meditate on any insights that I get from that or that I have coming up for me, and I have prayer points that I pray on every single day. I pray for the world, I pray for things that come up in the news, I pray for my family, I pray for my work family and my colleagues. I begin those prayers with a gratitude prayer, and thank you, and an affirmation that the day is going to be good, and that there will be blessings in the day, so I do some affirmations. That's how I start my day.*

### Reflection Questions

- ◆ Is there anything in your morning routine that you can identify is just "for me"? If there is, what do you do and why? If not, do you hope to add something that might help you feel more grounded before you start your day?
- ◆ Karen reads spiritual and inspirational-type writings and uses meditation as a part of her morning routine. If you could find one quote, prayer, inspirational saying or mantra that you looked at to set your intention for each morning, what would it be?

---

### LovingKindness Meditation

The following script is a guided lovingkindness meditation which uses thought and visualization techniques to evoke positive emotions. Research studies provide evidence that *engaging in lovingkindness mediation can increase mindful attention and self-acceptance, promote positive relations with others and foster good physical health* (Shapiro, Jazaieri, & De Sousa, 2002).

*Become comfortable in your chair or cushion, sitting with a relaxed but straight, posture, with your shoulders relaxed. Allow your hands to rest comfortably in your lap. Gently close your eyes Settling into awareness of the body and the breath.*

*Feeling into our body right now, noticing what's here. Open to whatever is to be experienced in the body in this moment. Connecting to the breath . . . noticing the wave-like movements of the belly . . .*

*In this practice, we'll be cultivating loving kindness.*

*We all have within us, this natural capacity for lovingkindness. Or friendship that is unconditional and open . . . gentle . . . supportive.*

*Lovingkindness is a natural opening of a compassionate heart . . . to ourselves and to others. It's a wish that everyone be happy. We begin with developing lovingkindness toward ourselves . . . allowing our hearts to open with tenderness,*

*Now, allow yourself to remember and open up to your basic goodness. You might remember times you have been kind or generous. You might recall your natural desire to be happy and not to suffer. If acknowledging your own goodness is difficult, look at yourself through the eyes of someone who loves you. What does that person love about you? Or, you may recall the unconditional love you felt from a beloved pet . . .*

*It may help to use the imagination and to picture yourself as a young child standing before you . . . perhaps 4 or 5 years of age . . . if that allows tender feelings of kindness to flow more easily*

*And, as you experience this love . . . notice how you feel in your body. Maybe you feel some warmth . . . or heat in the face. A smile . . . a sense of expansiveness. This is lovingkindness, a natural feeling that is accessible to all of us . . . always. Resting with this feeling of open, unconditional love for a few minutes*

*Letting yourself bask in the energy of lovingkindness . . . breathing it in . . . and breathing it out . . . inviting feelings of peace and acceptance . . .*

*So, beginning now to wish yourself well by extending words of loving kindness to yourself. I'll be offering as guidance the phrases that I've chosen to use in my own practice. You're invited to alter these phrases and choose whatever words express your wishes of loving kindness toward yourself and others.*

*And now, offering these words in your mind for yourself . . .*

*May I be filled with lovingkindness*
*May I be held in loving kindness*
*May I feel connected and calm*
*May I accept myself just as I am*
*May I be happy*
*May I know the natural joy of being alive*

*Now you can open the circle of lovingkindness by bringing to mind someone who is dear to you. Someone whom you care about and who has always been supportive. Reflect on this person's basic goodness, sensing what it is in particular that you love about him or her. In your heart feel your appreciation for this dear one, and begin your simple offering. . .*

*May you be filled with lovingkindness*
*May you be held in lovingkindness*
*May you feel my love now*
*May you accept yourself just as you are*
*May you be happy*
*May you know the natural joy of being alive*

*Now bring to mind a "neutral" person. This is someone you might see regularly but don't know well . . . It might be a neighbor, a grocery store clerk Bring this person to mind now, and repeat the words of loving kindness. . .*

*May you be filled with lovingkindness*
*May you be held in lovingkindness*
*May you feel my love now*
*May you accept yourself just as you are*
*May you be happy*
*May you know the natural joy of being alive*

*And now, if it's possible for you, bring to mind someone with whom you've had a difficult relationship. Perhaps it's someone you don't like to feel sympathy or compassion for. Seeing if it's possible to let go of feelings of resentment and dislike for this person. Reminding yourself to see this person as a whole being . . . deserving of love and kindness. As someone who feels pain and anxiety . . . as someone who also suffers. Seeing if it's possible to extend to this person the words of loving kindness in your mind. . .*

*May you be filled with lovingkindness*
*May you be held in lovingkindness*
*May you feel my love now*
*May you accept yourself just as you are*
*May you be happy*
*May you know the natural joy of being alive*

*Now, allow your awareness to open out in all directions . . . yourself, a dear one, a neutral person and a difficult person . . . and of all beings . . . humans and animals living everywhere . . . living in richness, poverty, war, peace, hunger, abundance . . . Aware of all the joys and sorrows that all beings experience. . .*

*May all beings be filled with lovingkindness*
*May all beings be happy*
*May all beings awaken and be free*

> *May all beings be happy*
> *And now, bringing this practice to a close by coming*
> *back to extend kindness to yourself. Sitting for a while and*
> *basking in the energy of loving kindness that may have been*
> *generated here.*
>
> Source: Veterans Affairs Department, Fresno, California www.fresno.va.gov/docs/Transcript_Lovingkindness_Meditation_.pdf

## Breathing

Breathing is a tool you can use to calm your regulatory system. As Dr. Bessel Van Der Kolk, internationally renowned expert on trauma and author of *The Body Keeps the Score* (2014), explains, "When we inhale we stimulate the sympathetic nervous system or SNS which makes the heart increase. Exhaling stimulates the parasympathetic nervous system PNS, which decrease how fast the heart beats. In healthy and calm individuals, the inhale and exhale are steady and a good heart rate measures well-being" (p. 269). Learning how to breathe can help you recover and manage small or large stressors. As discussed previously, when your body is stressed, hormones are released that propel you into a fight, flight or freeze mode. In order to manage your stress, taking deep and mindful breaths can benefit you emotionally. It can help you feel calm, develop self-regulation skills, provide access to your "thinking brain" rather than only the reactive part of your brain and prevent stress chemicals from circulating around your body.

*If you practice breathing daily, it can become a part of a routine choice you have available in your personal self-care toolkit.* It can be done anywhere and does not cost anything. Research studies examining the impact of breathing have identified many benefits, as described in the following textbox.

## Breathing and the Neural Highway . . .

While researchers are still investigating the biological impact of controlled breathing on the stress response system, we have learned in studies conducted with mice that there is a relationship between the circuit of nerves that connect the breathing pacemaker region of the brain (the part of the brain involved in the pace of breathing) with the part of the brain that is responsible for arousal, attention and panic (Yackle et al., 2017). The working hypothesis/theory applying this animal research to humans is that there is a "neural highway" between these two areas in the brain and changing the pace of a person's breathing (slowing it down through belly breaths) can reduce their brain's biological panic response.

**Research on breathing (with people) has shown the following benefits:**

♦ Controlled breathing techniques can reduce heart rate, blood pressure and cortisol levels, as well as improving mood and lowering perceived stress (Perciavalle et al., 2017).

♦ Diaphragmatic or "belly" breathing, which involves taking deep breaths to expand the lungs into the diaphragm rather than the ribcage, is especially beneficial, as it encourages a full exchange of incoming oxygen with outgoing carbon dioxide (Bernardi et al., 1998).

**And the benefits of breathing can be realized in a short amount of time:**

♦ Emotional exhaustion from job burnout has been reduced from even one day of participating in breathing exercises (Salyers et al., 2011).

♦ A breathing training course lasting six weeks has led to a significant decrease in anxiety (Chandla et al., 2013).

**To learn how to belly breathe, see the following videos:**

◆ For Adults: www.youtube.com/watch?v=kgTL5G1ibIo

◆ For Children: "Belly Breathing with Elmo": www.youtube.com/watch?v=_mZbzDOpylA

*Practice by following this simple ritual:*

◆ Sit up or stand up straight.

◆ Take a long, slow deep breath through your nose and then release all the air through your lungs.

◆ Next, take in a deep breath through your mouth and into your lungs and slowly release the air.

◆ Focus on your breathing for at least two minutes, noticing how your body responds.

◆ Try deep breathing at work for a moment, when stuck in traffic or anywhere you need to refocus.

---

### Deep Breathing to De-Escalate a Triggering Response

*Ten seconds of deep breathing will allow your brain to calm enough to allow you to take a more responsive and non-reactive approach in your interactions with adults and children.*

After taking some deep breaths, educators are better equipped to ask themselves, "What is this person communicating to me about how they feel and what they need? How can I respond in a supportive manner that leads them to feel visible, listened to, safe and cared for?"

Creating a pause through breathing and body awareness, educators can take a moment to imagine the situation through another person's (child, parent, colleague, supervisor or. . .?) perspective and, in doing so, strengthen their skills and ability to express empathy in communication with others.

Fawzia Saffi, a site supervisor in a Head Start center on the west coast, is a proponent of deep breathing to reduce her stress. She explains, "When my stress levels go up, I don't want to react, I want to be professional and so I breathe in and calm myself at that moment."

Alexandra Morales has been an early childhood educator for 40 years. She works in the classroom as a coach and trainer specializing in social-emotional learning. Alexandra practices meditation and deep breathing and has seen significant health benefits as a result. She uses an app named *Calm* to guide her in learning how to slow down and take deep breaths during the day at work and then again at night when listening to calming stories:

> *Meditation is a big thing for me. My blood sugar level was 8.3 a year ago. And then I was like, "Okay, you need to meditate, you need to calm down." Because I had a lot of stress in one year. It (my blood sugar) went up high and I know that was stress related. It wasn't diet related because I've already gotten rid of certain things. I've cut out sugar for 150 days. In four months, I was able to bring my sugar level down. I was able to do that because I sat in that chair every single day and turned on Calm.com and I was breathing . . . the lady guides you through the breathing and I do it also in the evening before I go to bed. I turn on the app and what's called, Bedtime Stories. And before you go to bed, that helps me relax and take some deep breaths. I have learned how to deep breathe.*

Monique Lee, a preschool director and teacher working in a very small private Catholic school attached to an elementary and middle school, teaches deep breathing to her students so everyone in the classroom can use breathing as a strategy to calm themselves down and do what she describes as "calm our bodies and calm our minds". Monique uses body awareness to notice when she is starting to feel angry, and as soon as she perceives stress signals, she begins to guide the students to breathe along with her. In this way, she is not only supporting the children to develop self-regulation strategies, she is modeling a positive way to manage stress *and* guiding them back to regulation through co-regulation. All this is learning while having fun together:

> If I feel myself getting angry, we're all human . . . you know, they know how to push those buttons. And I say, "Boys and girls, teacher needs to take a deep breath." So we do our deep breathing. And I'm like, "Just breathe with me. Just calm our bodies, calm our minds. Okay, now I'm feeling better. Now, let's focus on what we need to get done." So we can move on to whatever it was we were trying to do. We do a lot of deep breathing in my class. The children all know to breathe. And during circle time, we'll do animal breaths. We'll take a deep breath. Sometimes it's a cat. So I'll say, "All the way in. Breathe, breathe, breathe." And then we're lifting up our hands and we'd all say, "Meeeoooooow" to let it all out. Or we pretend to be a snake. And sometimes we can be a bear where you have to take a very deep breath all the way to your belly and then "Ahhhh" to blow it out. We'll do it three times. And then I talk to them. "How did that make your head feel? Do you feel like all that oxygen went into your brain? Do you feel calmer?" That helps when a situation does arise that is stressful or if I have a child who has a little meltdown. I'll just say, "Why don't you come breathe with me?" And they might say, "Oh, I don't want to." I respond, "Just put your hand right here" (on their belly). I'm breathing and then pretty soon, they're breathing with me and we're calming down together. So that's a way I help the children with their stress and it also helps me because I'm breathing with them and I can keep calm as well.

## Disrupting Mind-Loops

*Self-care is . . . treating myself gently, the way I talk to myself mentally, to be supportive and not to be punitive . . . my suggestion would just be to take care of yourself as though you're taking care of your inner child because that's really what you're doing*
—Heidi Schulz, Early Elementary Site Supervisor and Preschool Teacher

Dr. Charles Harris is a site principal who works within an early childhood department in a large urban school district. He serves as an instructional leader for three child development centers and supports the curriculum and instruction, operations and day-to-day management of the sites. When asked about his self-care strategies, he emphasizes the importance of disrupting negative self-talk—the "mind-loops or negative tapes in your mind"—because they have a powerful impact on our emotional stress and well-being. Disrupting mind-loops is not an easy endeavor but instead takes a "diligent effort". Dr. Harris disrupts his mind-loops by making sure that every day there is something he wakes up to that is inspiring to him:

*Mind loops are the negative tapes in your mind, you know, "Oh, I'm stupid", "Oh, I'll never do anything right", "Oh, I'll never lose weight", "Oh, this world is going to hell in a handbasket and it's never going to change", all that stuff . . . you need to find some ways to work with your mind because our mind is so powerful. When it causes us emotional stress, our body listens to it, unfortunately. I mean, every part of us gets affected by how we think. We have eye gates, we have ear gates, we have mouth gates. We need to protect all those to keep them sacred. We have a thought gate. All those gates, we have to keep them sacred. That's a constant diligent effort. What you gravitate toward on a daily basis will really, really change how you see the world, and so just even getting up and doing something that inspires you or doing an art project that inspires you, having something inspiring for yourself every day that gets you out of those mind loops.*

Elena Aguilar, author of *Onward: Cultivating Emotional Resilience in Educators* (2018), encourages educators to "intervene" in their thinking in order to interrupt cycles of negative thinking. Before educators can change their unproductive thoughts, they need to understand what is harmful and inaccurate about them. Although Aguilar uses the term "distorted thinking/distorted thoughts," we replace this with the phrase "Stuck Points" (Resick, Monson, & Chard, 2017), which is being effectively used in cognitive processing therapy for individuals impacted by trauma, a term we believe is more resilience focused and growth oriented. Following are the most common patterns in "Stuck Points" thinking, the "mind-loops" that require our diligent efforts to notice and then disrupt:

| *Stuck Point* | *What It Looks Like* |
| --- | --- |
| Binary Thinking (Either/Or) | Jessenia frequently uses words such as "always" or "every" or "never". A situation is either good or bad, right or wrong, excellent or terrible. There is no nuance or middle ground. "My director *always* criticizes me." |
| Jumping to Conclusions | Carmen draws conclusions about an interaction or situation without having sufficient information or sometimes without having *any* facts. Despite her knowledge gap, she makes negative assumptions and feels confident in concluding how others feel about her. She often predicts negative outcomes about things to come in the future. "My principal is coming in to observe me this week. I know she is going to give me a bad evaluation." |
| Unrealistic Expectations | Chris gets upset very easily when things in his life don't unfold in the way he thinks they "should" be. He has uncompromising rules and expectations and blames himself and others for things that are out of their control. He is relentlessly hard on others and himself. He often uses the word "should". "I'm not a perfectionist, I just have high standards." |
| Disqualifying the Positive | Khadija focuses on and expands the negative aspects of people, environments, interactions and experiences. She ignores or disqualifies positive evidence. |

| Stuck Point | What It Looks Like |
| --- | --- |
| | After her supervisor gave her a compliment she says, "No, I am really not that good at it, I just was lucky today."<br>Khadija is at her work party celebrating a birthday. She says to her colleague, "Looks like this agency does not value us because they bought the Costco cake." |
| Overgeneralizing | Lori takes one form of evidence and uses it to make sweeping conclusions.<br>Her site supervisor tells her about a community training on social-emotional learning in young children and she thinks, "How rude! She thinks I don't know how to teach." |
| Catastrophizing | Karla is convinced that everything will go wrong. She always imagines the worst-case scenarios and warns her colleagues about them. She tells herself that situations are extraordinary and intolerable.<br>"My annual review is Monday morning and I know it will be the worst day of my life." |
| Emotional Reasoning | Anisha believes that her feelings represent reality, and she makes projections based on the feelings she has.<br>"I'm feeling anxious about the new curriculum, it's never going to work." |
| Personalization | In Sofia's mind, everything is about her and relates back to her, especially when it's negative. She convinces herself that all bad news is the result of her actions and/or directed toward her. If something does not work, she concludes, "It must be my fault."<br>When she is raising her hand and is not called on while participating in training, she thinks, "It's because they think I'm stupid and I don't have anything interesting to share." |

*Source*: Adapted from Aguilar (2018, pp. 76–77)

Aguilar encourages educators to "unlock the door to resilience" by identifying and disrupting the thoughts that "don't serve you" and then redirecting energy toward "*crafting new stories . . . to live into*" (p. 80).

### Reflection Questions

◆ Have you ever been caught in a mind-loop or a Stuck Point thinking pattern that caused you to have a narrow perspective or a behavior that adversely impacted you or others?

◆ How might a Stuck Point thought pattern influence your beliefs about yourself, others and the world? How might these Stuck Points keep you from moving forward? (Resick et al., 2017)

◆ To break the mind-loop/stuck points, you can't do the same thing you always do. You have to walk a new path every day in order to build a new habit of thinking and responding. What strategies have you tried or could you try to break a pattern of a mind-loop and/or stuck point thought pattern?

## Visualizations

Visualization techniques are used to create mental images of a desired feeling, life experience or outcome. Visualizations are one strategy for disrupting distorted thinking and, as Elena Aguilar (2018) encourages, crafting the story you want to live into . . . now and for your future.

Jennifer Andrews, who works with early educators in her job at a state department of education, frequently uses visualizations to help her envision her workplace—where there are many stressors—as an environment where her relationships can be "smooth and easeful". She imagines herself as someone with creativity, energy and value, all aspects of a powerful story she crafts to guide her daily beliefs and actions and steer her toward her future. She explains:

*Visualization is something I do by myself and I usually do it as part of my meditation but sometimes I visualize when I'm gardening or out in nature. I focus on my heart space and then*

*I visualize myself as someone who has value and someone who has a lot to offer to the world. I will visualize myself doing my work and visualize my relationships at work being smooth and easeful. I visualize myself having energy or having creativity and ideas for the projects that I have. So it's envisioning my relationship to my work and to my colleagues and the people that I work with in my mind.*

Linda Jones, an administrator at a county early childhood agency, uses visualizations in a different way. Whenever Linda has an interaction with a child or an adult that she does not feel good about—an interaction that was unsuccessful for any reason—she uses visualizations to prevent herself from sinking into self-doubt and stuck-point thinking. Linda visualizes moments when she *was* successful in a similar type of interaction with a parent, a child or a colleague, an exercise that keeps her focused and productive and moving in a "good direction". She explains how she begins this visualization:

*When I am with a child or parent and the situation is not going the way that I would like it to, I think about times when I <u>have</u> been successful with a child or parent, but also with staff members. I think about times when I have been successful to get myself confident to move in a good direction.*

---

### Try One of These Visualizations . . . Or, Create One of Your Own!

#### Liquid Quiet

♦ Visualize "quiet" as a thick, clear liquid, filling your head with peace and quiet.

♦ See it pouring slowly down your body, filling you with the clear liquid until you feel like a liquid ball.

♦ Once you're in this zone, breathe deeply and stay in this position for a few minutes.

**Ball of Yarn**

- Picture a small ball of yarn holding all of that residual tension from the day.
- Find the tip of the yarn and imagine it slowly unrolling. The strand gets longer and longer, and you can actually feel your tension unwinding.
- When the yarn is completely loose, you can relax and enjoy the night.

**Serene Beach Scene**

- Visualize yourself lying on a white sandy beach, complete with clear blue skies and gently lapping waves.
- Imagine your body sinking into the chair and feel the warmth of the sand on your feet.
- Let go of any tension, soften your eyes, and continue to breathe with the rhythm of the rolling waves.

Source: Melissa Eisler (2018) https://mindfulminutes.com/ease-anxiety-with-visualization-techniques/

## Affirmations and Treasure Maps

Karen Tapia, uses a variety of self-care practices—including *focusing on her values and the sense of purpose driving her work*, posting affirmations in her home and creating treasure maps—to craft a story that represents all that she wants to "live into." For Karen this really is a process of reclaiming and "crafting a new story" for her life, one where she is a strong and resilient thriver who is dedicated to replacing the abuse and oppression she experienced in her earliest years with a life that is focused on love. Karen explains how at a very young age she developed leadership skills because of the need to protect herself and her siblings from the abuse of her father:

*I was the leader in my family. I'm the oldest child of three girls, in a family of domestic violence and sexual abuse from my father. . . . I have always been the leader of the family, not my mother, myself. My mother came to <u>me</u> for counseling all the time. When I was 11 years old, I had to watch my younger sisters like a hawk to make sure they were safe from my father. . . . I'm also the problem solver and peacemaker because there was a lot of fighting that went on between my mother and my sister who has bipolar disorder before she was diagnosed. . . . I am the cleanup committee, I am the mother, I am the counselor, I am the caretaker. And, I am the protector of children and families and caretakers. And it has just been a pattern over and over and over again in my life. And wherever I go, that pattern exists in early childhood settings too. I am not complaining about those roles, because they shaped me into who I am and many leadership skills that are good, but I do have to watch that I take care of myself and not fall back into dysfunctional patterns around these identities.*

Karen also integrates *affirmations* into her daily self-care practice. She writes them out on paper and then hangs them up in places in her home that she walks by each day. This ensures that every day she reads these affirmative messages that remind her of the life she desires and reinforces that she has the opportunity and responsibility to co-create it. She explains:

*I put little affirmations on my refrigerator and mirror that I walk by every day. I just try to remind myself to stay in that positive frame of mind. I have a lot of sayings everywhere. One says, "She decided to live the life she always imagined." It's a reminder that we wake up every morning, and we can decide what life we want to live. We can imagine it and we can take action also towards that. We are active participants in what comes next in our lives. I believe that with Creator. We are co-creating that life. It's not like we do it ourselves, but we can co-create the actualization of what we imagine. If we're imagining horrible things today . . . that may actually feel like the outcome at the end of the day, or we're setting ourselves up for it not to be a very wonderful day. Instead, we can imagine the life that we've always wanted. We always have a choice of how we frame our life, even the things that may not feel good at the moment we can choose to think differently about them, and at some point look back on that moment and realize what a valuable lesson that challenge was or really a gift for our growth.*

Karen creates *treasure maps* (sometimes people call these vision boards) to be visual/graphic representations of her affirmations, visualizations and the life she wants to create for herself. Her treasure map is a representation of "the treasure in her heart"; her hopes and dreams. Although there are an endless number of ways to create these boards/maps, Karen adds pictures she cuts out along with inspirational sayings to poster board. Over time, she is able to see her progress, which is motivating as she notices that she is able to take some of her imagined changes and see them actually happen in her life. She describes what this process looks like for her:

*The treasure map is just another way of visualizing. I visualize what I want. I make little treasure maps, and I put them up in my home. They're like gold. They show me what I want to do. It's like the treasure that's there in your heart, the dreams that you have that you want to become a reality in this world. It may be for yourself and it may be what you feel like your life purpose is. You cut out pictures and you put them on a board, a poster board, and you quote little sayings, little affirmations on there like "I live large", or "Today, I'm grateful for the life that I have, and I am thinking about the life I am becoming", or "Resources are flowing to me." Maybe you have a picture of money or maybe it's a bunch of friends or people in that picture, but you're picturing what you want in your life, and when you walk by that every single day . . . you're helping to keep in your mind what you want for your life.*

*Thinking about my self-care, my treasure map includes a beautiful bed with flowers all around it with a woman who is lying very reposed. It says, "Quiet and restful sleep" because I don't sleep well at night. I've put a picture of a bunch of vegetables in a garden and put "Healthy Eating" so I will*

*remember to do that. The interesting thing is when I look at the Treasure Map I started in January, many of those things have already happened. They're in my life now.*

## Karen Tapia's Treasure Map

### Exercise

Exercise is an important element of self-care for many early childhood educators. Angelica Chacon, an infant toddler specialist, goes to the gym to get more physical strength; she explains, "I do things that help my posture" and to "work out many demons". Strengthening her posture, Angelica describes, is a metaphor for the progress she has made in her adult life fighting the impact of internalized oppression as a Chicana Latina who grew up in "the barrio in East Los Angeles", a metaphor that reflects her strength and personal pride. She explains:

*I go to the gym. Because I know that that in my growing up experience I held stress in my body, I didn't always know how to get it out. When I started being around people of the dominant culture, because I grew up in the barrio in east Los Angeles, I remember when I went away to college just observing folks walking around and I always got this sense, they seemed to not walk with shame, there was just a rhythm in their walking and their postures that just seem to be, I don't know, like they didn't have to hide. And I felt that I carried negativity in my body and in my posture. And so at some point in my young to older adult life, I started getting more physical strength. And I began to notice later in life that I felt that my carriage was getting stronger and I liked how that felt. And so I go to the gym and do things that help my posture because it's one way that I—it's my self-care. It's self-comforting to me when I can feel my posture is strong and upright and it's a metaphor for my personal pride. And I've used the gym a lot to work out many demons.*

For Angelica, exercise is not just an activity she participates in to support her health, going to the gym and improving her posture is a deeply meaningful process that is transformative on many levels. Strengthening her posture represents her personal effort to disrupt historical cycles of oppression that impact Latinx individuals like herself and to participate in her own healing engagement and reclamation of positive esteem and identity.

Our family recently went kayaking for my birthday, and I realized that it's critical that we find someone to paddle through life with.
—Anh Tham, Early Childhood Mentor Teacher and Coach

## Giving Yourself Permission

Many early childhood educators report that they often focus their attention on caring for others and spend little time caring for themselves (for various reasons we have discussed in this book, including structural and internalized oppression, collectivist and group-oriented cultural beliefs, experiences of poverty and trauma, among other factors). Audre Lorde, a leading African American poet who wrote about issues of race, gender and sexuality from a social justice, intersectional and liberation perspective, described *caring for herself as an act of political warfare*. Social justice activists have a keen awareness of the need to embody self-care as an act of preservation so they have the energy to sustain their efforts despite the toll it takes on them physically and emotionally. Audre Lorde's words have inspired many people who have faced intersecting forms of oppression to claim or re-claim self-care—to in essence, "give themselves permission" to embrace caring for themselves as a radical and very political act.

"Black women are often the pillars of their community, literally, where we're tasked with taking care of everybody in our families, taking care of people who are not in our families but are in our villages. And we're often given the messaging that taking care of ourselves is selfish and that putting ourselves first takes away from the community. So when I read Audre Lorde's quote . . . what I read is that taking care of myself should be a priority, that there is nothing wrong with putting myself first and making sure that I am healthy. Because I am no good to anybody else when I am not good to myself. Black women . . . many of us are poor, many of us are working ourselves into graves, early graves particularly, and many of us put everybody before ourselves. . . *saying that I matter, that I come first, that what I need and what I want matters, I think is a radical act* because it goes against everything that we've been conditioned to believe . . . chronic illnesses like obesity, like heart disease, like diabetes, are killing Black women in droves. So when we say that our health matters and that we want to live as long a life as possible through self-care, it means that we're going to the doctor, it means that we're going to the gym, it means that we're eating healthier, if that is what it takes to preserve our health. Jada Pinkett Smith . . . said something that mirrors how I feel about self-care. 'You cannot be good to other people if your health is declining. You cannot be good to other people if you're miserable. You cannot be good to your children if you have them, to your spouse if you have one, to your job and your career if you are not emotionally and mentally and physically healthy' . . . prioritizing self-care and prioritizing health allows you to be a better member of your community. And I think that is especially important for Black women when we take on so much of other people's loads." (Mirk, 2016)

Michelle Peters, an early childhood special education teacher working for Head Start in Colorado, takes a different approach in describing how she gives herself "permission" for self-care. For Michelle, to find time for self-care and prioritize it in her life, she has learned to give herself permission to allow some small things to "fall through the cracks," a trade-off she describes as "actually okay" as long as she maintains her focus on bigger, more important things like her family's happiness and the time they spend together:

*To me, self-care means that it is okay to do things for myself and to not be giving my kids attention or maybe letting them watch TV or play on the Xbox longer than I would have liked for them to, so I can have a couple of quiet moments. I'm traveling so much during the day between different schools and working with so many different people that it is exhausting. I find that I come home and because I'm up so early in the morning, I need a nap . . . I realized that's actually okay. If I am spending a couple of minutes to take a nap or read a book or just sit and watch a ridiculous TV show or read People magazine, then that is perfectly okay. And if dinner . . . isn't homemade, then that's okay . . . as long as we are happy as a family and we are spending time together and everyone is getting what they needed, there are certain things that can fall through the cracks.*

## Strategies for Self-Care That Focus on "Tuning OUTward"

*Credit*: Alice Blecker

## Connecting to Nature

Many early childhood educators find spending time in green spaces/nature to be an important element of their self-care and restorative healing practices, an association that is documented in many research studies (Berman, Jonides, & Kaplan, 2008; Bratman, Hamilton, & Daily, 2012; Kaplan, 1995; Mayer, Frantz, Bruehlman-Senecal, & Dolliver, 2009; Park et al., 2007). For example, Fatima Ahmad has a very demanding and stressful job working as an administrator serving children ages 18 months to five years of age. Most of the children in her Head Start program are families experiencing homelessness, and they have experienced trauma in their earliest years. Because of the population she works with, Fatima has learned a lot about the neurobiology of stress and different trauma-informed strategies she can use to "ground" herself when her stress response system has been triggered. She finds that "hugging trees" is something she can do as a self-care strategy that is also accessible and non-threatening for the children and allows her to regulate herself while also co-regulating the children as she encourages them to follow her lead. Fatima chuckles a little as she shares:

> *I love to hug trees. Which sounds crazy, but it grounds me. Sometimes we take the children for a neighborhood walk and when we are walking with the children we say, "Look at the flowers, look at the trees, give a hug to the tree."*

---

### Grounding

Grounding is the process of bringing your focus to what is happening in your body internally or within your immediate surroundings in order to interrupt the body's stress response reaction and/or your worried thoughts. Grounding strategies allow you to calm your nervous system and disrupt the release of neurochemicals throughout your body. Re-focusing on your body and what you're physically feeling allows you to shift your mind away from anxious or stressful thoughts and focus on the safety and security of the current moment. Examples of grounding strategies include:

- ◆ Deep breathing
- ◆ Hold onto something and squeezing it tight
- ◆ Stomping your feet on the ground
- ◆ Being in nature
- ◆ Repeating a mantra (special saying or quote).

There are *people, places, activities or objects* that can help ground us. This menu of "grounders" is unique for each person.

---

Elsa Karlsson, an early childhood special education teacher, lives in Alaska, which provides her with many opportunities to care for herself in nature while walking and hiking, an experience she describes that "fills your soul". For Elsa, part of the thrill of this form of self-care is the always-present possibility for risk and danger. Whether being charged by moose or approached by a brown bear, Elsa is attuned to the beauty of her surroundings while also monitoring the environment at all times. *This hypervigilant awareness—the hyper-focus of her body in motion and all of her senses—is part of the restorative experience* for her, as she finds that hiking in places where such inherent dangers are not present "lacks excitement":

> *My main number one self-care is walking and hiking. We live in Alaska. It is a very beautiful place. I live up on the foothills of a mountain so we have bears and moose and you always have to watch that when you're out walking and hiking. Just to be outside, it's so beautiful, it just kind of fills your soul. Walking fast for an hour or hour and a half if I can, to just get that rhythm, it's kind of walking meditation I guess. I don't use music or anything because I always have to be able to hear the bears. I also can't just totally zone out anywhere because the moose can come out. Some of the trails I walk are pretty tight and we have a lot of brown bears and black bears here. So you always have to be aware. I don't carry bear spray when I walk by my home but I do when I hike in the mountains and so far I haven't had any issues. But moose, I've been charged a lot and that's scary. But as long as you're aware and if you see them ahead of you, I'll just turn around and walk another way. So I don't use music when I walk. I just walk and breathe. And I think that's absolutely most effective for me.*
>
> *Recently, I was in Minnesota to visit my family and it was kind of nice walking where I didn't have to worry about anything. And yet, when I came back, I thought, it kind of lacked excitement compared to walking here in Alaska where you always have to be aware. And it's so incredibly beautiful*

*here. It's so soul filling. It's not just the activity of walking . . . it's filling your soul with all this beauty around you.*

### Reflection Questions

♦ Some individuals' sensory systems seek input to regulate, restore and renew. Elsa has a sensory system that becomes restored and engaged when she seeks input such as new adventures, risk taking or even exhilarating situations that pose danger. As you reflect on yourself, are you sensory seeking or sensory avoiding? Do you seek risk or danger, or are you risk and danger avoidant?

---

Dr. Ming Kuo is a researcher at the University of Illinois Urbana-Champaign who has studied the effects of nature on humans for over 30 years. A review of the scientific literature reveals that nature has a systematic and very positive impact on humans' physical and emotional health, and this holds for individuals across socioeconomic groups. Some of the findings include:

♦ When people look out and see a green landscape, even from indoors, their heart rate decreases and their brain activity shifts from sympathetic nervous activity (fight or flight stress response) to parasympathetic nervous activity (tend and befriend). In fact, just looking at pictures of nature can help people to calm their central nervous system activity and reduce their blood pressure. Just the visual is enough to have this positive impact on reducing stress. As a result, looking at nature and greenery has a systematic and positive physiological impact on humans.

♦ There are also dozens of positive long-term health outcomes that are associated with people's contact with nature. For example, there is a connection between greenery and health markers for obesity, hypertension and diabetes. There is also evidence suggesting a relationship between greenery and the strength of our immune systems. After people spend several days in nature, researchers find measurable increases in what are known as natural killer cells. Kuo explains:

◆ *After a three-day weekend in a forest preserve—that boosts natural killer cells on average by 50%. And a three-day weekend in a nice urban area, it turns out, doesn't do anything for your natural killer cells. And then, if I come knock on your door 30 days later after your three-day weekend, and I say, can I have another sample of your blood, please, and you give it to me, it will show that you are still roughly 24, 25% above your baseline number of natural killer cells. So it's a big effect, and it lasts for a really long time.*

◆ Kuo has found in her laboratory research that spritzing people with phytoncides—essential aromatic compounds that we associate with being in the woods—even if people are not in the forest can lead to positive changes in people's natural killer cells and in their bloodstream.

Given the empirical research findings, Kuo explains that *nature is like a "multivitamin. You can get different benefits from different kinds of exposure".*

Source: Hidden Brain Podcast (August 19, 2019) www.npr.org/2019/08/12/750538458/you-2-0-our-better-nature; Taylor and Kuo (2006, 2011)

## Connecting With Others. Cultivating Community

*We need to move the self-care conversation into community care. We need to move the conversation from individual to collective. From independent to interdependent . . . to challenge the privilege and Western language of self-care and instead consider ourselves and our work as requiring political self-care within webs of communities and collectives of caring.*

(Clark, 2017)

*For me, there's this piece of community that is a big part of me feeling connected and joyful in the work that I do and in life . . . staying connected with folks that I've known forever, and then I get that boost and that joy from connecting with kids.*
—Matthew Davis, Preschool Teacher

Research studies document that our relationships, social networks and sense of belonging within families and communities provide us with many positive benefits that reduce our stress and increase our quality of life. There are different ways that educators use social connections to buffer their stress inside and outside of work. For many, culturally responsive self-care is most authentic to them when it has a community-relational focus, as individual-oriented practices are not meaningful given their cultural backgrounds and beliefs. Subsequently, we highlight several self-care strategies that emphasize social connections that early educators find helpful for them.

## Social Connections Buffer Stress

Having social connections is advantageous to our health. Our social networks and personal relationships provide three types of support that buffer our stress:

◆ Support through tangible or material assistance (e.g., receiving a dinner, a ride to a medical appointment or participating in a spiritual healing ritual)
◆ Informational support by providing us with advice, guidance and information
◆ Emotional support through expressions of empathy, care and reassurance.

The process works like this: We perceive that our social networks and social connections will provide us with aid in times of stress. This strengthens our internal belief that we have the ability to cope with our stressors. And this, in turn, leads us, in times of stress, to perceive the situations we face as less threatening (Wethington & Kessler, 1986; Cohen, Gottlieb, & Underwood, 2000; Cohen, 2004).

Receiving support can also buffer the impact of stress by providing us with distractions, offering solutions and/or by facilitating healthy behaviors, including exercise, nutrition, personal hygiene and rest (Cohen et al., 2000; Cohen, 2004). In the stress buffer hypothesis, social support only benefits health when under stress.

Participation in a range of social relationships and perceiving oneself as being part of a community (Brissette et al., 2000) promote positive psychological/emotional states. Feeling a sense of belonging and connection to community can promote positive thoughts and emotions. Having a positive outlook can improve health by increasing health-promoting behaviors such as eating nutritious meals and reframing from unhealthy coping mechanisms often associated with negative emotional states like substance abuse (Cohen, 2004). Participation in a large range of social relationships also provides individuals with a broader range of information and resources that can influence their health behaviors and their ability to effectively navigate health care services in addition to avoiding high-risk situations (Cohen, 2004).

Though positive social interactions can improve and support health and well-being, research suggests that negative social interactions can create stress and therefore deteriorate health (Cohen, 2004). For example, individuals who experience persistent conflicts with spouses/partners, family members and friends have been shown to have compromised immune system functioning, as they are more than twice as likely to develop the common cold (Cohen, 2004).

## Using Social Connections at Work to Buffer Stress

Many early childhood programs that prioritize self-care create processes that encourage staff to ask for help/relief when stress is too high for staff and they are at risk for being reactive and unproductive. In these programs, educators know it is not only OK to ask for help from their supervisor or colleagues, they understand that it is essential to do so to allow them to take a minute or two to calm down through deep breathing, counting to ten, taking a walk down the hall or another de-escalation strategy. Creating this type of system allows educators to work proactively and to draw on their relationships as sources of coping and support. In this way, connection with others is a stress-reduction strategy; relationships support co-regulation and help staff to remain professional and supported.

Connie Wright currently works with a state department of education on the east coast of the United States, providing grants, funding and technical assistance to different early childhood programs serving vulnerable populations. Because her career has focused on serving trauma-impacted children, families and communities, she has participated in a wide range of trainings focused on self-care and trauma-informed practices to support resilience and healing in early childhood settings. She has noticed over time that discussion of self-care is too often focused on individuals with little to no focus on the power of connections with others, "taking care of each other" and community in responses to stress. She explains this as problematic:

> *Self-care is important but when you're working with children in schools, with families, and with other teachers, taking care of each other is a very important part of self-care. . . . All of the trainings have been helpful to learn not just to take care of myself but to recognize what other people need also. Working with young children and families, especially those experiencing trauma, we need to not only take care of children, we need to take care of our coworkers as well.*

Thinking back to her first teaching job, Connie shares what it looks like to bring a relationship/community focus to thinking about stress management and self-care in an early childhood program. Teachers not only learn to develop body awareness for themselves when they are experiencing stress, they also learn to keep a caring eye on their colleagues and to offer help in moments when they perceive them to be overly stressed or triggered. She recalls how, at her previous site, all of the staff used a code message ("You have a call") to offer help to one another if they noticed someone looked stressed. Using this code was a way for adults to communicate their need for support without frightening or worrying the young children. She explains how this worked:

> So one thing that we did was to talk about what our hot buttons are and our triggers. This helped us as teachers to start to recognize when our coworkers were really starting to get to their limit. We wanted to make sure everybody was receiving what they needed. We had a code that we used if we saw that a teacher might need a little support, we would go up to them and let them know they had a phone call and we would ask them if they wanted us to "take a message" or if they wanted to "take the call". And if they wanted to take the call, that meant they needed help right now and they really needed to excuse themselves to go get themselves together. If they said, "Can you take a message?" that meant, "I'm still okay. I got this. But, thanks for checking." And that way we never made a child feel like they really got the best of the teacher. Sometimes kids can feel like "the teacher got angry with me and had to leave" and that just adds to that child's concerns. As teachers, we don't want to make them feel bad because our goal is just to help them so we don't want to add to their stress.

Another relational strategy Connie uses for stress-reduction and self-regulation at work is to ask a trusted colleague to partner with her and create a safe reflective relational space where she can talk through and process her feelings about a frustrating

Using a Code Word to Check in With a Colleague
*Credit*: Alice Blecker

or upsetting situation or interaction. She emphasizes that what she finds *most helpful is to have someone listen to her—to provide a "sounding board", not to offer solutions or advice.* The characteristics

Connie describes are similar to the process of reflective supervision without a formal supervisory relationship. Having access to this type of connection supports her to remain calm and professional even after very challenging moments at work. There are limitations to what she can say in these conversations, so this strategy has important limitations. However, talking with a co-worker offers certain benefits that she does not experience with others who do not understand her working context. Connie provides this contrast, describing that she feels "heard" in a different way with co-workers.

> *I don't ever want to lose my cool at work. Not only because I don't think it's professional, but I also don't want others to feed off that energy. So, I want to remain calm so that others remain calm. Sometimes I'm better at it than others, but I tend to talk through things. That makes me feel better. I like to talk it through and process it. So I do have a couple of good coworkers that I trust completely that when something is really bothering me, they understand I need to calm down and I need to process things so we just allow each other to talk through those things . . . I just say, "I need to talk about this and just make sure I'm not overreacting. . . ." That's how I process. Some people need quiet, they need to be alone for awhile. I need to talk it through. . . . Sometimes I try to talk with my husband but he doesn't understand it so he's just kinda staring at me. It's not the same. Or he has a solution, and I didn't want a solution. I just wanted a sounding board.*

---

### Name It to Tame It

Research shows that merely assigning a name or a label to what we feel calms down the activity of the emotional circuitry in the right hemisphere of our brains. When we tell the story of what happened to us with a trusted adult, it can help us with many different skills:

- ◆ Self-regulation—communicating the story of what we have been through, being heard and sharing what we feel can help calm down the intensity of our emotions.
- ◆ As telling the story can help us calm, it also helps us begin to piece together the events so that we can begin to move from a narrow view to gaining perspective of all sides.
- ◆ Through the support of another adult helping to calm us, we are then able to solve a problem with empathy and logical reasoning and find solutions that are not harmful to ourselves or others.

Think back to Connie. When she experiences stress at work, she finds it helpful to talk with one of her few trusted colleagues who will listen to her tell her story about how she is feeling, someone who can attune to her and understand the context of what she is saying. She feels "heard". In contrast, when she spoke with her husband, he provided her immediately with a solution to her problem. The response from her husband did not support Connie to name her emotions and/or feel as though she were in the presence of somebody who understood and empathized with her so she that she feels "heard". When Connie is feeling stressed and upset, she doesn't want or need a solution; instead, what she desires is a "sounding board": someone who allows her to "name it to tame it".

Source: Daniel J. Siegel, M.D., and Tina Payne Bryson, Ph.D., *The Whole-Brain Child* (2012)

## Drawing Upon Social Connections Outside of Work to Decrease Stress and Support Self Care

Many early educators find it energizing and healing for them to connect with others as a form of self-care.

*Joining and/or creating communities outside of work* is a really important approach to engaging in self-care for many. Linda Jones believes it is powerful and healing to participate in communities outside of work and describes these experiences as central to her self-care. One of these groups is her church community; another was a women's group:

> *I attend weekly services and I feel like being a part of my church community is really helpful to me because I'm around like-minded people that I have a relationship with. I also participated in a women's group called "Create a Beautiful Life" and that was a big, big support in being able to even consider and think about what I wanted for my life. Before I joined the group, whatever happened in my life, I was just going along with it . . . one of the greatest things that this group allowed me to see was how I could create the life I wanted. As women, we don't do that very often. If someone does do this, they learn so much from it and I think they can get a different life and a different perspective.*

---

### What Are the Different Ways You Reduce Your Stress and Take Care of Yourself?

*I love rollerblading to music on a local trail.*—Audrey Graham, Home Visitor/Early Intervention Provider

*Screaming in the car by myself.*—Fatima Ahmad, Head Start Director

*I like to hula hoop in the morning for ten minutes before work.*—Emily Taylor, Preschool Teacher

*Relax at home with my pets and a good book and a tall glass of wine.*—Melanie Pinto-Garcia, Behavior Technician

*Asking strangers on the street if I can pet their dog.*—Caroline Johnston, Preschool Teacher

*Giving myself permission to not do anything.*—Michelle Peters, Early Childhood Special Education Teacher

*Three months ago, I told my daughter, "Okay on Satur-day, I have to go to a training" but it wasn't true. I went to breakfast by myself, I went to catch up on work, I went shop-ping and it was so good. The whole day.—Mariana Reyes, Head Start Supervisor*

## Spotlight on Practice

Sarah Nadiv is the Director of the Global Center for Childhood Trauma and Resilience and Direc-tor of Business Development at Childhood Education International, a 127-year-old nonprofit with the core tenet that children's education is deeply intertwined with equal-ity, justice and human rights. An expert in infant and early child-hood mental health, her clinical background has galvanized her to ensure that research drives policy and practice. Ms. Nadiv has worked with teachers, child care providers, administrators, mental health providers and families for over 15 years. Her strategy for self-care professional development incorporates the following features:

- ◆ Setting the stage for self-reflection by guiding a self-reflection practice.
- ◆ Describing the value and necessity of self-care.
- ◆ Creating space for participants to imagine and describe their vision for their future.
- ◆ Creating a list of goals and action steps that will allow par-ticipants to realize their dreams for the future.

◆ Reflecting on a typical day, identifying the sources of stress and examining how their daily activities are aligning with their overall goals for themselves.

◆ Exploring the obstacles in their path to success and identifying what they can do or stop doing to reduce stress and create more space to reach their goals.

◆ Identifying manageable steps to reach their identified goals.

◆ Examining the physical, mental, spiritual and social supports participants need to complete their action steps.

◆ Culminating in the creation of a self-care action plan rooted in participant's vision for their future. Strategies for self-care are provided and discussed with participants.

◆ Incorporating a wide variety of self-care techniques throughout the training, including breathing techniques, meditation, song, community building and movement.

*Next, we introduce the Health and Wellness Toolkit* (see Figure 3.1). It is designed to help you explore the balance

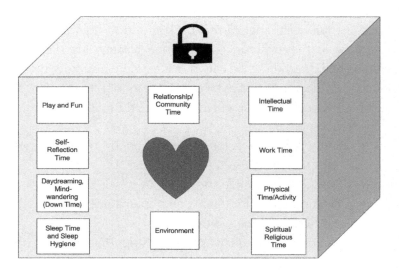

**FIGURE 3.1** Health and Wellness Toolkit

between stress and culturally responsive and restorative self-care activities that provide you with enough energy reserves to cope effectively with day-to-day stressors and support you to live a healthy and positive life inside and outside of work. We designed this tool to support you to think about healthy and balanced care for your mind, your body and your spirit.

## Examples for Each Category in the Health and Wellness Toolkit

The following are examples of the types of activities that fall into each of the categories listed previously. These are just examples and do not reflect all of the activities you might list for each of these categories. We provide some examples to inspire you to think about your own *Health and Wellness Toolkit*. We encourage you to consider your strengths as well as gaps or areas you need to attend to. You will see that many of these categories overlap and are not mutually exclusive. Each person's wellness toolkit will be unique, reflecting the activities/strategies that are culturally responsive, meaningful, healing and helpful to them, and these are likely to change not only in different contexts but also over the course of time. As discussed throughout the book, not all of these categories will be culturally and/or personally relevant for every educator.

---

The goal is for each early educator to explore and discover the self-care strategies that are the most helpful and genuine for them at a specific moment in time and to remain open and nimble to changing strategies as desired and/or needed in different contexts.

---

◆ *Sleep Time and Sleep Hygiene*—Each person's body needs a different amount of sleep. Only you will know what you need to feel rested and restored.

◆ *Physical Time (Exercise, Nutrition and Physical Health)*—How much physical activity one needs is individual, but it is recommended by the CDC to have an average of 150 minutes of mild to moderate exercise per week. Examples: walking, running, swimming, yoga, hiking, dancing.

◆ *Intellectual Time*—Activities that help grow the mind and knowledge are such things as reading, taking classes, going to school, searching the internet, watching a documentary: pre-frontal cortex activities that stimulate your thinking mind and support you to gain new knowledge.

◆ *Environment*—We can think about the environments that help us feel safe and restored. For some, it is outdoors in nature; others prefer to be inside. You might thrive with predictable routines or prefer to be unpredictable and to go with the flow. Some like physical objects of beauty around them and some need things in order. Others may lean toward an environment where there is space to get away, and then on the opposite side are those who are restored when surrounded by friends or family. It may be if you are introverted, you prefer quiet and more reflective environments and more time alone. If you are more extroverted, you may get energy from being social.

◆ *Relationship/Community Time*—Surrounding yourself with those who restore your energy, provide support and who care about you can help buffer toxic stress. When we choose to be with others who drain us or promote stress, this can add to our already existing stress. Some of these relationships are in our control and others are out of our control. For this section, think about what you have control over. Examples: being around friends who listen and support you; having relationships that challenge your thinking in a positive way; spending time with those who are fun, joyful and restorative; being with people who are healthy or help you grow and become a stronger person.

◆ *Play and Fun Time*— Activities that are enjoyable and done for fun rather than as a task to be completed or for practical purposes. Examples: dancing, listening to music, going out with friends, arts and crafts, creative cooking, going on adventures, travel, exploring something new, taking a class. Think of a child who is caught up in the moment with an activity where they are playing and having fun. It can be learning, praying, watching a sunrise, participating in an activity or eating a family meal: an experience that makes your heart leap with joy and sends the happy hormone serotonin through you, buffering the stressors in your mind and body.

◆ *Daydreaming, Mind-Wandering and Down Time*—The opposite of paying attention is daydreaming, letting your mind wander while exploring ideas or creative thoughts. This activity allows the brain to live in a creative mode that often allows for new ideas and insights. Examples: lying on a blanket while looking at the stars or clouds; lying in bed and letting your mind wander; walking, running or writing and thinking of ideas or talking out loud with someone who allows you to explore creative ideas.

◆ *Self-Reflection Time*—This refers to time for tuning inward and reflecting on our life. So much time is casting the spotlight of our attention outward that focusing inward can keep us in tune with our emotional state and well-being. Examples: counseling, therapy, talking with a friend, journal writing, praying, meditation, yoga, mindful walks.

◆ *Work Time*—Who needs to explain this one! How much you work and how stressful and restorative it is sometimes falls in or out of your control. However, what choices do you have to minimize the work stressors you may face? Examples: taking vacation days, saying no to tasks if you are able, prioritizing, not volunteering unless you have the energy.

◆ *Spiritual/Religious Time*—Many people find that believing in a higher power or sharing values/beliefs within a religious community or having spiritual beliefs and practices grounds them in something greater than themselves. There are thousands of religions and different spiritual practices throughout the world.

*Make a list of all the restorative activities and strategies that are genuine and meaningful for you (left column) and any new strategies you would like to add (right column).* If you identify several strategies and you plan to integrate them into your life on a monthly basis, you will increase your likelihood of preventing burnout, compassion fatigue and secondary traumatic stress.

| List the restorative activities you use | List strategies you could begin to use | Ideas of how to begin to build a new strategy |
|---|---|---|
| **Sleep and Sleep Hygiene** | Less phone and TV usage before bed to promote better sleep. Go to bed at a routine time. Less sugar and/or caffeine before bed. | Downloading Forest app will help me reduce my phone usage. Stop eating at 7 pm since I go to bed at 9. Only have caffeine before 12 noon. |
| **Physical Activity** Walking during my break or lunch. | Zumba class after work at the community center. | Download and post Zumba schedule and circle classes that I will attend 2× per week. |
| **Intellectual Stimulation** | If I get to bed earlier and do the one under environment, "Go to bed earlier and have my children go to bed on a more predictable routine so that I have some quiet, reflective and safe space to myself before bed", then I would have time to read. | Download Super Soul Sunday podcast topics that interest me. |

| List the restorative activities you use | List strategies you could begin to use | Ideas of how to begin to build a new strategy |
| --- | --- | --- |
| **Environment** Taking a bath, which is my only safe and quiet space to get away in my home. Everyone knows during bath time not to bother me! Pictures of my loved ones that make me realize how lucky I am. | | Notice flowers in my neighborhood to give me a connection to nature and beauty. |
| **Relationships/ Community** Talking with my best friend. Spending time with my mom and brothers regularly. Spending time with my children and partner. | Reducing time with friends that cause me stress. | Carve out an hour to start each weekend to make plans with loved ones either by phone or in person. |
| **Play and Fun** Dancing. Scrapbooking. Cooking. | | |
| **Daydreaming and Mind-Wandering** | Long walks alone to think and dream on weekend. Take five minutes before I go in to work and before I go in the house to have some thoughtful reflection and a mindful moment. | Sit in my car during my lunch hour and listen to music. Walk five minutes before work and after I get home. |
| **Self-reflection** Write in my journal. Meditation. | Go to bed earlier and have my children go to bed with a predictable routine so that I have some quiet, reflective and a safe space to myself before I fall asleep. | Buy a journal. Create new evening routine schedule and post in kitchen. Have a family meeting to roll out new schedule and routine. |

*(Continued)*

(Continued)

| List the restorative activities you use | List strategies you could begin to use | Ideas of how to begin to build a new strategy |
|---|---|---|
| **Work**<br>Asking my supervisor to help me prioritize my tasks since it feels overwhelming at times.<br>Saying no if I am able to or not volunteering to say yes to everything—being more careful. | Use my vacation time for a wellness day off to restore and do things I enjoy. | Schedule one day off and plan for (a) gardening, (b) walk through nature and (c) cooking a beautiful dinner all by myself! Say no to one request this week. |
| **Spiritual/Religious** | | |

Referring to the previous category descriptions, put an X next to the strategies that you engage in regularly. *These are your Wellness Self-Care strengths.*

| | |
|---|---|
| Sleep | |
| Physical Activity | x |
| Intellectual Stimulation | |
| Environment | |
| Relationships | x |
| Play and Fun | |
| Daydreaming and Mind-Wandering | |
| Self-Reflection | |
| Work | x |
| Spiritual/Religious | |

Next, we want you to identify your *Wellness Self-Care gaps.* Put an X where you need to place greater attention.

| | |
|---|---|
| Sleep | x |
| Physical Activity | |
| Intellectual Stimulation | |
| Environment | x |

Relationships
Play and Fun
Daydreaming and Mind-Wandering
Self-Reflection
Work
Spiritual/Religious                                    x

Now it's time to think of some *new strategies you would like to work on adding* to your daily and weekly self-care plan to create more balance in your life for healthier outcomes and restored energy.

*Following are some small things I can add this next month to my self-care routine. These are self-care strategies I can engage in daily and/or weekly to support my self-care plan. Some examples might include the following:*

1. Go on a walk after work to have a chance to connect with the outdoors/nature.
2. Light a candle and say a gratitude prayer before bed.
3. Cook a dish from my childhood to reconnect with my family and cultural background.

---

### What Do You Put in Your Health and Wellness Toolkit?

Teachers and others who work in early childhood have so many different ways they find helpful to manage their stress and care for themselves in individually and culturally genuine ways. Throughout this book and reflected subsequently is evidence that self-care is different for each of us, and your health and wellness toolkit will be a unique reflection of your intersectional identities, interests, family and cultural backgrounds.

*Every job is stressful but this job is a very physical job, it's mental and physical stress. And so I try to do things to relax myself.*

*Sometimes I go **do my nails** like I did yesterday and then I just sit there and listen to the jazz music. I love to do my nails, even though I don't do them all the time, but it makes a huge difference for me. I also like to exercise, go for a walk and just **taking a shower is self-care for me**.—Natalia Suarez*

*I like to **work on classic cars**, I have a 1968 Lexus Camaro that is a constant work in progress. And I'll go with my buddy ... he's got a couple cars that he's working on and I'll go and help him. I also like **doing absolutely nothing,** going to the couch, turning on the TV, and do absolutely nothing and just sit there watch a movie, watch a series, watch a show, whatever it is and just do nothing. That is self-care for me. —Martin Fuentes*

*When I come home, I like to listen to music on the way, that is the only thing sometimes that calms me down. I distract myself, **music from Afghanistan, my country or Indian songs**. Something I like the most to keep me calm. When I am at home, if something stressful comes to my mind, I will get out of my home and I put my music on and I go for a long walk.—Fawzia Saffi*

*I love to do art and music. I dabble in watercolor, I love to paint and listen to spiritual music or worship music. I do the painting with the music. I just recently took a stained glass class and made a beautiful window of a tree – to remind myself to keep growing and stretching, this medium was definitely a stretch for me. I play a little bit of guitar, but mostly I just love to sing. I sing all the time. I sing in the shower, I sing in the car, I sing on the way to work. I sing Celtic music and I also like to sing Christian worship music that has really positive words in it. It's like I'm singing affirmations. I also like to just make up a song ... I believe that we get our songs from nature and from the Creator, and so it just comes through you. You open your mouth and start singing and there's really not words to it, it's just a way of **singing through the spirit**. In our Native American tradition, **many of the traditional songs came out that way and the sounds are called it vocables**. The meaning comes*

> from singing the song in a worshipful and celebratory way, not from words.—Karen Tapia
>
> For my body, I do **acupuncture** and **yoga** besides **massage**.—Charles Harris
>
> I really like to think about **home improvement.** I like thinking about decor and design. I also really love cake shows ... how they design them. There's a beginning, a middle and an end. I just love that it's so satisfying to me to think about that stuff, to see that stuff, to be part of just, I just, I don't know what it is, but it's very satisfying and I like that.—Joyce Darbo
>
> I **pay attention to what I eat and what I drink**. I'm like boiling vegetables in chicken broth and adding strips of chicken or meat or something and then having whole wheat bread or corn tortillas or something like that. Just getting back to the basics of what food is. And it's really because when I'm stressed I don't want to eat. I don't want to put anything in my stomach. I must hold stress in my stomach.—Angelica Chacon

## Summary

*"Who are you?" said the Caterpillar.*

*. . . Alice replied, rather shyly, "I—I hardly know, sir, just at present—at least I know who I WAS when I got up this morning, but I think I must have been changed several times since then."*

*—Lewis Carroll*

When educators' stressors are buffered with wellness and culturally responsive caring routines, their energy is restored and renewed. Creating an authentic self-care "toolbox" with a range of strategies that are genuine, accessible and helpful helps educators to have more reserves to pull from to build and maintain positive and attuned relationships with children and adults, to remain self-regulated and calm during triggering moments and interactions, to support their own body awareness and prevent the release of stress chemicals that can damage their health. They can also transform their classrooms, programs and organizations by implementing trauma-informed and healing-oriented practices that buffer stress for children and families and contribute to a positive working climate for themselves and their colleagues. As you see evidenced in the educators' narratives, participating in meaningful self-care activities on a regular basis can be transformative, liberating and healing.

*So saying the rosary brings me peace. It makes me be able to sit and stop. And I think that's been harder for me to do this year at least, to just be with my thoughts. And that's been helpful too in a sort of reflective trance, to be able to be there and kind of let go and just feel like, "I'm here and present." And I think that's what it's been like even going to the cemetery when I feel like I can't focus. And it's this grassy patch on a hill where you can see the bay in all its glory and it's beautiful and it just feels like peace. I can no longer care for my father, so I care for his grave, I can no longer massage him, so I massage the soil, I can clean the tombstone, I can just be. I can visit others and feel grounded in a different connection that I carry beyond that space when I leave. Being with my daughter does this too. Her spirit full of so much peace and curiosity gives me perspec-*

tive and a new view and appreciation for all that is around me. I can gaze at her and feel full of hope and gratitude in the same breath. On that hill, alone or with my daughter, we're in the middle of everything, and in our own private world.

I grew up with four industrial sewing machines in our garage or in our little back room that my mom had for most of my life. Just constantly buzzing. But I never touched a sewing machine until I was 30 because I was always terrified I was gonna take out a finger. My mom had these different injuries that she would get. And we are very much a worst-case scenario, worry all the time, kind of family . . . like everything that could possibly go wrong will go wrong, which doesn't really help. But the last few years I've been trying to learn how to sew and it has become something really relaxing for me. But what gets in the way of doing so is usually time. Feeling that I can take that much time away from my family. Swimming is also something I love to do, and that's been mostly challenging to get out to do it. Symptoms of depression haven't helped . . . to really do much of what I'd typically like to do, or even move my body some days, but learning that I can dip my toe and not do it all as I might have typically aimed for, lightens the load a bit. I now mostly get in the water because I go with my daughter. And that's when I'm like, "Let's just go swim" and so it might not be laps, but let's put on a swimsuit and get wet. Why not? Even if it's water balloons or just going to the beach and sticking our feet in for a bit, and just finding something in between. It doesn't have to be everything, but those moments are what makes it all worth the "doing of things"—the being, simply being is necessary for the doing. And being in water, or creating something with my hands for those I love, well that's, what feeds me.

I hope that I do not give up when I feel tired and instead, that I am able to refocus and reenergize and regroup with *what brought me to the field and what drives me in the work I do. It's important to me to stay connected to those we're here to serve and support—to allow my values to lead me and never lose sight of all the caregivers and children who got me here, and not get lost in this system. When I reflect on my earliest memories, I find that my childhood caregivers, Lupe, my Nina Rosie, my sisters and Tia, keep me rooted in my purpose, and because they were family and friends, they continue to be a part of my life. I hope that just as my caregivers kept stories for me, that I can learn from and share the stories of caregivers back so that we can shape the system to work for us, and not get lost in it.*

*I find that while I entered the field because of my passion and commitment for children, unfortunately, many of the current systems in place are not designed with the caregiver in mind but are patchwork attempts to support the workforce and then prepare children for school. As policies are implemented, oftentimes the humanity is lost. Our systems perpetuate a constant self-doubt for caregivers and often create unnecessary stressors for an already oppressed and undervalued population. And in general, we simply do not value people who are not financially contributing to society—children and elders—which means, we also don't value those who care for them.*

*Many of the current policies were created without the heart of the children in mind, policies that take that precious time and energy that is created through the bond and the beauty of caregiving and they mechanize it . . . to make children ready for school instead of preparing the school and our homes for the children entering them. We are not here to break children's spirits so they can conform. I pray that I don't get caught in that system, but continue to chisel away at it, and downright break it apart as needed.*

*I focus on self-care for the children. And the role we have to help create a space that just allows them to be whoever they are becoming and to appreciate them in their full selves and everything that they bring to this world. I was talking with somebody recently about how I feel sometimes that— and especially in watching my daughter grow up—I feel like we're constantly trying to crush children's spirits in an effort to conform or to meet whatever standards we feel they need to meet. And I just want to honor the spirits that they come with. I just hope that we can always show kids respect and the dignity that they deserve and the families that they come from and with too. Just honoring everything that they bring with them and not making them feel like they need to either be someone else or conform to a certain system.*

*We must remember that our communities have been caring for our children since the beginning of time and the systems we create and live with should continuously lift them up so that we can all lead fulfilling lives, with strong roots and resilient wings. This is what caregiving is at heart.*

### Reflection Questions

♦ Which people in your life help you gain perspective like Doménica has with her daughter?

♦ Does time ever impact your self-care routine, like not feeling like you have time?

♦ Doménica talks about how she feels like we are constantly trying to crush children's spirits in an effort to conform or meet standards we put on them. If you were to imagine you have an inner child, what message would your adult side of you say to your inner child about self-care?

# 4

# Case Studies

## Applying Ideas Throughout the Book to Your Practice

How can we teach and learn from one another about culturally responsive self-care strategies? How can I apply the ideas I'm learning throughout this book to my own practice?

**Key Topics Covered**
- Case study #1. Anh Tham, Mentor Teacher and Coach: "True Self-Care Requires Fighting For It"
- Case study #2. Monique Lee, Large Family Child Care Provider: "I Know to Just Be Aware of My Heartbeat"
- Case study #3. Angelica Chacon, Infant Toddler Specialist: "I Worked Hard to Find Peace With the Situation While Maintaining My Integrity and My Pride and Honoring Knowledge of My Ability"
- Case study #4: Maria Sandoval, Assistant Director in a Small School: "Something That Stressed Me out at First Was Not Being Aligned With Some of the Values of the School, but Then I Found My Own Way"

♦ Case study #5: Nelena Alegre, Mental Health Consultant With Head Start: "Knowing That There's a Larger Picture at Play. That Belief Has Gotten Me Through All of the Trauma That I Have Witnessed and Experienced Working in Early Childhood Education"

## Case Study #1. Anh Tham: "True Self-Care Requires Fighting For It"

*Self-Care = healing both my body and my self-worth. Knowing my value and that I am loved. I believe that self-care means being truthful about my own experience. Talking about my suffering, and pain. I often listen to everyone else's pain and empathize with others, but I don't feel that I have that same permission to share my own pain. —Anh Tham*

*My name is Anh Tham. I am a mentor teacher, a coach, and I'm responsible for helping educators to self-assess, identify their strengths and growth areas. I also facilitate peer to peer, supervisor to staff and team to team interactions. I work with administrators and teachers in creating and maintaining an environment that is conducive to learning for children and families. I help to create an environment for educators to learn from and reflect with each other. I sometimes fill in as supervisor when a leadership team is not around or when an emergency arises or licensing visitors arrive. I stand in and support wherever I can help.*

*So I've been in three countries and two of them, I've been in a non-dominant culture. I moved from Vietnam to France when I was five years old. I moved from France to the United States when I was eleven years old. My fluency is in three languages, for example, Vietnamese I am about first grade level. My French about three years old-ish. I am losing them now as I'm not using it. And then my English, I am learning English. I've come to identify as American and am sometimes shocked when others try to differentiate and categorize. I am reminded of my Asian-ness when others call me "Chinese" (I'm not Chinese) or when I become the resident expert when I'm out with a group of (non-Asian) friends at an Asian restaurant. If pushed, I realize that if the choices are to be "white woman" or a "woman of color", I choose "woman of color", but that is not how I primarily self-identify. I was raised in San Francisco so there was a lot of diversity around me. I am realizing more now that my cultural background gives me compassion to work with the families and staff in my program, especially as they acclimate to a new culture, finding their voice, recognizing their need to feel safe with their own home language. (1)*

*My current stress at work . . . I feel like I have to be available for a lot of people all at once (2), especially this year. I'm the only coach here this year and I feel very guilty for supporting some of the classrooms and then neglecting others. I understand that I'm only one person, but I care about educators. I know their work is incredibly hard. Part of my stress is also the overlapping of responsibilities (3) and the fact that they are always changing (4). Sometimes I'm a coach, sometimes I'm the supervisor, sometimes I'm a parent and I'm bringing all these hats into the situation. I'm thankful for them and however, it's just a lot of work. And the changing priorities of our organization. One year we want to focus on CLASS (Classroom Assessment Scoring System Tool) and the next year we're focusing on high quality teaching and that can be stressful. Another piece of stress is that my agency does not recognize my 10 years of experience while I was running a family child care. Prior to that I was teaching for 15 years and they will count that but not the 10 years of family child care. So that kind of discourages me about what our agency believes about early learning.*

*Talking about it helps a lot. I feel like when I'm talking about it with a trusted coworker, it cuts the stress about 50%. Really talking about it, expressing my emotions. I also journal. I find the journal helps me so much because it slows me down, it coordinates my writing and my feelings and my thoughts. I talk about it with my husband sometimes. When I don't talk about it, I yell at my own children. So I'm learning about myself as well. Before going in the house when I park the car, I take a break like five minutes or ten minutes before I go in and I pray. I sometimes treat myself to a Boba drink. It helps me to get a Boba drink and take some time to myself before I go in the house or talk with my husband and share my day.*

*I take care of a lot of people and things (children, families, educators, activities, food, house, moving, packing, cleaning, etc.) Oftentimes, it is too much and exhausting. I am so busy caring for others (because I am generous, sacrificial and creative) yet, I neglect myself (5) (I name those characteristics even though I am very uncomfortable sharing it out loud, but I think it is important, especially as a woman, to name our strengths). I repressed my pain of being overwhelmed and my over-looked feelings. I suffered in silence. The questions I asked myself were:*

◆ *Who is taking care of you Anh*
◆ *What does it mean to be taken care of?* (6)

*I used to have this belief that it is selfish to have self-care* (7). *I know now that it's not selfish but I'm finding out my heart still believes that it is selfish. I'm trying to work on that right now. And I think it comes from a place where culturally I was raised to think about other people. I was thinking about how we're constantly thinking about community, for the good of community. For example in my childhood when we sit down to eat a meal, we children could not start the meal unless the oldest person started the meal. And then even the last piece of food, we could not take the last piece unless the elders offered it to you, or you made sure to check in with everyone else if you wanted the last piece. The way we serve meals, we each have a bowl of rice and the main dish is always in the middle and it's for everyone. You don't scoop it and put it on your plate and that's it. It's more like you take it one bite at a time, so that's different. So we all again, like we were always thinking about community, making sure that others have enough and you take one piece at a time.*

*I think that extends from thinking about other people in the community for the good of others, be in relationship with others so that we could work together. That was very important. And then again, I think that's my identity as an Asian American woman. You're raised to have this value where community is super important, whereas now I appreciate learning about how to be independent and I'm trying to marry the two. I'm trying to balance and knowing who I am apart from my community and who I'm raised to be. I know self-care is so important, I think is critical, but I'm still working on the heart piece to change and be more intentional. Put myself on the schedule. Make an appointment with myself.*

*I feel like my background has given me a sensitivity for the staff I work with now. For example, I grew up in a culture where we're*

*constantly in a community because we lived in close quarters. So rela-*
*tionship building for community is a top priority. We look out for what*
*others think, and how we are going to get along with others. And this*
*background influences my work. I noticed many of our Asian staff were*
*not speaking out about what they believe or think in our staff meetings.,*
*Most of them would wait until the end to chime in. So as a coach, I try*
*to bring that piece out, "What do you have to say?" I try to make sure*
*all of our staff have a voice in our meetings.*

*For me, self-care is being in solitude or in quietness.(8) That replen-*
*ishes me. It is about sitting and being with yourself or going and con-*
*necting with nature. I have this rock that I sit on and I write in my*
*journal or just be. Away from my phone, away sometimes even from my*
*journal. Just to be with myself with nothing. And that seems to really*
*replenish me. And I think about it and I pray. I think solitude is the one*
*that fills me, being in solitude. I don't know why I don't do it more often.*

*Another self care strategy I use is breathing. I found that the breath*
*is so powerful. Just being able to breathe, it slows down my blood pres-*
*sure and calms all my thoughts, my mind. I have a picture of breathing*
*in my office to remind myself to breathe. I often pray or give myself*
*affirmations just recognizing that I am loved. I don't know what it is*
*for me but when I am focusing on the idea that I am loved, it fills me up.*
*It reminds me why I'm here. I have everything I need to do my work or*
*live life. So I'm working on a lot of like changing my mind, being able*
*to reduce the stress in my mind. I de-stress by reading, sometimes spir-*
*itual books. I go out with friends, I watch movies with my family, we*
*cooked dinner together. I like to garden. I love having people come over*
*to my house, having gatherings. I'm part of a small group at church,*
*being connected to community. That's powerful too. And especially*
*I want to be around friends that are funny, you know? We all need*
*laughter. I just want to be around people who laugh and enjoy making*
*jokes. Joyful people. I need to be around joyful people. (9)*

*I used to think of self-care is having chocolates, a pedicure,*
*and massage, wine and cheese but now I believe that true self-care*
*requires fighting for it. I needed to fight against my own idea of what*
*a mother, wife, professional should be. I am aware of the need to fight*

*against others' expectations of me. On one hand, I try to be a super-woman, doing things by myself and doing it all, but I can't. Accepting my limits is the most responsible thing I can do as a traveler on the road to self-care. I have learned to take a breath, to eat, and receive a hug from a friend. I believe taking care of the self is a big part of being human.*

## Reflecting on Mentor Teacher and Coach Anh's Story

1.  In reading this story, how do race, culture, gender impact your daily life? How do you manage these stressors? What strengths do you have that help you cope?

2.  Anh says she has to be available to a lot of people at once. Have you been faced with this same situation?
    ◆ *How do you prioritize taking care of others when there are so many needs at one time?*
    ◆ *How do you build in protected time to spend with those you are helping?*
    ◆ *How do you handle emergencies when they arise?*
    ◆ *Do you ever say "no", and how do you do that?*
    ◆ *How do you give the same attention to yourself as you do to others?*

3.  Have you ever been faced with overlapping (too many) responsibilities on your plate at work?
    ◆ *How do you prioritize your work?*
    ◆ *Do you take work home, and does it come into your personal life? How does that impact you? Others?*
    ◆ *Where do you set boundaries?*
    ◆ *How do you balance the work responsibilities with personal time and activities to restore your stress?*

4.  Change—Anh talks about how things are always changing. Change seems to be a part of daily life. Yet some of us welcome change and some of us find it stressful.
    ◆ *Do you like change?*
    ◆ *What kinds of change restore your energy?*
    ◆ *What kinds of change create more stress for you?*

- *When is change welcome? At work? In your personal life?*
- *How do you prepare others for change (children, co-workers, supervisees, supervisors)?*

5. Could you relate to when Anh says, "I am so busy caring for others (because I am generous, sacrificial and creative) yet, I neglect myself."
   - *Does your pendulum swing more to you caring for others?*
   - *Does your pendulum swing more to you caring for yourself?*
   - *Or do you have a balance between caring for others and yourself?*
   - *How does this impact you (physically, socially, emotionally, mentally and/or spiritually)?*
   - *What, if anything, would you like to do differently? Why and how would this change impact you?*

6. Anh asks herself, "Who is taking care of you Anh?" "What does it mean to be taken care of?" Let's reflect on those same questions for you:
   - *Who is taking care of you?*
   - *What does it mean to be taken care of?*
   - *How do you take care of yourself?*

7. Where do your values, perceptions or beliefs fall related to the statement "It is selfish to have self-care"?

8. Which do you prefer to restore your energy—being with others or solitude?

9. Which, if any, of these self-care strategies do you use that Anh mentions she finds helpful:
   - *Breathing*
   - *Reading*
   - *Going out with friends*
   - *Watching movies with family*
   - *Prayer*
   - *Focusing on the idea that "I am loved"*
   - *Being around joyful people.*

## Case Study #2: Monique Lee: "I Know to Just Be Aware of My Heartbeat"

*Self-Care = I can have up to 25 or 30 conversations a day with parents, and then you've got the all-day conversations with children and new teachers. And then you have your husband and your kids. So, really creating a morning ritual that was all for me, and a time of my own reflection, and that was my morning bath, without question. A 30-minute bath in the morning was my luxury. —Monique Lee*

I've been a large family child care provider for 19 years serving children between the ages of newborn to 12 years old. I'm the oldest child of two parents that suffered mental illness. My father was diagnosed bipolar, much later in life, and had some suicidal tendencies. My mother suffered depression and was an alcoholic. I advocated for her to have a liver transplant, which was successful, and now she's sober. I was a caregiver to both my parents and that therapeutic piece has been a lot of my life experience and I bring that into my family child care practice. Having that experience of being really sensitive on the social-emotional piece is very important for me when working with children and also using my formal education by understanding, the development over the course of a lifespan from infant, toddler, pre-K, and then K through elementary, as well as my own experience as a parent, as a foster adoptive parent, and being a therapeutic parent.

Establishing loving, supportive relationships is critical to me. (1) Being present, emotionally present in the moment, with my interactions and trying to really make sure my communication is clear. So when somebody says something, or I'm talking with a parent, I listen. I will ask questions. If they need emotional support, I build safety and security for them. And I think, how much love can I provide to these families so they trust me? I mean they're trusting me with their most precious thing, their child. I feel very blessed and honored to have that privilege, to know the families and learn about their own cultural lenses, and support that and respect that in my family child care program. (2)

*I don't have a lot of stress working with families. But I do remember one family I worked with a decade or so ago, where the second child was having some facial scratches occur while in my care, and we could not figure out where this was happening. I requested a parent conference so we could talk about it. We, the child's parents and I, were trying to figure it out because we have 100% supervision of the children at all times. The father started to become very upset with me because there was no identifiable answer to explain the scratches on his son's face. As he was talking, he started to share his own experience of being in a family child care, which was a very negative experience for him. And he was carrying some of that bias with him into our relationship, which he started to acknowledge. And actually, what we identified in our conversation was that it was the older sibling, when hugging the younger sibling, his fingernails were—not intentionally—but they were gliding across the younger son's face (the child's older sibling was also in care with me). And so, once we discovered that, we were able to work with the older sibling to help him learn how to touch the younger sibling in a gentle manner, both at home and in the family child care environment. So that was stressful for me, because I was listening to the father's experiences and trying to empathize with his own background experiences where he had suffered. I knew that what he experienced was not happening in my practice. I was trying to support him emotionally but also help him not to make assumptions about his son's experiences in my home. Still to this day, almost 15 years later, we're very good friends, and his children are now going to college. But this story highlights how one of the stressors in my job is related to listening. (3) Because I don't always know a parent's history, where they're coming from, and just recognizing that I may not have all the information as to what their needs and goals are for their child, and this is both important and difficult at times. But, I try to remind myself to just meet the parent where they are at, and be okay with that. Another stressor I experience is managing my own family because of my children having special needs, and me being a foster parent advocating for them as well, simultaneously, while also supporting the children in my care can create stress for me.*

*What I've learned over the years is that when I start to feel dysregulated, my heart starts to race. And I have learned to just be aware of my heartbeat. When it starts to go fast, that is a trigger for me to stop and say, "Wow, something's bothering me or not feeling right. And I wonder what that is about?" So I kind of go through a quick check in with myself to consider what is going on in my mind that's making me feel anxious. Once I identify it, I start to make a plan as to what I want to do with that feeling. A lot of times, just sitting, breathing or removing myself out of wherever I'm at, and just taking a short break or washing my hands works really well. Or, talking to whomever I'm with at the time, and just checking in, "You know, I'm feeling this way, I'm seeing this. Are you seeing that, too? How do you feel about that?" Just sharing feelings and observations with them helps.* (4)

*To reduce my stress and care for myself, I love playing with my two dogs, and I like taking walks with my husband in the evenings and we reflect on our day together. Nature is really helpful. I also enjoy having a beautiful environment. That's very important to me, a very organized environment in my family child care home. I like to bring the outdoors inside with plants and flowers . . . fresh flowers.*

*Time management is the thing that I have to really be conscious about. You know, when is that time of day that I have for myself, and how I want to utilize that time? At the beginning of the day, I need to manage my meal times; how I eat, what I eat, how much I eat, as well as physical exercise. And then, I have to plan for how I want to end my day. I like to start it kind of slow and I like to end it kind of slow as well.* (5)

## Reflecting on Family Child Care Provider Monique's Story

1. How do you set loving and supporting relationships as a part of your self-care plan? Who do you define as the people in your life that are supporting and grounding you and filling your bucket up (the people who help to restore your energy)?

2. When you reflect on the day, how much time do you spend thinking of the future or the past? Or are you usually focused on the present moment? How do you find

time or be with yourself where you are fully present in the moment? What does "being fully present" look like in your life?

3.  Does listening to or empathizing with others ever cause you stress? How do you cope with that? How do you listen with compassion without getting burned out or taking on others' pain?

4.  Do you use any of the same strategies that Monique uses to destress?
    a.  Walking her dogs (animals)
    b.  Spending time with her partner
    c.  Being outdoors/in nature
    d.  Bringing outdoors indoors
    e.  Creating a beautiful work environment
    f.  Time management
    g.  Organizing the tasks in your day
    h.  Fresh flowers
    i.  Physical exercise
    j.  Managing your food/eating
    k.  Start the day slow . . . end the day slow.

## Case Study #3. Angelica Chacon: "I Worked Hard to Find Peace With the Situation While Maintaining My Integrity and My Pride and Honoring Knowledge of My Ability."

*Self-Care = The awareness and the validity of honoring the self, that we are deserving of feeling better, of taking care of ourselves. We're deserving of acknowledging the need that we experience hardships and that those hardships are worthy of being recognized as something we can learn from and overcome because it makes us wiser for the process of rolling through it. And we are so deserving of growing. —Angelica Chacon*

*My name is Angelica Chacon. I work as an infant toddler specialist and I teach infant-toddler child development to care providers. I also do technical assistance which is to observe providers in their practice and then I meet with them for reflective practice in order to help them reach their goals with the families or the children they are working with. I do this for both English-speaking and Spanish-speaking center-based care providers and for family child care providers. I've done this work for fifteen years. The other thing about me is I'm Chicana Latina and I often see things through a race equity lens.*

*The first way that I bring this to the folks I work with is through language as most of the providers I work with are Spanish-speaking. I also get to know them. Primarily, they are immigrant status folks, and I let them know I'm second generation. For example, once I worked with this particular family child care provider who has a way of being where her opinions come out as forceful. Some people in professional development circles describe her as somewhat troublesome. I worked to see who she is and what motivates her and I have learned that she has a heart of gold. I once observed her take a toddler's hand and pull him with her (I know that hand motion is looked upon negatively by many including outside evaluators who come into her program to rate the quality of her classroom). On one of my visits, I took a picture of her hand on his. I felt that it was essential that I could not walk out with integrity if I did not address her pulling on a child's hand but I also had a goal of wanting to help her really see it for herself. So, I decided to use a photo and I just*

*asked her, "What do you see?" And she said, "I'm pulling on his hand."*
*And then I said, "What were you wanting to do?" And she told me.*
*I had a sense of her intention and I just let her know, I said, "I know*
*you, and I know what your intention was. And the fact that you work*
*with people who will be coming and doing assessments, I want you to*
*know that this could give you a lower score." And so I said, "Let's look*
*at how else you could do what you were hoping to do with him. What*
*do you think?" And she said, "Oh, I could tell him that I wanted him*
*to come over here." And I said, "Yes. And if he didn't come?" And then*
*she didn't know what to say. So then I gave her some suggestions for*
*several ways she could encourage him to go where she was wanting him*
*to go with her. I helped her to see some other options . . . I wanted her to*
*hear that she's pulling on a child's hand. And, I wanted it to come from*
*a place of respect, and care, and honoring her as a professional, as an*
*individual, as a human being. I wanted to support her work with chil-*
*dren because she's Spanish-speaking, she's immigrant status, she's a*
*provider, she's female, she's all these things and she could help children*
*think positively about people in those positionalities. So I just saw all*
*this benefit from going the extra mile and getting creative and my work*
*was all from a place of positive-based intention.*

*The things that create stress for me in my work? I'll tell you, I've*
*grown quite tired of my professional peers who are of the dominant*
*culture whom I feel do not understand the extra mile I have to go to*
*be heard and the unique perspectives I bring from my cultural back-*
*ground. Many of them do not have a single clue and I have to work*
*really hard sometimes when situations happen to not lose it. One*
*example is an experience I had with Monica, a very respected toddler*
*teacher in our community. Monica is monolingual English-speaking*
*and White. She doesn't have any specific infant-toddler training in her*
*background. One day Monica approached me and asked if I wanted a*
*position to mentor, Christina, a Chicana infant-toddler teacher work-*
*ing in Monica's program. I said, "Yes, I would be honored." And then*
*two weeks later, Monica said to me, "You know, I've thought about it*
*again, and I think I want to be Christina's coach." I couldn't believe it.*
*I'm the one who has fourteen years of experience with infant-toddler*

providers. *I'm bilingual. And, I am Chicana. Between the two of us, I was the best person qualified to coach a Latina infant teacher given my experience, expertise in working with toddlers and because of the cultural continuity. Monica's treatment of me was not only a professional insult, it was also a racialized insult. I mean, how could she not see the cultural continuity and what an opportunity it would be to offer that to an infant-toddler teacher in her program? How could she not see that? It was like my expertise and background were invisible to her. I worked hard to find peace with the situation while at the same time maintaining my integrity and my pride and honoring knowledge of my ability.* (1)

*To manage the stress of this situation, I journaled a lot.* (2) *At this time, I was studying race equity pedagogy for the infant-toddler field in a graduate degree program and I was living my own example of why that lens is needed in this field. So I had academic information and concrete evidence that racism exists in the educational field. I had validation. I also had the support of my supervisor to process the experience. The fact that she is White was also helpful. Processing the experience of invisibility with my supervisor helped me.* (3) *I felt validated, heard, and understood by somebody from the dominant culture. Ultimately, the agency funding the mentor position was consulted and they advised that the position should go to an individual with infant-toddler care training. So, in the long run, I became Christina's coach.*

### Reflecting on Infant-Toddler Specialist Angelica's Story

1. Angelica reports that one of her stressors is that she has *"grown quite tired of my professional peers who are of the dominant culture whom I feel do not understand the extra mile I have to go to be heard and the unique perspectives I bring from my cultural background"*.

   ♦ *Does this story ring true for you?*
   ♦ *Have you experienced stress because you identify with the non-dominant culture?*
   ♦ *How does this impact you emotionally, physically, at work and/or at home?*

2. Angelica says she journals to help her cope. Have you ever used journaling as a self-care strategy?

3. Angelica also took some time to talk with her supervisor who is White to share with her how she feels. *"Processing with my supervisor the experience of invisibility helped me."*
   ◆ Have you ever processed a stressor with your supervisor?
   ◆ *Do you have an example when it helped?*
   ◆ *Do you have an example when it was not helpful?*
   ◆ *Why was it helpful or not helpful?*
   ◆ *What strategies did you use to make it helpful or not helpful?*
   ◆ *What strategies did the supervisor use to make it easier to reflect and feel supported, and what did they do specifically when it was not supportive?*

4. Gloria E. Anzaldúa (2009, p. 309), was a scholar who grew up on the Mexico–Texas border and used her lived experiences of social and cultural marginalization to write about the experiences of individuals who navigate borders and experience a sense of being "in-between". She wrote, "I am visible—see this Indian face—yet I am invisible. I both blind them with my beak nose and am their blind spot. But I exist, we exist. They'd like to think I have melted in the pot. But I haven't. We haven't." How does this quote relate to Angelica's story? Do her words resonate with your lived experiences? If so, in what way?

## Case Study #4: Maria Sandoval: "Something That Stressed Me out at First Was Not Being Aligned With Some of the Values of the School, but Then I Found My Own Way . . ."

Self-Care = *What really helps is doing physical exercise . . . also, taking care of sleep hygiene and trying to go for a coffee.* —Maria Sandoval

*My name is Maria Sandoval and I am from South America, but I am currently living and working in California. I work as an assistant director and teacher in a small independent school. Half of the students are subsidized by the state and half of the students pay tuition on a sliding scale. It's a diverse classroom, socioeconomically, culturally, and linguistically. In my role, I am responsible for administrative tasks and I work with our small team of teachers in building inquiry skills linked with emergent curriculum. I also substitute teach.*

*On a typical day, when I wake up I try to do yoga and go for a run. If I'm teaching or subbing early, I download an app with a 7 minute workout. I try to do this before going to school. It makes me more focused. When I am teaching, I usually get there at 7:30. I greet the other teachers and then I ask the head teacher what role she wants me to be in. It's a free-play based school, so I'm typically there from 8–11:30 in the areas they choose. I prefer being outdoors in the playground because I work better in the outdoor spaces, so if this is something I can do, I prefer doing that. Then there is a 15 min bathroom/do what you want to do break at 9 or 10, which we rotate. At 11:30, it is circle time. At lunch, I sit with the younger children who are about 3–4 years old. Then it's naptime, which is a slow transition. Even though the classroom is big, it's for 24 children, so the space is something that we need to be mindful of. The cots are close together. I help set up the cots and support children in naptime. I sit next to them and pat their backs, though the school's approach is to let the children put themselves to sleep. Then I take a 30 minute lunch break. I try to do this outdoors. Sometimes other teachers join and sometimes I do it by myself. After half an hour, I go back into the classroom and start setting the tables with another teacher. I do a bit of cleanup, and then when the children start getting up, we do a walk in the playground. When the children all wake up, we do some sort of play-based activity. I do a head teacher check-in before she leaves at 3:30. I'm usually the one who talks to parents, and so when the parents come, around 4:30, I always try to say something positive. By 5:30 all the children and teachers are gone and I am by myself. There are always one or two parents who are late, though. And then I clean up the last few things. I like that moment, because it's my moment of unwinding. I put away toys, sweep, do things you don't think about too much, and I go back to the office to check emails. (1) Then, by 7, I go back to home. At home, I try to cook; sometimes I pick my husband up and we go home together, cook, watch Netflix and go to sleep.*

*Something that makes me stressed is pickup time. I like to be close to parents and to have close relationships, but stress comes from multitasking. At pickup, when parents are asking detailed questions, they are not taking care of their children at that time. I am not either, as I am focusing on my own language and getting the information across to the parents. So it's like a grey area. When this happens, with parents and children with needs, the multitasking stresses me out. . . . Some parents are really demanding and they trust us so much. This wouldn't happen in my home country. I talk to them and find out how they do things at home, but they ask, "What <u>should</u> I do?" I don't have an answer. For me, there's sometimes a bit of a language barrier and sometimes a different validation of the teacher role.*

*Another thing that used to stress me out was not being aligned with some of the values of the school. Like naptime. Here [in the United States], we are expected to have a "loving disengagement" and to avoid eye contact, because the idea is that this is going to improve their autonomy . . . I don't have my own kids but I was really uncomfortable about this. I used to get stressed out—not because the moment of naptime was stressful, but I considered what the school was telling me, and then found my own way, my own style. There is more physicality and more oral communication here, and that is a big cultural difference. When I go back to my family in South America, I see my sister with her children and they are . . . it's a big difference in the amount of talk. . . . She gets children involved but in a way that's less verbal. I learned a lot about parents here and cultural differences. (2)*

*Space is also a stress—when it's more cramped, children struggle to get their own space. The amount of toys is not enough and children are still struggling how to move their bodies. My stress is anticipatory stress ( . . . this will be conflict for sure!). It doesn't work as well when it's a small space ("You're bumping me!"). Also, I have in some sort of way, this distance, this cultural space. I'm usually really close to children but now I'm trying to be less close—I'm in the middle and need to step back, and I'm still working that out. . .*

*When I talk to my friends who are teachers in South America, they say it's different. Lunchtime, for me, in my own culture is a space to unwind, but I unwind with others and wish I could always have a lunchtime with coworkers. But sometimes when I sit on the porch— yesterday this happened—a teacher was **working** next to me, and I didn't want to interrupt her but I felt it was a bit disrespectful. It's a space for unwinding but she was working. I thought "OK lunchtime!" but then your colleagues just put their headphones on. But [I understand] there are space constraints. Now I know that everyone has their own way of unwinding. (3) Everyone here in this area [in the United States] is working so much. Nobody can take time for going on a 3 hour hike on the weekend, so everyone is working. Back home, nobody works on the weekend. Only if you work in finance, maybe.*

*Outside of work, what really helps [to destress] is doing physical exercise. I'm enrolled in a yoga center. It helps because I'm paying, so I'm going to go. Also, taking care of sleep hygiene. When I sleep less, I'm not as good at taking care of things. I also try to spend time with other people. When I'm stressed I try to go for a coffee. I get what I used to call a "school phobia" on Sunday, that feeling that "I need to teach" or "I have a long day ahead" so it helps to do something fun Sunday evening. (4) Another thing that works is taking what I need to do and breaking it into steps and taking a visual agenda, and I used to journal a lot. What doesn't help is to keep talking about work all the time. Some days I feel that venting with my husband is helpful but it is not really helpful. Working on weekends doesn't help. . .*

*I used to think self-care involved a more school-based approach. If the school is not committed to self-care, you can do it yourself, but it would be better if the school is committed. We don't have self-care as a centerpiece of the school but it would be a great thing to do. (5) We have had a lot of [teacher] absence lately, getting sick more than normal, so this is a signal about the immune system. We all know that preschool teachers have really low salaries. Fortunately, our school is not a public school and receives a lot of private funding, so we are doing better, but it is a very stressful position. It would be more fair if we were able to choose something more healthy, like part time work as this would allow us more years in the profession. But the shortage of teachers is very high, so how can we make this work? Make the roles more flexible? Teachers can also be mentors—so perhaps have non-classroom time but a full time position. There may be other roles, but we need to be creative with that. I don't have an answer but working part time is not an option if you need to pay for your family and pay your rent . . .*

*At a certain point I was stressed out and I talked with my boss and said, "I feel rushed. All the time. Is there a way we can put a break on some of the things? Maybe we are rushing everything . . . I need to be in another role where I can stop, reflect a bit more, etc." So she said, "You can move to this [assistant director] role." (6) This was an important part of my professional decision. I cannot be in a classroom for 8 hours. I wanted to be half-time or part-time. For many teachers who have been around a while, we ask them if they would like to be part-time, but this is a bit of social justice issue. When you are working part time the salary is lower so only people who are wealthy can do this.*

### Reflecting on Assistant Director/Teacher Maria Sandoval's Story

1. Maria finds peace in cleaning up after the children and other teachers are gone.
   ◆ *Are there tasks or times at work that are grounding for you? What are they?*
   ◆ *Where and when else might you find times to reflect and destress during the workday?*

2. Maria mentions the challenges of cultural differences between her home country and the United States: in the ways people de-stress, in the language, the ways people interact with children and the expectations of teachers. Have you experienced differences between your belief systems and the expectations of your job?

   ♦ *Have these differences caused challenges for you at work? How so?*

   ♦ *What would you like for others to understand about your background and culture?*

   ♦ *What would you like to understand more about others' differences?*

3. When Maria wants to unwind during breaks at work, she wants to be social with her colleagues. However, her colleagues don't necessarily want the same thing.

   ♦ *How do you communicate norms with your colleagues at work? Do you understand each other's values, needs and ways of unwinding?*

   ♦ *Does your workplace make space for or encourage this discussion? If so, how?*

   ♦ *If not, how might you approach your colleagues to have these conversations?*

4. Can you relate to the "school phobia" Maria feels on Sunday?

   ♦ *Do you have routines or practices you engage in during the evenings, weekends or other times off which prepare you mentally, emotionally and physically for when work begins again? If so, what are these?*

   ♦ *What else might you adopt from Maria's self-care practices to prepare for work?*

5. Some workplaces make self-care a centerpiece; others do not. How would you describe your workplace?

   ♦ *In what ways does it address stress and/or encourage self-care?*

   ♦ *What would you like to see?*

6. When Maria spoke to her boss about her stress, she was able to negotiate a different role at her work.
   - *Have you self-advocated at your job? If so, how? What was the outcome?*
   - *If not, how might you approach your supervisor about your needs? What sorts of barriers or challenges do you think you might encounter?*
   - *Draft a script you might use to talk about your challenges and advocate for your needs with your colleagues or boss.*

## Case Study #5. Nelena Alegra: "Knowing That There's a Larger Picture at Play. That Belief Has Gotten Me Through All of the Trauma That I Have Witnessed and Experienced Working in Early Childhood Education"

*Self-Care = A lot of activities . . . like dancing, hiking, spending time in nature. It's having close connections with friends, being able to talk about anything that's on my mind or in my heart. It's being reminded of the joys in life, like feeling loved by people, love for animals, love for nature. Just having my tank refilled with the love that I see and experience in the world. And, my spiritual beliefs are kind of the overarching thing that can help me in my day to day interactions. —Nelena Alegra (1)*

*My name is Nelena and I am a therapist. I worked for two and a half years with Head Start as a mental health consultant. In the classroom, I remember feeling the general sense of chaos . . . this sense of a lack of control of all these things happening all around me and not being able to know what to tend to first, which child to take care of, which one needed the most care in the moment. It felt like a triage situation where I would see the chaos erupt in the room and I would have to find which particular child needed the most attention in the moment. And maybe that was crying, maybe that was hitting or throwing or trying to break something, maybe it was hiding in the corner and just looking scared or just completely spaced out and not being fully present. And I would look at all of these different reactions and have to immediately make a decision of where I needed to put my energy and effort. There were periods of calm in the classroom and then something would happen that would cause all of this reaction all at the same time, and I would feel a general sense of overwhelm, overstimulated, pulled in so many directions, and needing to make split second decisions, all while maintaining my sense of calm. And then individually while doing play therapy with the children, I would have experiences where children wouldn't want to leave the play therapy room to go back to the classroom. So they would throw toys around or they would try to hit me or hurt themselves or they would just start to make a mess. They would start crying. They would cling to me, they wouldn't let me put them down. I had to abide by the rules and I could only keep them for a certain amount of time until they had to get back to the classroom. All these are different pressures that I would feel.* (2)

*In those situations, what was breaking me down was the emotional trauma—the vicarious trauma—of hearing what was happening to some of these children, like the abusive situations they would have at home or the bad foster situations they were in or other bad life situations they were experiencing. And there were times when I felt completely helpless, like when I had suspicions of sexual abuse or physical abuse happening and I was doing everything I could and making the report to CPS, they were investigating, everything was done that I possibly could, but it still felt like it wasn't enough or it wasn't going to go anywhere.*

*I felt helpless and out of control. And in those times I called my therapist friends and I told them I needed help. I just needed somebody to be with me and just to get me out of that moment. I would feel a sense that "I'm powerless and terrible things have happened in the world and there's nothing I can do about it." That was always the worst feeling for me. These were the times that I needed a different layer of self-care: When I felt that sense of helplessness to the difficult, horrible things that happen in the world. And when those started coming up, that was when I really started to lean on my deeper sense of how I make meaning in the world.* (3)

*My father's from Mexico and he's mostly Indigenous. I grew up with this lineage that taught me a lot about spirituality and the way to make meaning of the world, a sense of karmic justice, that there's a reason things happen, not necessarily a good reason, but just that it's essential to a part of a life path not that everything that happens is good, but that it's an essential part of one's life path and it's something that will ultimately make us grow as human beings, as spiritual human beings. When something happens that makes me feel out of control, it gives me a sense of control knowing that there's a larger picture at play. It makes me feel like I don't have to be personally in control of every-thing because there is something larger out there that I believe in.* (4)

*That belief has gotten me through all of the trauma that I have witnessed and experienced working in early childhood education. It has gotten me through the feeling that I'm not going to be good enough to heal everybody. I'm not going to be able to take care of everybody; but, as a therapist, as a healer, I have this pressure inside of me and this desire to heal everybody. And of course that's not possible. And that's what often leads to burnout is realizing we can't heal everybody. What keeps me from reaching that burnout is that I trust in this larger sense of control in the world and know that I personally don't have to have control over everything. And so then I can just do everything I can and that feels like it's enough.*

*For me, a barrier to self-care is the pressure to feel like I'm supposed to be the healer so I shouldn't be the one needing to be taking so much time to heal. I need to be healing other people so it can sometimes feel like a pressure to prioritize other people and other people's health and healing over my own. I don't struggle with that as much now, but I used to. Now I know the importance of putting on your own oxygen mask before somebody else's. I absolutely believe that and practice it 100%. (5)*

*When there's a lot of things pulling at me at once, or children's reactions that are just grating on my nerves, things that are just making me feel frazzled and frustrated when those things come up, my spiritual beliefs or general sense of making meaning in the world helps me in this regard. I take a step back and say to myself in my head, "Zoom out." (6) And it's my way of taking a step back, breathing, taking the bigger look at what is happening and remembering, "This isn't going to bother me in an hour. What's bothering me so much right now is not going to matter in a day, in a week or even in an hour." And that helps me to let it go.*

*The other thing that really helps me is I think oftentimes when things happen to us, we tend to take them personally and feel like the world revolves around us; this sense of believing in something greater than us helps me to remember that the world doesn't revolve around me—it's not about me and it helps me to not take it personally. For example, when the children are driving me crazy and I feel like they're just pushing my buttons to try to get a reaction out of me, I can remind myself they are just needing something and they don't know how to communicate it. (7) It's not about me, they're not just trying to piss me off. It's that they're struggling with something and maybe it's because they had a really bad night of sleep the night before or maybe something happened to them at home or somewhere else, and they're just having a hard day themselves and it's not about me. And when I can take a step back, zoom out, remember that it's not about me, and not take it person- ally . . . so much of that stress releases, and then I'm just able to focus on the child and what they need. I apply that idea to everything, especially in my relationships. It's not the world conspiring against me. It helps me to let things roll off more easily. I think my biggest sense of self care is to let things roll off of me in the moment so that it doesn't even build up to the point where I need to do other activities like dancing or hiking. The relief is that I don't even let those stressors build up in the first place.*

## Reflecting on Mental Health Consultant Nelena's Story

1. Nelena defines what self-care is for her. Which strategies do you relate to that she uses?
   - *Dancing*
   - *Hiking*
   - *Spending time in nature*
   - *Having close connections with friends*
   - *Being able to talk about anything that's on her mind or on her heart*
   - *Being reminded of the joys in life, like feeling loved by peo- ple, love for animals, love for nature*
   - *Having her tank refilled with the love that she sees and experiences in the world*
   - *Her spiritual beliefs help her in her day-to-day interactions.*

2. Nelena mentions "*I remember feeling the general sense of chaos . . . this sense of a lack of control of all these things hap- pening all around me and not being able to know what to tend to first, which child to take care of, which one needed the most*

*care in the moment."* This can happen to all of us working in the field of early childhood.

- ♦ *How do you cope in the moment when things all around you feel chaotic?*
- ♦ *What strategies do you use to calm yourself in the moment when you cannot leave the situation?*

3. Nelena mentions vicarious trauma and the idea of being exposed daily to others' (children, coworkers, families) trauma or traumatic experiences and stories. Have you experienced this in the workplace?

- ♦ *How does this impact you?*
- ♦ *How do you release the emotional stress from being exposed to others' traumatic stories or experiences?*
- ♦ *Do you have a person or like Nelena, a therapist, to help you?*
- ♦ *Who supports you when you are faced with daily exposure to trauma?*

4. Nelena says, *"My father's from Mexico and he's mostly Indigenous. I grew up with this lineage that taught me a lot about spirituality and the way to make meaning of the world, a sense of karmic justice, that there's a reason things happen, not that everything that happens is good but that it's an essential part of one's life path and it's something that will ultimately make us grow as human beings, as spiritual human beings. When something happens that makes me feel out of control, it gives me a sense of control knowing that there's a larger picture at play. It makes me feel like I don't have to be personally in control of everything because there is something larger out there that I believe in."*

- ♦ *Do you have a cultural belief/saying/mantra passed down from your family that is a part of your practice that helps with self-care?*
- ♦ *What other cultural values or beliefs were passed down that support your self-care practice?*

5. Have you ever experienced the same barrier Nelena has faced: *"For me, a barrier to self-care is the pressure to feel like I'm supposed to be the healer so I shouldn't be the one needing to be taking so much time to heal. I need to be healing other people so it can sometimes feel like a pressure to prioritize other people and other people's health and healing over my own"*?

   ◆ *Do you have a belief that you should not be helping or taking care of yourself? Where did this belief come from?*

   ◆ *How does it serve you now? What would you like to believe?*

6. One of Nelena's self-care mantras to calm herself in the moment of chaos and stress is *"take a step back and say to myself in my head, 'zoom out'."*

   ◆ *Do you have a mantra or saying that calms you down in the moment?*

7. When Nelena is faced with children with behaviors that challenge her, she uses a coping strategy where she says to herself *"They are just needing something and they don't know how to communicate it. It is not about me."*

   ◆ *When children have dysregulated behavior and your buttons are being pushed emotionally, what do you do to calm yourself and consider what they are communicating to you—the need or feeling underneath the behavior—so you don't become reactive?*

# Conclusion

*People travel to wonder at the height of the mountains, at the huge waves of the seas, at the long course of the rivers, at the vast compass of the ocean, at the circular motions of the stars, and yet they pass by themselves without ever wondering.*

—St. Augustine

*As stressful as it is being in the ECE field, at the end of the day, I can say that I've been able to go to sleep and just think how grateful I am to be a part of helping families' lives. Because a lot of other jobs you don't get that rewarding feeling . . . so as stressful as it gets, I always come back to the fact that this is a job that makes me happy. It's very fulfilling for me. So, despite what I've gone through, I can say that I don't regret it at all.*

—Whitney Carr, Site Supervisor at a Child Development Center

The early childhood educators' narratives throughout this book highlight how culturally responsive self-care is explicitly tied to broader issues of social justice for young children, their families and communities and the early childhood workforce at the heart of our field. Self-care must be acknowledged as a critical element of high-quality programs in early childhood and understood to be a foundational pillar of equity for our field. Two critical truths are clear: Early childhood educators face inequitable and stressful conditions on a daily basis that impact their professional work, and early educators play a profoundly important role in the lives of young children and their families during the most critical years of their development. Valuing and integrating self-care, healing and wellness into the policies and practices of programs, agencies and throughout our early childhood systems is urgently needed. Not doing so is untenable given the consequences significantly impacting the health, quality of life and well-being of the early childhood workforce.

Despite the stressors they face inside and outside of the workplace, the *early educators' stories woven throughout this book make visible their extraordinary strengths, ingenuity, creativity, resistance, resilience, coping and commitment to the work they do* despite the inequitable conditions they face.

## Nepantla: A Site of Transformation, Struggle and Equilibrium

Nepantla is a concept used often in Chicano and Latino anthropology, social commentary, criticism, literature and art. It was first used by the Nahuatl-speaking people in Mexico (Aztecs) during the 16th century to mean "in the middle of it", or "middle", representing the feelings and consequences of their experience being colonized by the Spaniards. It represents a concept of "in-between-ness". Nepantla has also symbolized:

◆ The response of Indigenous peoples who were conquered by the Spanish to create their own "in-between" culture where they blended parts of both cultures maintaining at least parts of their culture through subtle and subversive acts of resistance

◆ An imaginary world that encompasses historical, emotional and spiritual aspects of life

◆ A borderland and being at literal or metaphorical crossroads

◆ A tool for political change—individuals who live within two different cultural contexts become levers to inspire change

◆ People's painful experiences, including a sense of invisibility, a loss of control and transition in life

◆ A "liminal" space representing the time between the "what was" and what is coming "next." It is a place of transition, waiting and not knowing. Liminal space is where transformation takes place, if we learn to wait and let it form us (Bernal & Alemán, Jr., 2017).

Gloria Anzaldúa (2002) describes Nepantla as a site for "transformation". She explains, "As you make your way through life, Nepantla itself becomes the place you live in most of the time—home. Nepantla is the site of transformation, the place where different perspectives come into conflict and where you question the basic ideas, tenets, and identities inherited from your family, your education, and your different cultures. Nepantla is the zone between changes where you struggle to find equilibrium" (p. 548).

We draw on the idea of Nepantla to reflect the diverse and culturally situated beliefs and varying practices educators describe in their concepts of the "self" and the actions and inactions they take with intentionality to enact an ethic of care for themselves and others. The stories throughout this book reflect the essence of Nepantla: tensions, borderlands, transitions, a fight for political change, imagination, joy, resistance, pain, invisibility, loss of control, literal and metaphorical crossroads between "what was/is" and what is possible for coming "next", all evidenced in the authentic and complex lived experiences that are realities for educators working in early childhood in the United States today.

The road to self-care is a personal and collective dynamic journey filled with tensions, struggle, resistance and liberation. As Patel (2016) states, "Learning is fundamentally about transformation. It is coming into being and constantly altering that being; it is a subjective and often messy act" (p. 76).

We encourage each one of you to honor your authentic path to self-care, healing and wellness as you wind through peaks and valleys of self-awareness, self-compassion and transformation.

## The Butterfly Looks for a Safe Place to Lay the Eggs: The Life Cycle Begins Again

Having come through a full metamorphosis—where strength was born of pain and struggle . . . fighting to emerge from its chrysalis, the butterfly fortifies its wings, giving it the ability to

**FIGURE 5.1**

*Credit*: Alice Blecker

fly far and wide, and now prepares to lay its eggs and spawn the life-cycle to begin anew (Figure 5.1). Each species of butterfly searches for the specific plant types that provide the nutrition its caterpillars will need to grow. Once found, the eggs are sites of growth and energy. The cycle of rebirth continues.

Early educators shed old beliefs and behaviors in a transformative learning process, a dynamic cycle that moves through discomfort and struggle toward increased understanding, personal strength and the opportunity to "spread their wings and take flight" in search of a place to land. An environment where they can engage in the work that fuels them so deeply—supporting young children and families. An environment that provides educators with the specific nutrients, the conditions they need to prioritize and advance their personal and professional health, engagement and well-being. Environments where an educator's transformative learning also becomes a ripple of hope that inspires others to see this metamorphosis is a possibility that is open to them.

*The brilliance of people always astounds if we can only get out of the way and shine the light on them . . .*

## Onward...

We hope this book will spark new ideas, inspire conversations and generate new practices and, most importantly, encourage every-one in early childhood to keep learning about what it means to authentically care for themselves so they can continue to engage in the work they love without negative consequence for their physical or emotional health, happiness or overall well-being. The ideas we offer should be considered a living document. We hope readers will adapt what works, extend the content to meet their specific needs, discard what doesn't serve them and continue to create and innovate. We close with an inquiry and an appeal: *What is one bite-sized action step you can take today to care for yourself?*

*Now with self-care something being intentionally talked about, I feel like I recognize it much more in little things that we do. I think I also recognize things that I did as a child a bit more and why. I think it's just made me more aware of myself... there was a song that keeps coming up in one of my playlists, Maria Lando, and it made me think so much of what I grew up with... "Maria doesn't have time to rest her eyes. She doesn't have time to take a lunch break. She doesn't have time to have dinner. She*

*doesn't have time to sleep, she can't rest her eyes . . . she is suf-
fering, ella de andar sufriendo, she only works, sólo trabaja, and
Maria's work serves others . . . ella sirve a otros." It's a beautiful
song. But it made me think of just how much I was raised with
that idea. A lot of people are. And we miss seeing the songs we
sing ourselves to give us strength through it. We miss seeing how
we dance and breathe life and love into ourselves. My mother's
life was full of days that blurred together, from work to raising a
family of five children, while being apart from her own parents
and the world she knew. She created her own world, where we
could have the privilege and freedom to just be. What a gift.*

*I think it's time to say, "It's okay to take time for ourselves."
To write our own lyrics to another beautiful song. . .*

# Resources on Self-Care for Educators

## Self-Care Cards

**Self-Care Cards—A 52 Card Deck by Cheryl Richardson**
Fifty-two prompts that challenge you to take a specific action to engage in self-care.

**Self-Compassion Deck**—50 Mindfulness Based Practice Cards by Christopher Willard Psy.D., Mitch Abblett Ph.D., Timothy Desmond

## Books

*Buddha's Brain: The Practical Neuroscience of Happiness, Love & Wisdom* **by Rick Hanson, Ph.D.**
Dr. Rick Hanson combines ancient teachings with modern neuroscience to describe how individuals can rewire their brains over time to achieve better emotional balance and greater peace of mind.

*Hardwiring Happiness: The New Brain Science of Contentment, Calm, and Confidence* **by Rick Hanson, Ph.D.**
Dr. Rick Hanson suggests the brain has a negativity bias that causes it to act like Velcro for negative experiences. He adapts concepts from neuroscience into easy and practical guided practices in positive thinking to overcome the negativity bias and improve well-being and a sense of inner peace.

*The Mindful Brain: 12 Revolutionary Strategies to Nurture Your Child's Developing Mind* **by Daniel Siegel, Ph.D.**
Dr. Daniel Siegel explores how children's brains develop and mature. Applying these principles of neuropsychiatry to everyday caregiving, Dr. Siegel describes how caregivers and educators can turn day-to-day struggles into opportunities for development and growth.

*The Mindful Child* **by Susan Kaiser Greenland, J.D.**
Susan Kaiser Greenland adapts mindfulness-based stress reduction techniques for children and walks caregivers through how to teach children to engage with mindfulness.

*Mindful Games: Sharing Mindfulness and Meditation with Children, Teens and Families* **by Susan Kaiser Greenland, J.D.**
*Mindfulness on the Go* **by Jan Chozen Bays, M.D.**
Twenty-five simple meditation practices designed to be used anywhere and anytime.

*Sitting Still Like a Frog: Mindfulness Exercises for Kids* **by Eline Snel**
*Trauma-Sensitive Mindfulness Practices for Safe and Transformative Healing* **by David Treleaven, Ph.D.**
Dr. David Treleaven introduces a trauma-sensitive approach to mindfulness meditation, discussing both research and providing tangible modifications to mindfulness practices.

*The Way of Mindful Education: Cultivating Well-Being in Teachers and Students* **by Daniel Rechtschaffen, M.F.T.**
Daniel Rechtschaffen discusses how educators can introduce mindfulness in their classroom, program, center or school and provides resources and lessons that can be directly implemented by educators.

# Apps (Mobile Applications)

**Headspace**—www.headspace.com

Headspace is a free app and website that gives users access to quick and easy "bite-sized" guided meditations. The app provides exercises targeted to stress, sleep, focus and anxiety, among many other themes.

**Insight Timer**—https://insighttimer.com

Insight Timer is a free app that provides a free course on meditation and guided meditation exercises for stress reduction, relaxation and sleep. In addition to guided meditation, users can use the timer page to customize the duration and background music/sounds.

**Breathe2Relax**

Breathe2Relax is a free iPhone, iPad and Apple Watch app that walks users through the steps of diaphragmatic "belly" breathing to control stress and promote relaxation.

**Calm**—www.calm.com

Calm is an app for meditation and mindfulness. It provides guided meditations, sleep stories, music and soundscapes to promote relaxation and sleep and video lessons on movement and gentle stretching.

**Stop, Breathe & Think Adults**

The Stop, Breathe & Think app sends daily reminders for users to stop and take a moment for a self-check-in. Users are able to indicate how they are feeling during their check-in, and the app then provides a quick guided meditation exercise targeted to the indicated emotions. The premium subscription option also includes daily journaling prompts.

**Forest**

The Forest app encourages users to disconnect from their smart-phones to focus or just take a break. The app plants a virtual tree that grows while the phone is not in use. Users can set a timer, and if the phone is picked up before the end of the designated time the virtual tree will die. As the tree grows, users earn coins that can be used to have trees planted in real life.

# Videos

### Self-Care Is Radical

www.ted.com/talks/raymonda_reese_self_care_is_radical

Mental health clinician Raymonda C. Reese discusses the differences between self-care and community care and teaches how to create spaces for people to support ourselves and those around us.

### Why We All Need to Practice Emotional First Aid

www.ted.com/talks/guy_winch_the_case_for_emotional_hygiene?referrer=playlist-the_importance_of_self_care

Guy Winch discusses the importance of practicing "emotional hygiene" by taking care of our emotions and our minds with the same dedication we give our bodies.

### The Power of Vulnerability

www.ted.com/talks/brene_brown_on_vulnerability?referrer=playlist-the_importance_of_self_care

Brené Brown discusses her research on human connection and our ability to empathize, belong and love.

# Websites

### Center for the Study of Social Policy: Strengthening Families (www.strengthening.families.net)

"Taking Care of Yourself: For Early Care and Education Providers"—https://cssp.org/wp-content/uploads/2018/08/Self-Care-for-ECE-Providers.pdf

## Self-Care Assessments and Exercises

https://socialwork.buffalo.edu/resources/self-care-starter-kit/self-care-assessments-exercises.html. This link provides self-care resources. They are intended to supplement the basic self-care plan. There are several self-assessment checklists and measures that can help you examine different aspects of your present well-being. With self-care exercises and activities from menu planning to tips to reduce stress, this page is filled with activities and resources to promote good self-care.

## ACEs Connection

www.acesconnection.com/g/practicing-resilience or home page: www.acesconnection.com/

ACEs Connection is a social network that supports communities to accelerate the global ACEs science movement, to recognize the impact of adverse childhood experiences (ACEs) in shaping adult behavior and health and to promote trauma-informed and resilience-building practices and policies in all communities and institutions—from schools to prisons to hospitals and churches—to help heal and to develop resilience instead of traumatizing already traumatized people.

# References

Aboagye, M. O., Qayyum, A., Antwi, C. O., Jababu, Y., & Affum-Osei, E. (2018). Teacher burnout in pre-schools: A cross-cultural factorial validity, measurement invariance and latent mean comparison of the Maslach Burnout Inventory, Educators Survey (MBI-ES). *Children and Youth Services Review, 94,* 186–197.

Acharya, S., & Shukla, S. (2012). Mirror neurons: Enigma of the metaphysical modular brain. *Journal of Natural Science, Biology and Medicine, 3*(2), 118–124. doi:10.4103/0976-9668.101878

Adams, R., Boscarino, J., & Figley, C. (2006). Compassion fatigue and psychological distress among social workers: A validation study. *American Journal of Orthopsychiatry, 76*(1), 103–108. doi:10.1037/0002-9432.76.1.103

Aguilar, E. (2018). *Onward: Cultivating emotional resilience in educators.* San Francisco, CA: Jossey Bass.

Alexander, M. (2010). *The new Jim Crow: Mass incarceration in the age of colorblindness.* New York, NY: The New Press.

Anda, R. F., Williamson, D. F., Escobedo, L. G., Mast, E. E., Giovino, G. A., & Remington, P. L. (1990). Depression and the dynamics of smoking: A national perspective. *Journal of the American Medical Association, 264*(12), 1541–1545.

Anderson, V. D. (2005). Sociocultural contexts of African American families. In V. C. McLoyd, N. E. Hill, K. A. Dodge, & M. Putallaz (Eds.), *African American family life: Ecological and cultural diversity* (Vol. 2, pp. 21–44). Duke Series on Child Development and Public Policy. New York, NY: Guilford Press.

Anthias, F. (1998). Rethinking social divisions: Some notes towards a theoretical framework. *Sociological Review, 46*(3), 506–535.

Anthias, F. (2013). Intersectional what? Social divisions, intersectionality, and levels of analysis. *Ethnicities, 13*(1), 3–19.

Anzaldúa, G. (2002). *This bridge we call home: Radical visions for transformation.* New York, NY: Routledge.

Anzaldúa, G. (2009). La conciencia de la mestiza: Towards a new consciousness. In R. Warhol-Down & D. P. Herdyl (Eds.), *Feminisms redux: An anthology of literary theory and criticism* (pp. 303–313). New Brunswick, NJ: Rutgers University Press.

Aten, J. D., Topping, S., Denney, R. M., & Bayne, T. G. (2010). Collaborating with African American churches to overcome minority disaster mental health disparities: What mental health professionals can learn from Hurricane Katrina. *Professional Psychology: Research and Practice, 41*(2), 167.

Awanbor, D. (1982). The healing process in African psychotherapy. *American Journal of Psychotherapy, 36*(2), 206–213.

Azevedo, F. A., Carvalho, L. R., Grinberg, L. T., Farfel, J. M., Ferretti, R. E., Leite, R. E., . . . Herculano-Houzel, S. (2009). Equal number of neuronal and nonneuronal cells make the human brain an isometrically scaled-up primate brain. *Journal of Comparative Neurology, 513*, 532–541. doi:10.1002/cne.21974

Baer, R. A. (2003). Mindfulness training as a clinical intervention: A conceptual and empirical review. *Clinical Psychology: Science and Practice, 10*, 125–143.

Bailey, Z. D., Krieger, N., Agenor, M., Graves, J., Linos, N., & Basset, M. T. (2017). Structural racism and health inequities in the USA: Evidence and interventions. *Lancet, 389*, 1453–1463.

Barnett, J. E., Johnston, L. C., & Hillard, D. (2006). Psychotherapist wellness as an ethical imperative. In L. VandeCreek & J. B. Allen (Eds.), *Innovations in clinical practice: Focus on health and wellness* (pp. 257–271). Sarasota, FL: Professional Resources Press.

Beatty, B. (1995). *Preschool education in America: The culture of young children from the colonial era to the present.* New Haven, CT: Yale University Press.

Beauchamp-Turner, D. L., & Levinson, D. M. (1992). Effects of meditation on stress, health, and affect. *Medical Psychotherapy: An International Journal, 5*, 123–131.

Bell, Jr., D. A. (1995). *Brown v. Board of Education* and the interest convergence dilemma. In K. Crenshaw, N. Gotanda, G. Peller, & K. Thomas (Eds.), *Critical race theory: The key writings that formed the movement* (pp. 29–28). New York, NY: The New Press.

Bell, L. (2016). Theoretical foundations for social justice education. In M. Adams and L. Bell (Ed.) *Teaching for Diversity and Social Justice* (pp. 3-26). New York, NY: Routledge.

Berman, M. G., Jonides, J., & Kaplan, S. (2008). The cognitive benefits of interacting with nature. *Psychological Science, 19*, 1207–1212.

Bernal, D. D., & Alemán, Jr., E. (2017). *Transforming educational pathways for Chicana/o students: A critical race feminista praxis.* New York, NY: Teachers College Press.

Bernardi, L., Spadacini, G., Bellwon, J., Hajric, R., Roskamm, H., & Frey, A. W. (1998). Effect of breathing rate on oxygen saturation and exercise performance in chronic heart failure. *The Lancet, 351*(9112), 1308–1311.

Bishop, R. S. (1990). Mirrors, windows, and sliding glass doors. Originally published in *Perspectives, 1*(3), ix–xi. Retrieved from https://scenicregional.org/wp-content/uploads/2017/08/Mirrors-Windows-and-Sliding-Glass-Doors.pdf

Bonilla-Silva, E. (2013). *Racism without racists: Color-blind racism and the persistence of racial inequality in the United States.* Lanham, MD: Rowman & Littlefield Publishers, Inc.

Bratman, G. N., Hamilton, J. P., & Daily, G. C. (2012). The impacts of nature experience on human cognitive function and mental health. *Annals of the New York Academy of Sciences, 1249*, 118–136.

Brissette, I., Cohen, S., & Seeman, T.E. (2000). Measuring Social Integration and Social Networks In S. Cohen, L. Underwood, & B. Gottlieb (Ed.) *Measuring and Intervening in Social Support.* Oxford, UK: Oxford University Press.

Brown, A.M. (2017). *Emergent Strategy: Shaping Change, Changing Worlds.* Chico, CA: AK Press.

Buchanan, T., Bagley, S., Stansfield, R., & Preston, S. (2012). The empathic, physiological resonance of stress. *Social Neuroscience, 7*, 191–201. doi:10.1080/17470919.2011.588723

Buchanan, T., & Preston, S. (2017). Commentary: Social stress contagion in rats: Behavioral, autonomic and neuroendocrine correlates. *Frontiers of Behavioral Neuroscience, 11*, 175. doi:10.3389/fnbeh.2017.00175

Cacioppo, J. T., & Berntson, G. G. (1992). Social psychological contributions to the decade of the brain: Doctrine of multilevel analysis. *American Psychologist, 47*, 1019–1028.

California Department of Education (2016b). *Family Partnerships and Culture.* Sacramento, CA: Author. Retrieved from https://www. cde.ca.gov/sp/cd/re/documents/familypartnerships.pdf

Carnevali, L., Montano, N., Statello, R., Coudé, G., Vacondio, F., Rivara, S., et al. (2017). Social stress contagion in rats: Behavioural, autonomic and neuroendocrine correlates. *Psychoneuroendocrinology, 82*, 155–163. doi:10.1016/j. psyneuen.2017.05.017Casey, B. J., Tottenham, N., Liston, C., & Durston, S. (2005). Imaging the developing brain: What have we learned about cognitive development? *Trends in Cognitive Sciences, 9*(3), 104–110.

Cervantes, J. M. (2010). Mestizo spirituality: Toward an integrated approach to psychotherapy for Latina/os. *Psychotherapy: Theory, Research, Practice, Training, 47*(4), 527.

Chandla, S. S., Sood, S., Dogra, R., Das, S., Shukla, S. K., & Gupta, S. (2013). Effect of short-term practice of pranayama breathing exercises on cognition, anxiety, general well being and heart rate variability. *Journal of the Indian Medical Association, 111*(10), 662–665.

Cheon, B. K., Im, D. M., Harada, T., Kim, J. S., Mathur, V. A., Scimeca, J. M., . . . Chiao, J. Y. (2013). Cultural modulation of the neural correlates of emotional pain perception: The role of other-focusedness. *Neuropsychologia, 51*(7), 1177–1186.

Cho, S., Crenshaw, K., & McCall, L. (2013). Toward a field of intersectionality studies: Theory, applications, and praxis. *Signs, 38*, 785–810.

Clark, L. (2017). *Decolonizing self-care: Towards caring communities and self-preservation.* Retrieved from www.vawlearningnetwork.ca/ webinars/recorded-webinars/Towards_Caring_Communities_ decolonizing_selfcare.pdf

Cochran-Smith, M. & Lytle, S.L. (2009). Inquiry as a Stance: Practitioner Research for the Next Generation. New York, NY: Teachers College Press.

Cohen, S. (2004). Social relationships and health. *American Psychologist, 59*(8), 676–684.

Cohen, S., Gottlieb, B., & Underwood, L. (2000). Social relationships and health. In S. Cohen, L. Underwood, & B. Gottlieb(Eds.), *Measuring and intervening in social support.* New York, NY: Oxford University Press. Collins, P. H. (2015). Intersectionality's definitional dilemmas. *Annual Review of Sociology, 41*, 1–20.

Conkbayier, M. (2017). *Early childhood and neuroscience: Theory, research and implications for practice.* New York, NY: Bloomsbury Academic.

Cozolino, L. (2006/2012). *The neuroscience of human relationships: Attachment and the developing social brain.* New York, NY: Norton.

Craig, S. (2016). *Trauma-sensitive schools: Learning communities transforming children's lives, K-5.* New York, NY: Teachers College Press.

Crenshaw, K. W. (1991). Mapping the margins: Intersectionality, identity politics, and violence against women of color. *Stanford Law Review, 43*, 1241–1299.

Dallman, M. F., Pecoraro, N., Akana, S. F., La Fleur, S. E., Gomez, F., Houshyar, H., . . . Manalo, S. (2003). Chronic stress and obesity: A new view of "comfort food". *Proceedings of the National Academy of Sciences of the United States of America, 100*(20), 11696–11701.

Davidson, R. J., Kabat-Zinn, J., Schumacher, J., Rosenkranz, M., Muller, D., Santorelli, S. F., . . . Sheridan, J. F. (2003). Alterations in brain and immune function produced by mindfulness meditation. *Psychosomatic Medicine, 65*, 564–570.

Delgado, R., Stefancic, J., & Liendo, E. (2012). *Critical race theory: An introduction* (2nd ed.). New York, NY: New York University Press.

de Waal, F., & Preston, S. (2017). Mammalian empathy: Behavioural manifestations and neural basis. *Nature Reviews Neuroscience, 18*, 498–509. doi:10.1038/nrn.2017.72

Dhabhar, F. S. (2000). Acute stress enhances while chronic stress suppresses skin immunity: The role of stress hormones and leukocyte trafficking. *Annals of the New York Academy of Sciences, 917*, 876–893.

DiAngelo, R. (2016). *What does it mean to be White? Developing white racial literacy* (Revised ed.). New York, NY: Peter Lang.

Didion, J. (2006). *We tell ourselves stories in order to live: Collected nonfiction*. London: Everyman's Library.

Dube, S. R., Anda, R. F., Felitti, V. J., Edwards, V. J., & Croft, J. B. (2002). Adverse childhood experiences and personal alcohol abuse as an adult. *Addictive Behaviors, 27*(5), 713–725.

Dutton, M., Kaltman, S., Centers for Disease Control and Prevention, & Atlanta, G. (2007). *Longitudinal study of battered women in the healthcare system*.

Emmons, R. A., & Stern, R. (2013). Gratitude as a psychotherapeutic intervention. *Journal of Clinical Psychology, 69*(8), 846–855.

Engert, V., Plessow, F., Miller, R., Kirschbaum, C., & Singer, T. (2014). Cortisol increase in empathic stress is modulated by emotional closeness and observation modality. *Psychoneuroendocrinology, 45*, 192–201. doi:10.1016/j.psyneuen.2014.04.005

Fernández, L. (2002). Telling stories about school: Using critical race and Latino critical theories to document Latina/Latino education and resistance. *Qualitative Inquiry, 8*(1), 45–65.

Figley, C. (2002). Compassion fatigue: Psychotherapists' chronic lack of self care. *Psychotherapy in Practice, 58*(11), 1411–1433.

Frye, M. (1983). *The politics of reality: Essays in feminist theory*. Trumansburg, NY: The Crossing Press.

Gay, G. (2010). *Culturally responsive teaching: Theory, research, and practice* (2nd ed.). New York, NY: Teachers College Press.

Ginwright, S. (2018). The future of healing: Shifting from trauma informed care to healing centered engagement. *Medium*. Retrieved from https://medium.com/@ginwright/the-future-of-healing-shifting-from-trauma-informed-care-to-healing-centered-engagement-634f557ce69c

Glaser, R., Sheridan, J., Malarkey, W. B., MacCallum, R. C., & Kiecolt-Glaser, J. K. (2000). Chronic stress modulates the immune response to a pneumococcal pneumonia vaccine. *Psychosomatic Medicine, 62*(6), 804–807.

Goleman, D. J., & Schwartz, G. E. (1976). Meditation as an intervention in stress reactivity. *Journal of Consulting and Clinical Psychology, 44*, 456–466.

Gone, J. P., & Calf Looking, P. E. (2011). American Indian culture as substance abuse treatment: Pursuing evidence for a local intervention. *Journal of Psychoactive Drugs, 43*(4), 291–296.

Gootjes, L., & Rassin, E. (2014). Perceived thought control mediates positive effects of meditation experience on affective functioning. *Mindfulness, 5,* 1–9.

Gottlieb, D., Hennessy, L., & Squires, V. (2004). Burnout: Knowing the symptoms & learning how to care for yourself, too. *Child Life Focus, 6*(2), 1–4.

Halfon, N., Shulman, E., & Hochstein, M. (2001). Brain Development in Early Childhood In N. Halfon, E. Shulman, and M. Hochstein (Ed.) *Building Community Systems for Young Children.* Los Angeles, CA: UCLA Center for Healthier Children, Families, and Communities.

Hall, E. T. (1976). *Beyond culture.* Garden City, NY: Anchor Press.

Hammond, Z. (2015). *Culturally Responsive Teaching and the Brain: Promoting Authentic Engagement Among Culturally and Linguistically Diverse Students.* Thousand Oaks, CA: Corwin Press.

Han, S., Northoff, G., Vogeley, K., Wexler, B. E., Kitayama, S., & Varnum, M. E. (2013). A cultural neuroscience approach to the biosocial nature of the human brain. *Annual Review of Psychology, 64,* 335–359.Hanks, A., Solomon, D., & Weller, C. E. (2017). *Systemic inequality: How America's structural racism helped create the black-white wealth gap.* Center for American Progress. Retrieved from www.americanprogress.org/issues/race/ reports/2018/02/21/447051/systematic-inequality/

Harb, C., & Smith, P. B. (2008). Self-construals across cultures: Beyond independence—interdependence. *Journal of Cross-Cultural Psychology, 39*(2), 178–197.

Hassel, C., Tamang, A. L., Foushee, L., & Bad Heart Bull, R. (2019). Decolonizing nutrition science. *Current Developments in Nutrition, 3*(2), 3–11. doi:10.1093/cdn/nzy095

Heckman, J. J. (2008). The case for investing in disadvantaged young children. In First Focus (Ed.), *Big ideas for children: Investing in our nation's future* (pp. 49–58). Washington, DC: First Focus.

Heckman, J. J., & Masterov, D. V. (2007). The productivity argument for investing in young children. *Review of Agricultural Economics, 29*(3), 446–493.

Heckman, J. J., Moon, S. H., Pinto, R., Savelyev, P. A., & Yavitz, A. (2010). The rate of return to the HighScope Perry preschool program. *Journal of Public Economics, 94*(1), 114–128.

Heckman, J. J., Stixrud, J., & Urzua, S. (2006). The effects of cognitive and noncognitive abilities on labor market outcomes and social behavior. *Journal of Labor Economics, 24*(3), 411–482.

Heffron, M. C., & Murch, T. (2010). *Reflective supervision and leadership in infant and early childhood programs*. Washington, DC: Zero to Three Press.

Henrich, J., Heine, S. J., & Norenzayan, A. (2010). The weirdest people in the world? *Behavioral and Brain Sciences, 33*(2–3), 61–83.

Herculano-Houzel, S. (2009). The human brain in numbers: A linearly scaled-up primate brain. *Frontiers in Human Neuroscience, 3*, 31. Retrieved from www.frontiersin.org/articles/10.3389/neuro.09.031.2009/full

Hill, N.E., McBride-Murry, V., Anderson, V.D. (2005). Sociocultural Contexts of African American Families In V.C. McLoyd, N.E. Hill, and K.A. Dodge (Ed.), *African American Family Life: Ecological and Cultural Diversity* (pp. 21-44). New York, NY: Guilford Press.

Hill Collins, P. (2015). Intersectionality's definitional dilemmas. *Annual Reviews of Sociology, 41*, 1–20. doi:10.1146/annurev-soc-073014-112142

Holzel, B. K., Lazar, S. W., Gard, T., Schuman-Olivier, Z., Vago, D. R., & Ott, U. (2011). How does mindfulness meditation work? Proposing mechanisms of action from a conceptual and neural perspective. *Perspectives on Psychological Science, 6*, 537–559.

Jack, R. E., Blais, C., Scheepers, C., Schyns, P. G., & Caldara, R. (2009). Cultural confusions show that facial expressions are not universal. *Current Biology, 19*(18), 1543–1548.

Jobson, L. (2009). Drawing current posttraumatic stress disorder models into the cultural sphere: The development of the "threat to the conceptual self" model. *Clinical Psychology Review, 29*(4), 368–381.

Kaplan, S. (1995). The restorative benefits of nature: Toward an integrative framework. *Journal of Environmental Psychology, 15*, 169–182.

Kaur, A., & Noman, M. (2015). Exploring classroom practices in collectivist cultures through the lens of Hofstede's model. *The Qualitative Report, 20*(11), 1794–1811.

Kelly, J. (2013). *All aflutter*. Retrieved from https://mag.uchicago.edu/science-medicine/all-aflutter#

Kirmayer, L.J. (2007). Psychotherapy and the cultural concept of the person. *Transcult Psychiatry, 44*(2), 232–57.

Kitayama, S., & Uskul, A. K. (2011). Culture, mind, and the brain: Current evidence and future directions. *Annual Review of Psychology, 62,* 419–449.

Kohli, R. (2013). Unpacking internalized racism: Teachers of color striving for racially just classrooms. *Race Ethnicity and Education.* doi:10.1080/13613324.2013.832935

Kohli, R., & Solórzano, D. G. (2012). Teachers, please learn our names! Racial microaggressions and the K-12 classroom. *Race Ethnicity and Education, 15*(4), 441–462.

Koppelman, K. L., & Goodhart, R. L. (2011). *Understanding human differences: Multicultural education for a diverse America.* Boston, MA: Pearson, Allyn & Bacon.

Ladson-Billings, G., & Tate, W. (1995). Toward a critical race theory of education. *Teachers College Record, 97*(1), 47–68.

Leiter, M. P., & Maslach, C. (2004). Areas of worklife: A structured approach to organizational predictors of job burnout. In P. L. Perrewe & D. C. Ganster (Eds.), *Research in occupational stress and well-being* (Vol. 3, pp. 91–134). Oxford: Elsevier.

Levine, P., & Kline, M. (2007). *Trauma through a child's eyes: Awakening the ordinary miracle of healing. Infancy through adolescence.* Berkeley, CA: North Atlantic Books.

Liddell, B. J., & Jobson, L. (2016). The impact of cultural differences in self-representation on the neural substrates of posttraumatic stress disorder. *European Journal of Psychotraumatology, 7*(1), Article ID 30464.

Lieberman, A. (2018). *Video: Teacher stress and low compensation undermine early learning.* New America Foundation. Retrieved from www.newamerica.org/education-policy/edcentral/video-teacher-stress/?utm_medium=email&utm_campaign=Early%20and%20Elementary%20Ed%20Update%20433&utm_content=Early%20and%20Elementary%20Ed%20Update%20433+CID_85a589ff4e7d8e8eae2754a321ec3597&utm_source=Campaign%20Monitor%20

Newsletters&utm_term=Video%20Teacher%20Stress%20and%20
Low%20Compensation%20Undermine%20Early%20Learning

Lipsky, L. (2009). *Trauma stewardship: An everyday guide for caring for self while caring for others.* San Francisco, CA: Berrett-Koehler Publishers.

MacLean, C., Walton, K. G., Wenneberg, S. R., Levitsky, D. K., Mandarino, J. P., Waziri, R., . . . Schneider, R. H. (1997). Effects of the transcendental meditation program on adaptive mechanisms: Changes in hormone levels and responses to stress after 4 months of practice. *Psychoneuroendocrinology, 22,* 277–295.

Maltzman, S. (2011). An organization self-care model: Practical suggestions for development and implementation. *The Counseling Psychologist, 39*(2), 303–319.

Markus, H. R., & Kitayama, S. (2010). Cultures and selves: A cycle of mutual constitution. *Perspectives on Psychological Science, 5*(4), 420–430.

Martinez, M. E. (2001). "The Process of Knowing: A Biocognitive Epistemology". *The Journal of Mind and Behavior, 22*(4), 407–426.

Martínez, K. G., Franco-Chaves, J. A., Milad, M. R., & Quirk, G. J. (2014). Ethnic differences in physiological responses to fear conditioned stimuli. *PLOS ONE, 9*(12), e114977.

Maslach, C., & Jackson, S. E. (1986). *The Maslach Burnout Inventory* (2nd ed.). Palo Alto, CA: Consulting Psychologists Press.

Mathieu, F. (2007, March). *Transforming compassion fatigue into compassion satisfaction: Top 12 self-care tips for helpers.* Workshops for the Helping Professions. Retrieved from compassionfatigue.org

Matsumoto, D., & Juang, L. (2013). *Culture & Psychology.* Boston, MA: Cengage Learning.

Mayer, F., Frantz, C., Bruehlman-Senecal, E., & Dolliver, K. (2009). Why is nature beneficial? The role of connectedness to nature. *Environment and Behavior, 41,* 607–643.

McEwen, B. S. (2000). Allostasis and allostatic load: Implications for neuropsychopharmacology. *Neuropsychopharmacology, 22*(2), 108–124.

McEwen, B. S. (2006). Protective and damaging effects of stress mediators: Central role of the brain. *Dialogues in Clinical Neuroscience, 8*(4), 367–381.

McEwen, B. S., & Wingfield, J. C. (2003). The concept of allostasis in biology and biomedicine. *Hormones and Behavior, 43*(1), 2–15.

McLean, C., Whitebook, M., & Roh, E. (2019). *From unlivable wages to just pay for early educators.* Berkeley, CA: Center for the Study of Child Care Employment, University of California.

Milner IV, H. (2017). Where's the race in culturally relevant pedagogy? *Teachers College Record, 119*(1).

Mirk, S. (2016). *Audre Lorde thought of self-care as an "act of political warfare".* Bitch Media. Retrieved from www.bitchmedia.org/article/audre-lorde-thought-self-care-act-political-warfare

Mrazek, M. D., Franklin, M. S., Phillips, D., Baird, B., & Schooler, J. W. (2013). Mindfulness training improves working memory capacity and GRE performance while reducing mind wandering. *Psychological Science, 24,* 776–781.

National Center for Complementary and Integrative Health. (2017, September 24). *Meditation.* Retrieved from https://nccih.nih.gov/health/meditation.

National Research Council and Institute of Medicine. (2015). *Transforming the workforce for children birth-age 8.* Report. Retrieved from www.nap.edu/resource/19401/BirthtoEight_brief.pdf

Neff, K. D., Kirkpatrick, K. L., & Rude, S. (2007). Self-compassion and adaptive psychological functioning. *Journal of Research in Personality, 41,* 139–154.

Nicholson, J., Kurtz, J., Leland, J., Wesley, L. & Nadiv, S. (2021). *Creating and Sustaining Trauma-Informed and Healing Engaged Early Childhood Organizations and Systems.* New York, NY: Routledge Press.

Nicholson, J., Perez, L., & Kurtz, J. (2019). *Trauma informed practices for early childhood educators: Relationship-based approaches that support healing and build protective factors in young children.* New York, NY: Routledge Press.

Noddings, N. (2013). *Caring: A Relational Approach to Ethics and Moral Education* (2nd ed.). Berkeley, CA: University of California Press.

O'Brien, J. L., & Haaga, D. A. F. (2015). Empathic accuracy and compassion fatigue among therapist trainees. *Professional Psychology: Research and Practice, 46*(6), 414–420.

Ochsner, K. N., & Gross, J. J. (2008). Cognitive emotion regulation: Insights from social cognitive and affective neuroscience. *Current Directions in Psychological Science, 17*, 153–158.

Osei Aboagye, M., Jinliang, Q., Collins, A., Qayyum, A., Opoku Antwi, C., Jababu, Y., & Affum-Osei, E. (2018). Teacher burnout in pre-schools: A cross-cultural factorial validity, measurement invariance and latent mean comparison of the Maslach Burnout Inventory, Educators Survey (MBI-ES). *Children and Youth Services Review, 94*, 186–197. doi:10.1016/j.childyouth.2018.09.041

Ostafin, B. D., & Kassman, K. T. (2012). Stepping out of history: Mindfulness improves insight problem solving. *Consciousness and Cognition: An International Journal, 21*, 1031–1036.

Oyserman, D., Novin, S., Flinkenflögel, N., & Krabbendam, L. (2014). Integrating culture-as-situated-cognition and neuroscience prediction models. *Culture and Brain, 2*(1), 1–26.

Paley, V. (1993). *You can't say you can't play*. Cambridge, MA: Harvard University Press.

Pally, R. (2000). *The mind-brain relationship*. New York, NY: Other Press LLC.

Papadopoulos, I., Shea, S., Taylor, G. P., Pezzella, A., & Foley, L. S. (2016). Developing tools to promote culturally competent compassion, courage, and intercultural communication in healthcare. *Journal of Compassionate Health Care, 3*, 1–10.

Parham, T. A. (1999). Invisibility syndrome in African descent people: Understanding the cultural manifestations of the struggle for self-affirmation. *The Counseling Psychologist, 27*, 794–801.

Paris, D. (2012). Culturally sustaining pedagogy: A needed change in stance, terminology, and practice. *Educational Researcher, 41*(3), 93–97.

Paris, D., & Alim, H. S. (2017). *Culturally sustaining pedagogies: Teaching and learning for justice in a changing world*. Language and Literacy Series. New York, NY: Teachers College Press.

Park, B., Tsunetsugu, Y., Kasetani, T., Hirano, H., Kagawa, T., Sato, M., & Miyazaki, Y. (2007). Physiological effects of Shinrin-Yoku (taking in the atmosphere of the forest)—Using salivary cortisol and cerebral activity as indicators. *Journal of Physiological Anthropology, 26*, 123–128.

Park, D. C., & Huang, C. M. (2010). Culture wires the brain: A cognitive neuroscience perspective. *Perspectives on Psychological Science, 5*(4), 391–400.Patel, L. (2016). *Decolonizing educational research: From ownership to answerability.* New York, NY: Routledge.

Pennebaker, J. (2004). *Writing to heal: A guided journal for recovering from trauma and emotional upheaval.* Wheat Ridge, CO: Center for Journal Therapy Inc.

Perciavalle, V., Blandini, M., Fecarotta, P., Buscemi, A., Di Corrado, D., Bertolo, L., . . . Coco, M. (2017). The role of deep breathing on stress. *Neurological Sciences, 38*(3), 451–458.

Perry, B. (2014). The cost of caring: Understanding and preventing secondary stress when working with traumatized and maltreated children. In *CTA parent and caregiver education series* (Vol. 2, p. 7). Houston, TX: The Child Trauma Academy Press.

Perry, B., Pollard, R., Blakley, T., Baker, W., & Vigilante, D. (1995). Childhood trauma, the neurobiology of adaptation and use dependent development of the brain: How states become traits. *Infant Mental Health Journal, 16*(4), 271–291.Pienaar, J., & Van Wyk, D. (2006). Teacher burnout: Construct equivalence and the role of union membership. *South African Journal of Education, 26*(4), 541–551.

Pines, A., & Aronson, E. (1988). *Career burnout: Causes and cures.* New York, NY: The Free Press.

Porges, S. (2011). *The polyvagal theory: Neurophysiological foundations of emotions, attachment, communication, and self-regulation.* New York, NY: Norton.

Ray, S., Wong, C., White, D., & Heaslip, K. (2013). Compassion satisfaction, compassion fatigue, work life conditions, and burnout among frontline mental healthcare professionals. *Traumatology, 19*(4), 255–267. doi:10.1177/1534765612471144

Resick, P. A., Monson, C. M., & Chard, K. M. (2017). *Cognitive processing therapy for PTSD.* New York, NY: Guildford.

Rogers, K. (2011). *The brain and the nervous system.* New York, NY: Britannica Educational Publishing.

Rogoff, B. (2003). *The cultural nature of human development.* Oxford, UK: Oxford University Press.

Rogoff, B. (2011). *Developing destinies: A Mayan midwife and town.* Oxford, UK: Oxford University Press.

Rogoff, B., & Angelillo, C. (2002). Investigating the coordinated functioning of multifaceted cultural practices in human development. *Human Development, 45*(4), 211–225.

Rogoff, B., Coppens, A. D., Alcalá, L., Aceves-Azuara, I., Ruvalcaba, O., López, A., & Dayton, A. (2017). Noticing learners' strengths through cultural research. *Perspectives on Psychological Science, 12*(5), 876–888.

Rogoff, B., Najafi, B., & Mejía-Arauz, R. (2014). Constellations of cultural practices across generations: Indigenous American heritage and learning by observing and pitching in. *Human Development, 57*(2–3), 82–95.

Romero, S., Dickerson, C., Jordan, M., & Mazzei, P. (2019). "It feels like being hunted": Latinos across the US in fear after the massacre in El Paso. *New York Times.* Retrieved from www.nytimes.com/2019/08/06/us/el-paso-shooting-latino-anxiety.html

Ross, J. L. (1987). Cultural tensions in strategic marital therapy. *Contemporary Family Therapy, 9*(3), 188–201.

Rushton, S. (2011). Neuroscience, early childhood education and play: We are doing it right! *Early Childhood Education Journal, 39,* 89–94. New York, NY: Springer Science + Business Media, LLC. doi:10.1007/s10643-011-0447-z

Salyers, M. P., Hudson, C., Morse, G., Rollins, A. L., Monroe-DeVita, M., Wilson, C., & Freeland, L. (2011). BREATHE: A pilot study of a one-day retreat to reduce burnout among mental health professionals. *Psychiatric Services, 62*(2), 214–217.

Sanchez, I. (2019). *El Paso horror spotlights long history of anti-Latino violence in the U.S.* Retrieved from www.cnn.com/2019/08/05/opinions/el-paso-shooting-was-a-hate-crime-against-latinos-sanchez/index.html

Schaufeli, W. B., & Janczur, B. (1994). Burnout among nurses: A Polish-Dutch comparison. *Journal of Cross-Cultural Psychology, 25*(1), 95–113.

Schore, A. N. (2003). Early relational trauma, disorganized attachment, and the development of a predisposition to violence. In M. F. Solomon & D. J. Siegel (Eds.), *Healing trauma: Attachment, mind, body, and brain* (pp. 107–167). New York, NY: Norton.

Shapiro, S. L., Jazaieri, H., & De Sousa, S. (2016). *Meditation and positive psychology* (3rd ed.). Oxford, UK: Oxford University Press.

Shapiro, S. L., Schwartz, G. E. R., & Santerre, C. (2002). Meditation and positive psychology. In C. R. Snyder & S. J. Lopez (Eds.), *Handbook of positive psychology* (pp. 632–645). New York, NY: Oxford University Press.

Siegel, D. J. (2007). Mindfulness training and neural integration: Differentiation of distinct streams of awareness and the cultivation of well-being. *Social Cognitive and Affective Neuroscience, 2*(4), 259–263.

Siegel, D. J., & Bryson, T. P. (2012). *The whole-brain child: 12 revolutionary strategies to nurture your child's developing mind.* New York, NY: Delacorte Press.

Silva, K. G., Correa-Chávez, M., & Rogoff, B. (2010). Mexican-heritage children's attention and learning from interactions directed to others. *Child Development, 81*(3), 898–912.

Silva, K. G., Shimpi, P. M., & Rogoff, B. (2015). Young children's attention to what's going on: Cultural differences. In *Advances in child development and behavior* (Vol. 49, pp. 207–227). JAI. Cambridge, MA: Academic Press.

Smith, L.T. ( 2012). *Decolonizing Methodologies.* Dunedin, New Zealand: Otago University Press.

Smithsonian Institution. (n.d.). *Butterflies.* Retrieved August 2019, from https://www.si.edu/spotlight/buginfo/butterfly.

Solórzano, D. G., & Yosso, T. J. (2002). Critical race methodology: Counter-storytelling as an analytical framework for education research. *Qualitative Inquiry, 8*(1), 23–44.

Sorrels, B. (2015). *Reaching and teaching children exposed to trauma.* Lewisville, NC: Gryphon House, Inc.

Stein, P. T., & Kendall, J. (2004). *Psychological trauma and the developing brain: Neurologically based interventions for troubled children.* New York, NY: The Haworth Maltreatment and Trauma Press.

Stroud, B. (2010). Honoring diversity through a deeper reflection: Increasing cultural under-standing within the reflective supervision process. *Zero to Three, 31*(2), 46–50.

Suárez-Orozco, C., Casanova, S., Martin, M., Katsiaficas, D., Cuellar, V., Smith, N. A., & Dias, S. I. (2015). Toxic rain in class: Classroom interpersonal microaggressions. *Educational Researcher, 44*(3), 151–160. doi://10.3102/0013189X15580314

Substance Abuse and Mental Health Services Administration (SAMHSA) and the Health Resources and Services Administration. (n.d.). *Trauma.* Retrieved from www.integration.samhsa.gov/clinical-practice/trauma

Sue, D. W. (2005). *Multicultural social work practice.* Hoboken, NJ: John Wiley & Sons.

Sue, D. W., Capodilupo, C. M., Torino, G. C., Bucceri, J. M., Holder, A. M. B., Nadal, K. L., & Esquilin, M. (2007). Racial microaggressions in everyday life: Implications for clinical practice. *American Psychologist, 62*(4), 271–286. doi:10.1037/0003-066X.62.4.271

Sue, D.W. & Sue, D. (2013). *Counselling the Culturally Diverse: Theory and Practice* (6th ed.) Hoboken, NJ: John Wiley & Sons.

Sullivan, K. T., & Lawrence, E. (Eds.). (2016). *The Oxford handbook of relationship science and couple interventions.* Oxford, UK: Oxford University Press.

Suñer-Soler, R., Grau-Martín, A., Flichtentrei, D., Prats, M., Braga, F., Font-Mayolas, S., & Gras, M. E. (2014). The consequences of burnout syndrome among healthcare professionals in Spain and Spanish speaking Latin American countries. *Burnout Research, 1*(2), 82–89.Taylor, A. F., & Kuo, F. E. (2006). Is contact with nature important for healthy child development? State of the evidence. In *Children and their environments: Learning, using and designing spaces* (pp. 124–140). Cambridge, UK: Cambridge University Press. doi:10.1017/CBO9780511521232.009

Taylor, A. F., & Kuo, F. E. (2011). Could exposure to everyday green spaces help treat ADHD? Evidence from children's play settings. *Applied Psychology: Health and Well-Being, 3*(3), 281–303. doi:10.1111/j.1758-0854.2011.01052.x

Tuhiwai Smith, L., Tuck, E., & Yang, K. (Eds.). (2019). *Indigenous and decolonizing studies in education: Mapping the long view.* New York, NY: Routledge.

U.S. Department of Health & Human Services, Administration for Children and Families, Administration on Children, Youth and Families, Children's Bureau. (2018). *Child maltreatment 2016.*

Retrieved from www.acf.hhs.gov/cb/research-data-technology/statistics-research/child-maltreatment

U.S. Department of Justice. (n.d.). *Hate crime statistics*. Retrieved from www.justice.gov/hatecrimes/hate-crime-statistics

Valencia, R. (2010). *Dismantling contemporary deficit thinking: Educational thought and practice*. New York, NY: Routledge.

van der Kolk, B. A. (2014). *The body keeps the score: Brain, mind and body in the healing of trauma*. London, UK: Penguin Books.

Vega, W. A., Kolody, B., & Valle, R. (1988). Marital strain, coping, and depression among Mexican-American women. *Journal of Marriage and the Family, 50*, 391–403.

Waters, S., West, T., & Mendes, W. (2014). Stress contagion: Physiological covariation between mothers and infants. *Psychological Science, 25*, 934–942. doi:10.1177/0956797613518352

Wendt, D. C., Gone, J. P., & Nagata, D. K. (2014). Potentially harmful therapy and multicultural counseling: Bridging two disciplinary discourses. *Counseling Psychology, 43*(3), 334–358.

Wethington, E., & Kessler, R. C. (1986). Perceived support, received support, and adjustment to stressful life events. *Journal of Health and Social Behavior, 27*, 78–89.

Whitebook, M., King, E., Philipp, G., & Sakai, L. (2016). *Teachers' voices: Work environment conditions that impact teacher practice and program quality*. Berkeley, CA: Center for the Study of Child Care Employment, University of California. Retrieved from https://cscce.berkeley.edu/files/2016/2016-Alameda-SEQUAL-Report-FINAL-for-Dissemination-v2.pdf

Whitebook, M., McLean, C., Austin, L. J., & Edwards, B. (2018). *Early childhood workforce index—2018*. Berkeley, CA: Center for the Study of Child Care Employment, University of California. Retrieved from http://cscce.berkeley.edu/topic/early-childhood-work-force-index/2018/

Whitebook, M., Phillips, D., & Howes, C. (2014). *Worthy work, STILL unlivable wages: The early childhood workforce 25 years after the national child care staffing study, executive summary*. Berkeley, CA. Retrieved from http://cscce.berkeley.edu/files/2014/ReportFINAL.pdf

Witt, L. (2017a). Why decolonizing self-care fuels our resistance. *Wear Your Voice*. Retrieved from https://wearyourvoicemag.com/culture/decolonizing-self-care-resistance

Witt, L. (2017b). Putting ourselves first as Black women/Femmes is like returning to our first love. *Wear Your Voice*. Retrieved from https://wearyourvoicemag.com/identities/rachael-edwards-self-care

Wolfe, P. (2007). *Mind, memory and learning: Translating brain research to classroom practices*. Napa Valley, CA: Association for Supervision and Curriculum Development (ASCD).

Yackle, K., Schwarz, L. A., Kam, K., Sorokin, J. M., Huguenard, J. R., Feldman, J. L., . . . Krasnow, M. A. (2017). Breathing control center neurons that promote arousal in mice. *Science, 355*(6332), 1411–1415.

Yeh, C. J., Hunter, C. D., Madan-Bahel, A., Chiang, L., & Arora, A. K. (2004). Indigenous and interdependent perspectives of healing: Implications for counseling and research. *Journal of Counseling & Development, 82*(4), 410–419.

Zaki, J. (2019). *The war for kindness: Building empathy in a fractured world*. New York, NY: Crown Publishing.

Zhan, S., Zhang, W., Niitepold, K., Hsu, J., Haeger, J. F., Zalucki, M. P., . . . Kronforst, M. R. (2014). The genetics of monarch butterfly migration and warning colouration. *Nature, 514*, 317–321.

# Index

Page numbers in *italics* indicate figures; page numbers in **bold** indicate tables.

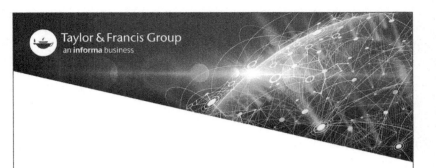

Made in the USA
Las Vegas, NV
02 July 2021